SCAPEGOAT

The Chino Hills Murders
and the Framing of Kevin Cooper

13-digit ISBN 978-0-9842333-7-3
10-digit ISBM 0-9842333-7-7

For David Alexander and Norm Hile

TABLE OF CONTENTS

During the fall of 2008, I was in the San Francisco Bay area on a book tour for *The Framing of Mumia Abu-Jamal.* The tour was arranged by Jeff Mackler, the executive director of the Mobilization to Free Mumia Abu-Jamal, and it involved about fifteen speaking engagements at different venues. Jeff told me that supporters of death-row inmate Kevin Cooper—whom I had not heard of—would be attending a number of these presentations, and that they would be asking me to write a book about Kevin's case. Indeed, two of Cooper's most dedicated supporters, Carole Seligman and Rebecca Doran, did just that.

Cooper had been convicted in 1985 of the brutal murders of Doug and Peggy Ryen, their ten-year-old daughter, Jessica, and eleven-year-old houseguest Christopher Hughes, and the attempted murder of the Ryens' eight-year-old son Joshua.

Jeff had gotten to know Cooper over the years, and had visited him about twenty times. Kevin's case was quite different from Mumia's, he said, in the sense that Mumia is essentially a political prisoner and Kevin was anything but.

When I decided to begin researching the Kevin Cooper case in early 2009, I had no pre-conceived notions about his guilt or innocence. Each case is different, radically so. My first step was to read and notate the trial transcripts, documents of over eight-thousand pages. I then read all the police reports, witness interviews and various newspaper accounts. Finally,

I read all of the appeals and the judicial rulings. By this time I was ready to begin interviewing various people involved in Cooper's trial and his subsequent appeals.

One problem in researching a crime nearly twenty-five years after it occurred is that a number of key people involved in the investigation and trial have passed away or have retired or have simply forgotten important factual details. Another obstacle is that, because Cooper technically still has appeals open to him, the San Bernardino County District Attorney's Office refused to discuss the case.

During the summer of 2009, I made arrangements to interview Kevin Cooper in a visitor's cell on death row at San Quentin. On several issues, particularly those regarding his criminal record previous to the Chino Hills trial, I found him protective and less than forthcoming. That was all behind him, he seemed to suggest.

On the other hand, I was taken by his equanimity and his resolve to prove he was wrongfully convicted of the gruesome Chino Hills murders. I could see that the many years he had spent on death row, instead of diminishing him, had turned him into a person worthy of the high regard that his supporters—and his attorneys at the Orrick law firm—felt for him. On death row, Kevin Cooper had finally grown up.

Contrary to popular belief, most of the nation's more than three-thou-sand-five-hundred death row inmates do not profess innocence. In fact, unlike Kevin Cooper, very few do. For those who do, the road to exonera-tion is a long, slow trek that usually fails. But it does succeed occasionally. Since 1973, when the U.S. Supreme Court allowed states to resume execu-tions, one-hundred-thirty-six death-row inmates have been exonerated. In the majority of those cases, the proof of the inmate's innocence was so convincing that the prosecutor dropped the charges rather than retry the case. In forty-five cases where there was a retrial, the inmate was acquitted.

There are two things that do link the Mumia Abu-Jamal and Kevin Cooper cases: Each was prosecuted by a district attorney's office hell bent on winning a death-penalty conviction; and neither defendant received a proper defense. What separates the two cases is that, while Mumia's trial was a mockery of the justice system's standards for a fair trial, Cooper's trial had the trappings of fairness—but was lost long before the trial opened. Two pre-trial developments caused this outcome: The San Bernardino County Sheriff's Department destroyed evidence that could have exonerated Cooper; and his public defender insisted on going it alone. Not many Davids actually slay Goliaths.

This then is a book about a gruesome murder case, painfully recounted; all quotes are from either documents or interviews I conducted doing my research. It is also a book about how justice can go astray. It is the true story of the Chino Hills murders, and the prosecution of Kevin Cooper, a prisoner who escaped once too often and found himself in the wrong place at the wrong time. Since 1985, he has been on death row at San Quentin asserting his innocence in failed-after-failed appeal while awaiting his execution.

CHAPTER ONE

Chino Hills

Five years after Mexico ceded California to the United States in 1848, the County of San Bernardino was formed out of the vast expanses of deserts and mountains of Los Angeles County.

In most ways it is the exact opposite of its glitzy neighbor to the west. While Los Angeles County is home to the City of Angels, Hollywood, Pasadena, Brentwood, Malibu, Bel Air and Westwood, a majority of Americans could not name any city in San Bernardino County other than the county seat itself. This is as it has always been, since the town of San Bernardino was so named on May 20, 1810 by Father Francisco Dumetz, a Franciscan missionary, to honor the feast day of Saint Bernardino of Siena.

What San Bernardino County lacks in national lore, it makes up for in size alone. It is the largest county in the continental United States, encompassing over twenty-thousand square miles that sprawl from the Riverside-San Bernardino area to the Nevada border and the Colorado River. It is larger than nine U.S. states and is larger in area than Maryland, Delaware, Rhode Island and Massachusetts combined. It is the only county in California to border both Arizona and Nevada.

The San Bernardino Valley is at the eastern end of the San Gabriel Valley, and, along with Riverside County, is part of the Inland Empire, so named to distinguish the region from the coastal areas of Los Angeles County. The San Bernardino Valley includes the cities of Chino, Chino Hills, Colton, Fontana, Grand Terrace, Hesperia, Highland, Loma Linda, Ontario, Rancho Cucamonga, Redlands, Rialto, San Bernardino, Upland, and Yucaipa.

Chino Hills is nestled in the southwest corner of San Bernardino
County. Its forty-five square miles of rolling hills border Los Angeles
County on its northwest side, Orange County to the south, and Riverside
County to the southeast. In 1771 the Spanish founded Mission San Ga-
briel and began using the area to graze the mission's cattle.

Developer Richard Gird bought the land in 1910, the same year he
founded the nearby city of Chino. During Prohibition the Carbon Canyon
Mineral Springs opened for business and the Los Serranos County Club
soon followed, drawing both day visitors from Los Angeles and bootleg-
gers to the isolated area.

By the mid-1970s, Chino Hills was still unincorporated with less than
twenty-thousand residents. About half of Chino Hills consisted of unde-
veloped grazing land for equestrian ranchers and dairy farmers. Over the
next twenty years the area experienced rapid development. When Chino
Hills was incorporated in 1991, its population had more than doubled to
forty-two thousand residents.

A somewhat worrisome aspect of life in Chino Hills is the presence of
a major state prison located just three miles away with over four-thousand
convicted felons. Over the preceding ten years, escapes had occurred with
unsettling frequency, ranging from eight to thirty per year.

The California Institute for Men sits in a barren southwest corner of
San Bernardino County, sandwiched between two state highways, in the
town of Chino. When it opened in 1941 it was known as "The Prison
Without Walls." Its first warden, Kenyon Scudder, believed in education
and rehabilitation. He took the title of superintendant and the guards –
all unarmed – were referred to as "supervisors." The only fence Scudder
allowed on the two-thousand-six-hundred acre property was a low barbed-
wire one erected to keep dairy cows from wandering through the prison
complex. In 1952 Doubleday published Warden Scudder's seminal work
on penology, *Prisoners Are People*. The 1955 movie, *Unchained*, was based
on his book. Chester Morris of Boston Blackie fame played the role of the
groundbreaking superintendent.

As California's prison population exploded in the 1970s – thanks in part
to the crackdown on drugs and the overcrowding that produced throughout

the state's prison system – CIM devolved to the traditional mode of simply incarcerating prisoners in maximum, medium, and minimum-security facilities.

The minimum-security area, the only holdover from the Scudder days in terms of appearance, sits in an open, grassy area with dorms, surrounded by a waist-high, chain-linked fence. Guards do not patrol its perimeter.

CHAPTER TWO

The Ryens of Chino Hill

he secluded area of Chino Hills that Doug and Peggy Ryen and
their two-year-old daughter, Jessica, and infant son, Joshua, moved
into in 1975 fulfilled a long-held dream for Peggy Ryen, joining a small,
close-knit community of Arabian horse breeders who operated adjoining
or close-by ranches. Their neighbors referred to their ranches along Old
English Road as the "Arabian Horse Center of Southern California."

From their hilltop house, the Ryens looked out over a maze of white
fences that hemmed in their and their neighbors' ranches. In the Ryens'
stables were more than a dozen white Arabian show horses, including their
champion stallion, Tutal.

Peggy had owned her own horses since she was twelve years old, gifts
from her twice divorced mother, Dr. Mary Howell. Peggy loved to train
horses and enter them in competitions near her mother's chiropractic
practice in Lititz, Pennsylvania, not far from Lancaster. As a teen she as-
pired to be become a veterinarian, but her mother persuaded her to follow
in her footsteps. Like her mother, Peggy attended the Palmer School of
Chiropractic in Davenport, Iowa, graduating in 1963 and then joined her
mother's chiropractic clinic in Santa Ana. Three-and-half years later, Peggy
opted to venture out on her own, opening her own clinic in Santa Ana. At
an alumni reunion at Palmer in 1970, Peggy Ann Howell met Franklin
Douglas Ryen, an ex-Marine who was in the final year of the school's
four-year program and who by now was separated from the woman he had
married in 1964. Doug, who descended from Norwegian ancestry, grew up
on the outskirts of Des Moines, Iowa.

At a Lutheran Church in Corona Del Mar, California, two months after Doug's divorce was finalized, Doug and Peggy were married on December 20, 1970. For eighteen months, Doug joined Peggy at her clinic, but when Peggy became pregnant they decided to sell the practice. They used the $10,000 proceeds to open their own clinic in Olympia, Washington. Peggy bought her first two Arabian horses and threw herself into training them. Jessica Kate Ryen was born in Olympia on November 9, 1972.

In Olympia, as they would be to an even greater degree in Southern California, the horses were an economic burden. The cost to maintain them strapped the couple for cash. At one point, Peggy was forced to tap her mother for money to buy hay. With Peggy's new responsibilities as a mother and her dedication to her horses, establishing the new chiropractic clinic fell mostly to Doug. With the practice failing to take hold, the Ryens reluctantly opted to close their Olympia clinic and accept Mary Howell's offer to join her successful and lucrative chiropractic clinic in Santa Ana in mid-1973.

The Ryens, thanks to a $5,000 down payment provided by Dr. Howell, bought a home in Santa Ana with a backyard big enough to hold the Arabians. By December Peggy had three Arabians in her backyard, one still in Olympia, and one in training about thirty-five miles away. Her mare was pregnant. In a post-Christmas letter to her half-sister Lillian Shaffer, she wrote, "We can't wait for our 'big mama' to have her baby…We're hoping for a filly (girl)—they sell for more."

The hand-written letter was on newly printed stationery inscribed "Ryen Arabian Ranch" that Doug had given her for Christmas. "Where we are now we should call it 'Backyard Arabians!' Look out a window and see a horse looking back at you—but we love it," Peggy wrote.

When the Ryens' neighbors in Santa Ana began to complain persistently about Peggy keeping her horses in her backyard, Dr. Howell bought a four-bedroom house in Chino Hills with six acres so the horses could be kept there.

In another letter to Lillian, this one written in May of 1974, Peggy brimmed with enthusiasm about her plans to breed and train Arabian horses. "Right now we are horse poor, but give us five years of our planned breeding program and we'll have only the best. It's so exciting! Finally, after all of these years of wanting I've got what I've always wanted."

She wrote about Doug and her watching their mare foal at 2:30 a.m and described the newborn as "a real pistol." They named him Barna-B, but "of course we call him Barny." She said because Barny was a full brother to their dark stallion, he would be for sale later on. "It's so much fun having a little one to train since our other youngests are two years old already. Jessa loves having one her size around."

In other news, Peggy mentioned buying a five-year-old Arabian stallion she named Scruffy, and arranging to impregnate one of her mares with the highly regarded stud, Sahara Prince, whose photo was on the back cover of the current Arabian horse magazine. "We'll have the foal next year. Can't wait to see his babies—we should make a mint when we sell that one."

Her other two mares were going to be bred to two top stallions also featured in that issue of the magazine. "These stallions are pure polish and really gorgeous animals," she wrote. "The dark stud's fee is $1,500, a real bargain. The blood line of our one mare is a very valuable cross and the foals are going for $20,000 or so. Untrained! But we won't sell that one—I'll show it next year."

Her other mare would be bred to the white stud shown in the magazine "and what a movin' machine we'll have from that cross."

With three foals on the way next year and one already born, the Ryens began ranch hunting. By now, Peggy was pregnant again. Several months after Dr. Howell moved to Chino Hills, a five-acre, a hilltop ranch directly above Dr. Howell's house came on the market. Doug and Peggy Ryen sold their home in Santa Ana and bought it. Peggy said that the property came with "a gorgeous barn and huge riding ring but rotten house! Oh well, we can always change that." The three-bedroom, two-bath house featured a sunken living room, a family room, and a Jacuzzi in the patio off the master bedroom. The Ryens would never get around to fixing up the well-worn house.

CHAPTER THREE

June 4, 1983

On Saturday, June 4, 1983, the Ryens and eleven-year-old Chris Hughes attended a potluck barbeque dinner with about a hundred other Arabian horse people and their families at the Chino home of George and Valerie Blade. George Blade made his living as a horse shoer, a service he had provided the Ryens for the past eight years. It was a BYOL affair. Doug and Peggy brought a bottle of pink Chablis. Earlier that afternoon, Chris called home to get permission to spend the night with his friend Josh. That night, the Blades' young son, Jason, pleaded with his parents to allow him to spend the night at the Ryens' as well, but he was not allowed to because his grandmother was visiting and it was already 9 p.m., an hour after his normal bedtime.

Around 9:30 p.m. the Ryens and Chris returned to the Ryens' rambling, split-level, pentagon-shaped home. After awhile, the children went to sleep, the boys in sleeping bags on the floor in Josh's room and Jessica in her room. Doug Ryen watched some television before joining his wife in bed, probably after 11 p.m. As was their custom, the couple slept in the nude in their king-size waterbed.

When Chris did not come home at 9 a.m. to join his family for church the next morning, his mother, Mary Ann Hughes, began calling the Ryens' house only to get repeated busy signals. At 11 a.m. she drove the short distance to the Ryens' house, went to the front door and knocked. When no one answered, she tried to open the door but found it locked. She walked around to the west side of the house and looked into the children's bedrooms but could not see or hear anyone. She called out several names but got no response. She noticed that the Ryens' station wagon was gone and then drove home to ask her husband to go take a look.

Bill Hughes, an agriculture professor at Cal Poly Pomona, got in his Audi and drove up to the Ryens' house. He went to the front door, but no one answered and the door was locked. Hughes went around to peer through a sliding glass door into the Ryens' master bedroom. He could not at first believe what he was seeing. "It was a very bloody scene and my first recollection was that this can't be blood, this is paint, makeup…I thought what kind of crazy game is this?"

Peggy Ryen was lying on her back naked in the middle of the room and Doug Ryen, also nude, was kneeling over by the edge of the bed. Both were covered in blood. Not far from Mrs. Ryen, Chris Hughes was lying on his stomach and Josh, drenched in blood and curled up in a fetal position, was near him. Josh was moving, but his eyes were glazed and the left side of his head was "gashed up." Josh had been left for dead with his throat slit from ear to ear, a hatchet blow to his head that fractured his skull, several stab wounds to his back that broke three of his ribs and collapsed one lung, broke his collarbone, and nearly severed his left ear. He had survived by keeping his fingers pressed to his throat to staunch the bleeding, and then going into shock for eleven hours until help arrived.

Hughes tried to enter through the glass door, but couldn't budge it. The door was unlocked, but in his panic, he was tugging it the wrong way. He yelled to Josh to open it. Josh tried to move but could not. Hughes ran around to another side of the house and kicked in the kitchen door. In the kitchen were the Ryens' Irish setter, their golden retriever, and three kittens playing on the floor. "I thought that was strange, that they were playing," Hughes recalled. As he approached the master bedroom he saw the bloodied, incredibly lacerated body of Jessica Ryen, sprawled across the doorway. He reached down and touched her and by her stiffness knew she was dead. He entered the master bedroom and called out to Josh. When Josh looked at him, Hughes asked him what had happened, but Josh could only mumble. He told Josh to just lie there.

Hughes checked his son and the Ryens for signs of life and found instead massive face and head wounds. Rigor mortis had set in. Hughes tried to call 911 from the Ryens, but both phones were out of order. He raced to a neighbor's house and asked Bob Howey to call the police and request an ambulance for Josh. Hughes, recalling that he was "somewhat in a state of shock," went home to tell his wife what he had seen while Howey went up to the Ryens to wait with Josh until help could arrive.

A crew of six from the Chino Fire Department—three paramedics and three firefighters—arrived and soon began treating Josh in the master bedroom about 12:30 p.m. Josh was lying on his left side, with his head turned toward the end of the water bed. Ruben Guerrero, a fire department medic, put some Vaseline on Josh's neck wound, then gauzed and bandaged it. He then rolled Josh over on his back and attempted to start an IV but could not locate a vein in his arm. Josh was manifesting numerous signs of being in shock: no bleeding from an open wound, no blood pressure and no pulse. His system had literally shut down, but he was able to raise eight fingers when Guerrero asked him how old he was. The medic tore Josh's pajama top off and cut his clothes away and washed away some of the blood and fecal matter on him with a white towel another medic removed from the master bedroom bathroom. The towel ended up on Peggy Ryen's leg.

As the medics were treating Josh, a firefighter was coming in and out of the master bedroom, providing treatment advice being relayed from the emergency room of Loma Linda University Hospital. In response, Guerrero placed anti-shock trousers—called a MAST suit—on Josh. Anti-shock pants are used to get any blood that is pulled to the lower extremities back up to the vital organs.

A little after 1 p.m., a helicopter arrived and air-lifted Josh to the nearby hospital, arriving there at 1:36 p.m. En route, an IV was started and an oxygen mask attached. Josh was given ten liters of oxygen a minute, a substantial amount.

At 1:50 p.m. Dr. Imad Shahhal, a neurosurgeon, began operating on Josh's head wounds as another team of surgeons began treating the wounds to his neck. Dr. Shahhal found Josh surprisingly responsive. As he shaved the boy's head he could see the fracture in Josh's skull. He cleaned and sutured the wound. Another surgeon, Dr. Larry Habenicht, inserted an endotracheal tube in Josh's windpipe to aid his breathing.

CHAPTER FOUR

A Massacre

San Bernardino County Sheriff's Department Deputy Paul Beltz was the first officer at the crime scene, arriving six minutes ahead of the paramedics. Dispatch had told him to go to 2943 Old English Road, a homicide scene with one survivor. Beltz, with his gun drawn, entered through the kitchen door. He soon saw Jessica sprawled in the bedroom doorway and checked her for vital signs. He stepped over her to enter the master bedroom. "I thought, my God, what in the hell have I come across. The walls were all white, but smeared with blood—I mean everywhere," he told a newspaper reporter from the *Daily Bulletin*. "It was like something you see in a *Helter Skelter* movie. That must have been one holy battlefield. I felt inadequate holding a handgun."

The murders had an uncommon viciousness to them, as if the killers meant not only to kill, but to send a message of payback or retribution. There would be no open caskets at these funerals. Each of the murder victims sustained numerous deep chopping wounds to the face and head and stabbing wounds to the body inflicted by a long knife. An ice pick was also used. Many of the wounds to Jessica Ryen were meted out post-mortem. The autopsy reports stated that more than one-hundred-forty wounds, twenty-eight fractures, and two amputations were inflicted on the four murder victims.

Forty-one-year-old Doug Ryen was found slumped kneeling against his bed, the victim of thirty-seven hatchet and knife wounds. Two of the hatchet blows fractured his skull. One of the knife wounds to his chest penetrated five inches through the right pleura cavity and then through the right lung. Another transected the left carotid artery causing extensive hemorrhage and arterial blood spraying on the wall behind the water bed. He sustained that injury on the opposite side of the bed from where his body was found, indicating he was mobile during part of the onslaught. Oddly, all four fingertips of his left hand were lightly touching the edge of the waterbed on his side of the bed. Another indication that the solidly built six-foot-two chiropractor had at least a few moments to attempt to ward off the attack was a severed finger on his right hand. The blow that amputated the finger was delivered with such force that the finger was propelled into a bedroom closet. Also suggesting that Doug actively resisted the attack were a number of defensive-type wounds slashed into both of his arms, one of them fracturing the ulna of his right forearm above his wrist.

Peggy Ryen, also forty-one years old, was positioned in the middle of the bedroom with her arms straight out, her left leg straight out and her right knee slightly bent inward, much as though she had been nailed to a cross. The blood drain pattern running from her right thigh to her right foot indicated to the medical examiner, Dr. Irving Root, that she was standing when she incurred that wound. He said the bruising near her nose indicated that she was alive for one to three minutes after being hacked in the left cheek. A smudge pattern on her left knee meant "she had to be elsewhere for a period of time" from where her body was found. During the attack, and while still alive, she suffered hatchet wounds to both her face and the back of her head and a stab wound to her left breast.

Her body was covered with smeared dried blood and what the deputy coroner, David Hammock, described in his crime scene report "as a number of loose hairs about the subject body, including some very long brown hair, both on the left thigh and, in particular, about the auxiliary areas and arms. These hairs are longer than the subject's own head hair."

Peggy sustained seventeen hatchet wounds to the forehead, face and chest and four separate knife wounds to her chest. She, too, showed signs of resisting the attack, with stab wounds on fingers of both hands and left forearm. The hatchet wounds exposed her skull to the bone and caused multiple skull fractures. The medical examiner listed thirty-three separate wounds, most of them delivered with great force and destruction.

Although San Bernardino County Sheriff Floyd Tidwell told the media that the killings were in no way "ritualistic," a good deal of staging could be inferred from the placement of both Doug and Peggy Ryen's bodies. It was as equally unlikely that Doug Ryen would have died kneeling with his fingertips barely touching the front side of the bed as it was for his wife to have died with her body splayed straight out in a T.

Jessica, who died with a clump of blond or light brown hair clutched in her fingers, sustained the most wounds, forty-six, and had the most defensive type wounds to her hands and arms. Her autopsy reported eight separate stabbing wounds to her right forearm and four to her right hand and wrist. The little finger of her left hand was cut to the bone. At four-feet-nine-inches and eighty pounds, she apparently sustained all those wounds before succumbing to having her forehead and face hacked in and her throat deeply slit. One hatchet blow to the right side of her mouth was delivered with so much force that it caused three of her teeth to dislodge from her gums.

A knife was dragged across her back and then inserted. Dr. Root said the bruising around the entry wound indicated it occurred early on in the assault.

In another display of staging, Jessica's chest was dotted with twenty puncture wounds most likely inflicted post-mortem with an ice pick in what the medical examiner described as showing "some type of pattern." Her head was twisted up so that her heavily mutilated face was visible.

Some of Jessica's hair was found on her mother's body. This led Dr. Root "to believe the mother was cradling her daughter at one point during the attack."

Chris Hughes endured twenty-six separate wounds, including a deep hatchet gash that ran from his eyebrows to the tip of his nose. He sustained numerous skull fractures. He was stabbed clear through his sternum. His hands, wrist and arms also revealed numerous defensive wounds: his left arm was nearly severed and the second finger on his right hand was attached by a flap of skin.

Theft did not appear to be a motive for the killings. In reviewing the crime scene the day the murders were discovered, Detective John Clifford saw no signs of ransacking. On a counter between the kitchen and the dining room, he saw coins and some bills in plain view next to Peggy Ryen's purse. Her purse contained over $40 in cash and numerous credit cards. There was also a small amount of cash in Doug's pants. Clifford also located a coin collection in a safety deposit box on the upper shelf of a master bedroom closet. Also visible in the bedroom was a jewelry box with jewels in it, as well as a video camera, stereo system, and a TV with a VCR. In a nightstand drawer less than five feet from where Peggy Ryen's body was laying, he found a loaded .22 Ruger pistol. In Doug Ryen's closet, about two feet from where his body was found, was a loaded .22 caliber Winchester Magnum rifle with scope attached. An unloaded Smith & Wesson pellet gun was on the bottom shelf of that closest. Doug Ryen's wallet was missing, but it would be found under the front seat of his pickup truck in late July. Only the Ryens' station wagon had been stolen. Their pickup truck, a 1976 Chevy Silverado with "Ryen Arabians Chino California" printed on the side, was still in the driveway with the keys in it.

CHAPTER FIVE

The Crime Scene

N *ot since the Tate-LaBianca murders in 1969* had California law enforcement been called to a more grisly crime scene than when the Ryen/Hughes murders were discovered on June 5, 1983. The white walls of the Ryens' master bedroom were spattered with an uncommon amount of blood and the victims' bodies were strewn about in grotesque positions, one of them clutching hair in her hands, indicating a fierce battle for their lives.

Four people had been murdered in a frenzied, vicious and stunningly quick attack and a small boy left for dead with a hatchet wound to his head, his throat slashed, and knife stabs in his back.

If any crime scene called for extraordinary care and preservation, this one did. It had already been contaminated by Bill Hughes when he entered the house and the master bedroom to discover the crime and by neighbor Bob Howey who stood by Josh Ryen until medical help arrived. Three paramedics assisted Josh in the master bedroom, accompanied by three firefighters.

Shortly after Josh was evacuated, the coroner and the medical examiner arrived at the scene to begin processing the bodies. As they worked, deputies moved about the room taking pictures and doing measurements prior to the removal of the bodies to the morgue.

Even with all that unavoidable intrusion, an entire scenario of how the murders took place could be recreated with diligent detective and forensic work. There was blood splatter on all the walls and the ceiling and on every object in the room.

The blood drops on the walls of the master bedroom had hit the wall from different directions. Some of the drops were big, some small, some roundish, some speckled, some looked like exclamation points, and all were going in different directions. While the bodies were still in the master bedroom, lab technician David Stockwell began scraping the blood drops off six separate sections of the walls and placed them all in one canister, mixing them together, making it impossible for anyone later to tell which drops came from which spots on the walls.

He followed the same procedure for cutting blood drops from parts of the bedding, mixing those samples together without noting what sections of the bedding each sample came from. When he was done cutting samples from the top bed sheet, he packaged the sheet in the same paper sack that contained the tourniquet the paramedics had used on Josh. No photos were taken of the sheet before the cuttings commenced.

The blood on the walls and ceiling, bed linens, furnishings, and carpet, coupled with the placement of the victims' bodies would have shown the approximate movements of each victim prior to death if these blood samples had been collected properly and later matched to the victims' blood types. Stockwell's collection procedures had destroyed this opportunity.

During the first two days following the discovery of the murders, what remained of the crime scene would be compromised beyond reconstruction when over forty San Bernardino County Sheriff's deputies, detectives and brass traipsed through the crime scene. During the first few hours of the investigation, as many as twelve sheriff's department personnel congregated in the master bedroom at one time. So did District Attorney Kottmeier and three deputy D.A.s from the San Bernardino District Attorney's office. The next day two local reporters were allowed to stand on the patio outside the master bedroom and shoot footage of the crime scene.

It would be the district attorney, not the lead detective on the case, who would order the tearing down of the crime scene at the Ryen house the day after the murders were discovered, saying he did not want "another Manson defense possible" in regard to the massive blood evidence. Asked in 2010 what he meant by this reference to the Manson case crime scene,

Kottmeier said he could not exactly remember, but that he did not want to "have a defense expert come in and say, 'Look what I found.'" He said he feared the defense "fabricating evidence."

A district attorney taking such a direct role that early in a murder investigation is virtually unprecedented. The normal practice is for a D.A. to wait until the police investigation develops evidence sufficient for an indictment to get involved. Kottmeier's inserting himself into this high-profile case by ordering the dismantling of the crime scene deprived both the sheriff department's investigators and later on Cooper's defense from ever being able to determine the movements of the victims or the order of their deaths. Such information was of crucial importance in answering the question of how many perpetrators were involved in the devastating assault.

Kottmeier was in such a rush to have the crime scene dismantled that he ordered the removal of the blood-splattered walls, doors, and furnishing while the crime lab team was collecting evidence in the master bedroom, halting that process in its tracks on the second day of the investigation. It was as though an entire sheriff's department had forgotten in unison the most basic rules of investigation and crime scene preservation.

In their needless haste, deputies preserved an insufficient amount of blood samples from the master bedroom and nearby hallway before the murder scene was torn down. The blood samples they did remove were not recorded properly to show their relationship to the victims' bodies. Other blood samples were disregarded or destroyed. For example, deputies noted blood on the refrigerator, a light switch, and on a beer can—blood that may have been left by one or more of the assailants—but none of this blood evidence was preserved or tested. Within hours of discovering the murders, deputies found one of the presumed murder weapons, a bloody hatchet, near the Ryens' house just off the only paved road leading away from it. In unsuccessfully dusting the hatchet for latent fingerprints, deputies destroyed the blood evidence.

Due to the botched crime-scene investigation, lead detective Billy Arthur never developed a workable theory of how the attack occurred, of how the house was entered or the order in which the murders took place, other than Chris Hughes, based on Josh's recollections, being the last to die.

CHAPTER SIX

Motive

Understanding motive is a key element in any murder investigation. Considering the raw rage that the Ryen/Hughes murders represented, the San Bernardino Sheriff's Department was not oblivious to the possibility that the Ryens had been targeted out of vengeance. Early on the investigation turned to delving into the private lives of Doug and Peggy Ryen, searching to find some plausible motive to explain the horrific deaths inflicted.

The first person of interest Sergeant Arthur wanted tracked down was Doug Ryen's first wife, Lucille Ann Sachs. He assigned Detective Acevedo to locate her. Acevedo used divorce records dating from September of 1970 at San Diego Superior Court to inform Arthur that she lived in Escondido, California. Interviewed, she was quickly cleared of suspicion.

Another early suspect was a seventeen-year-old girl who had worked for about a month at the Ryens' ranch cleaning out stalls and grooming horses until Peggy Ryen discharged her three weeks before the murders and withheld her last paycheck. She was viewed as a pot-smoking flake.

As early as two days after discovering the murders, deputies began interviewing neighbors, friends, and work associates of the Ryens, digging into their private matters, including reviewing all the Ryens' various bank accounts and credit card histories. They wanted to know if either of the Ryens was having an extra-marital affair, did they engage in group sex with friends or strangers in their Jacuzzi, did they do drugs, did Doug drink too much, did he gamble, were they pressed for money, did they owe anyone a lot of money, had they recently updated their wills, did they have any known enemies.

The interviews generated a hodge-podge of responses that portrayed the Ryens as a normal couple and dedicated parents beset with the usual tensions of any marriage, most of which stemmed from the financial drag operating an Arabian horse ranch brought on. The Ryens were hard-working but strapped for cash. They did not do drugs and did not engage in orgies despite their well-known practice of sleeping in the nude, and like thousands of other Californians, they had an outside Jacuzzi. Doug did go to Las Vegas a couple of times a year and, on occasion, he drank too much, but his gambling appeared moderate.

Doug's drinking emerged as a cause of concern. One seventeen-year-old neighbor told a deputy that on the nights when Doug would get drunk, Peggy would send the children to a neighbor's house to spend the night so that the children would not see him that way. She also said that too much drink could lead Doug to make "advances on women," as he had once to her. She said Peggy told her not to worry about it because that's the way Doug gets and her husband would not remember the incident the next day.

Doug's sister, Cindy Settle, who was just a year younger, described Doug in an interview: "He was a flirt. It's just his nature. He's happy, he smiles, he flirts. I'm a lot like him. Everybody says I'm a flirt too. We're just basically happy people—not for any particular reason—that's just the way we are. All through high school, all the girls loved him and their mothers did too. He was a charmer. I remember him telling almost all of my closest girlfriends that he loved them."

Other tidbits that popped out of these interviews were that the Ryens had recently settled an IRS suit by paying $6,000; the Ryens had redone their wills five months earlier, and that Doug was biased against Mexicans and Vietnamese.

The Ryens operated a chiropractic clinic in Santa Ana, but the focus of their lives was raising their children and operating their horse ranch. Peggy only worked at the clinic one day a week so she could be free to operate the ranch. She loved to train the horses and show them at competitions, usually held on Saturdays at the Carnation Ring at the Pomona Fairgrounds in Los Angeles County. According to the office manager at the clinic, Catherine Rhoads, the practice was doing "pretty well" and certainly better than the horse business. In his June 15, 1983 report, Homicide Detective Tim Wilson stated that Rhoads told him "the chiropractic business was doing financially better than the horse business and often times she would transfer money from the chiropractic account into the Ryen Arabian Horse account."

Asked by Wilson if either of the Ryens had a separate bank account that the other did not know about, Rhoads told him, "Dr. Peg did have a separate savings account unknown to Dr. Doug and the purpose of this account was so she could save up some money as she wanted to get some horse stud service from a special ranch up in Santa Barbara."

Aside from the unsupported possibility of extra-marital affairs, there were two primary theories investigators thought might explain the Ryens' horrendous deaths. In some way, perhaps through drugs available to them at their clinic or their horse ranch, a drug deal had gone bad or some transaction involving their horses had soured. Three weeks before the murders the Ryens repossessed a horse they had sold to a woman who lived in Los Angeles County. "The lady was quite upset over losing the horse," Deputy Dale Sharp noted in his June 7, 1983 report about an interview he had conducted with a friend of the family.

In a report filed by Detective Michael Hall the next day, he wrote, "I received information regarding an alleged $250,000 horse transaction that went awry." Hall's source was a woman in the Arabian horse circuit who had known the Ryens for the past eight years. She recounted Doug telling her four months earlier about the high offer he had received for a young stud horse named "The Boy," that had not yet been studded out. She said Doug told her the offer had been made by three or four men representing a horse-breeding syndicate based in Scottsdale, Arizona. When she ran into Doug three months later he told her "he had decided not to go through with the sale of the horse."

Hall asked her why anyone would pay $250,000 for a horse that had never been tested as a stud. She said this particular horse had "perfect lines for an Arabian horse with the small head, elongated neck, and there's other features."

Hall asked the woman to speculate about the horse's value now that the Ryens were deceased and the horse possibly sold at a probate auction. She said the value could drop to "the four digit range." That suggested the remote possibility that the Scottsdale breeders may have murdered the Ryens to save themselves over $200,000 in purchase fees, but the woman could not identify who they were.

The possibility of other enemies surfaced when a correctional officer at the nearby California Institute for Men, Donnie Eddings, wrote a memo to her superior stating that an inmate by the name of Luparello had confided to her that a Hispanic gang known as "A-Troop" had murdered the Ryens out of vengeance. The inmate told Eddings that earlier in 1983 the Ryens' chiropractic clinic in Santa Ana had been burglarized—which it had been—and Doug Ryen had either pressed charges against members of the gang or had testified against them. If anyone connected with the investigation pursued this lead remains unknown. (The Ryens' clinic was burglarized about three weeks before their murders. The suspects had been apprehended and the items stolen from the clinic—a typewriter, a copier and some other office items—had been recovered and subsequently identified by Doug at the police station. Doug had been scheduled to appear in court as a witness on June 3, but the trial had been postponed.)

In May of 1984, Sergeant Billy Arthur conducted an extensive tape-recorded interview with Caryn Rhiner at the homicide office. Rhiner had been hired by the Ryens as a babysitter about six years earlier, when Josh was three and Jessica five. From her, Arthur would learn intimate details about each of the Ryens.

Peggy Ryen originally hired her to babysit on Wednesdays when she worked her day at the clinic and Doug was running errands or home working on the ranch. Over time, as her duties expanded to taking care of the house and the horses when the Ryens were away for a day or more—sometimes for a week at a time—she became an integral part of the household, the one non-family person the protective Ryens would trust with their children. She felt as though she had a special relationship with the children and Doug and Peggy.

Arthur's first substantive question concerned how the Ryens secured the house when they were home. She told him they only locked the wooden front doors, but did not lock the kitchen door because it provided a direct route to the horse barn. They did not lock the sliding glass doors in the living room or the master bedroom. With all the windows around the house, Rhiner felt like she was in a fish bowl. Only the children's rooms had curtains. Arthur told her he felt the same way when he was in the house—exposed—and asked her if she had ever discussed the Ryens' reasoning for living so "open to the world?"

"Well, their whole attitude...was that it was a rural area...that they were way up on a hill and there was nothing around there, and they didn't really have to worry about that and then they had the dogs running loose all the time," Rhiner said.

The issue of the dogs was one of the most perplexing aspects of this case. How could intruders surprise the Ryens, who had loaded guns in their bedroom, without first setting off loud and persistent barking from the Ryens' dogs?

Doug was known to get out of bed in the middle of the night and shoot at coyotes with his rifle when he heard the dogs barking.

Rhiner explained that when she house-sat for the Ryens several weeks before the murders that Peggy had told her that they were bringing the dogs in at night due to the coyotes.

The fact that the dogs were in the house the night of the murders did not mean they would not have been barking if someone tried to enter the home. Rhiner, confirming what several others interviewed by detectives told them, said the dogs barked at her every time she came in the house and would keep barking until she shushed them, particularly an Irish Setter named Ruffy, whom she described as "a real big mouth."

Arthur asked her if the dogs were vicious.

"No. But they were real good watch dogs…they would have barked."

In addition to the Irish setter, there was a male golden retriever that liked to roam the canyons above the house. The Ryens bred him to one of their other dogs and had a mixed-breed puppy. The other dog was a mutt, a stray Peggy adopted about eighteen months before the attack.

Whether the dogs barked or not is not known. Josh said he did not hear them barking that night nor did he see any of them during the attack. Strangely, the dog that normally slept in Josh's room each night was not there when he was awakened by his mother's screams. None of the dogs was harmed. Larry Lease, who lived four-hundred yards down the road below the Ryens' house, was attending a mare birthing a foal at the time of the murders and he reported hearing no commotion.

One explanation for the dogs not barking would be that the home was entered through the sliding doors to the master bedroom, far enough away from where the dogs slept not to wake them. Another would be that the assailants had already entered the house before the Ryens and Chris returned and hid until everyone went to sleep.

Although, according to Rhiner, Doug was a heavy sleeper and difficult to awake in the morning, he had only been in bed for less than an hour when his home was breached. The defensive wounds on his hands and arms showed that he had at least a brief opportunity to fend off the attack. His ability to counter the attack may have been impeded by his blood-alcohol content. The pathologist estimated he had a blood alcohol level of .21, more than twice the level considered inebriated in California. A criminologist explained that the alcohol level in decomposing bodies could account for up to .10 of the reading, a factor that would drop Doug's actual alcohol level to .11 percent.

Doug's drinking was something that Rhiner brought up on her own when Arthur asked her if she had anything else she wanted to tell him. She responded, "Okay, uh, Doug's drinking." Arthur did not encourage her to pursue the topic, saying he thought they had already covered it sufficiently. "Well, what about what Peg used to say about it?" she asked him. He told her to go ahead.

Rhiner said Doug did not drink to the point where he was "staggering around," but his eyes would get red and he would "get real friendly." She said one time Peggy told her Doug's drinking was such a problem that she had considered leaving him, but stayed with him because of the children. She recounted an incident where Doug had driven the station wagon into a palm tree and said Peggy "was furious about that—really upset, and it upset her because she was worried about the kids."

Rhiner told him a spotlight illuminated the peak of the house near the Ryens' master bedroom and a light over the barn would turn on in response to movement.

Arthur also wanted to ask Rhiner about the house directly below the Ryens' house, the one Dr. Howell purchased prior to the Ryens moving to Chino Hills. When Dr. Howell put the house on the market in 1980, she allowed Rhiner and her husband to live there for two months. Arthur asked her if she could see the Ryens' house from there. She said she could only see it from the backyard patio. From there she could see only the peaked roof that jutted out a number of feet over the Ryens' living room. If she walked further into the backyard, she could see the top part of the living room window and the top part of the sliding glass door to the living room.

When Arthur asked her if she could see movement in the Ryens' house at night, she said you could not unless you climbed to the top of a bank of plants on the west side of the house and looked from there, something she said she had never done.

The big question Arthur wanted answered—so he asked it again in a different way—was could she see the Ryens' house from any vantage point inside the house below, suggesting she might have been able to see it from the northwest corner of the house next to the fireplace. "If you would see anything, you would see the roof," she answered.

Nor could she see the Ryens' driveway and their vehicles parked there.

CHAPTER SEVEN

Suspects

I n addition to the medical examiner's initial conclusion about multiple assailants, as well as the presence of blond or light brown hair in
Jessica's hand, the sheriff's department fielded a steady stream of developing evidence that pointed to three or four white men as the murderers.
One witness would even name one of the likely killers, her boyfriend, a
convicted murderer.

The first indication of multiple white assailants came from communications Josh Ryen provided to hospital personnel and a deputy sheriff in the
emergency room shortly after he arrived for treatment. Based on the input
from Josh, police logs from that day showed that law enforcement was
looking for three white men driving the Ryens' station wagon.

This possibility was soon supported by eyewitness accounts to the
sheriff's department. The next day, Linda Edwards, one of the Ryens'
neighbors, told Detective Tim Wilson that around midnight on the night
of the murders she saw what she thought was the Ryens' station wagon—a
white 1977 Buick with wood paneling and a luggage rack—driving away
from their house toward Peyton Road at a rapid rate of speed. She said she
thought perhaps there was an emergency.

Further down Peyton Road, Douglas Leonard was pulling out of a
driveway but had to wait for a station wagon barreling down the road from
the direction of the Ryen house. When the Ryen/Hughes murders were
reported the next day, Leonard informed Lieutenant Knadler of the San
Bernardino County Sheriff's Department that he and his wife had seen
a "young white male" driving a station wagon down Peyton Road at a fast

rate of speed. Leonard said the car was a "light color" station wagon with a luggage rack. His wife, Paula Leonard, said she "remembered thinking" that she saw three or four people in the car. She also recalled "wood grain" paneling and stated she thought it had a luggage rack.

Two hours after Josh was air-lifted to the hospital, a citizen, Ellis Bell, parked his pickup truck on Old English Road and saw a well-worn Estwing hatchet lying in the weeds on the dirt shoulder of the road. When he saw what appeared to be blood on it, he flagged down Sergeant Rick Roper as he was driving up Old English Road to go the Ryens' house. Roper noticed a sharp indentation in a nearby fence pole that suggested the hatchet had been hurled from the right side—the passenger's side—of the Ryens' station wagon as it made its way down to Peyton Road. Roper saw that there was both blood and hair on the hatchet's blade.

The hatchet was fourteen-inches long, made of tempered, forged steel. Its handle was covered in laminated, genuine leather strips that had a muted orange color. In unsuccessfully testing the hatchet for latent fingerprints, Roper used a Dura-Print substance that destroyed the blood evidence in the process. He subsequently sent the hatchet to Texas Tech University where the hatchet was processed with dyes and other chemicals that turned the orange leather to a charcoal color. Once again, no latent prints were discovered.

The next day, June 6, a day after the murders were reported, a citizen called the sheriff's department to report that she had found a blue shirt that appeared to have blood on it alongside Peyton Road, across the intersection from the Canyon Corral Bar. The bar is located down a steep, winding road below the Ryens' house. Deputy Scott Field was dispatched to collect the shirt. A sheriff's department log from that day referenced the recovery of the blue shirt at 2:41 p.m.: "On Peyton and Glenridge…Laurel Epler reports finding a blue shirt that possibly has blood on it. Unit 21D14 [Deputy Field's squad car] handling…Evidence picked up."

The discovery of the blood-stained blue shirt prompted Sergeant Arthur to order a search of the Peyton Road area the next day. That search netted a blood-stained tan T-shirt and an orange towel, which Deputy Field took into custody at 5:30 p.m. that day. The tan T-shirt was found in a ditch on the same side of the street as the bar. It was a medium-size, Fruit of the Loom T-shirt with a front pocket. Initial tests done by the San Bernardino County Sheriff's Department Crime Lab showed that the blood characteristics on the T-shirt were consistent with only Doug Ryen's profile. The finding of the second blood-stained shirt near the bar was a strong indication that at least two assailants had been involved in the Ryen/Hughes murders and had discarded the incriminating evidence.

Something else that clearly supported the multiple-assailant theory was the Ryens themselves. Peggy Ryen, as both a chiropractor and a horse trainer, was an exceptionally strong woman in her own right. And quite decisive, according to her older half-sister, Lillian Shaffer. On a cross-country trip to visit the Ryen family in 1979, Lillian saw a snake dangling from a ceiling crossbeam in the Ryens' master bedroom as she and Peggy walked into the room. "Peg went to the closet, got a rifle, and shot the snake on the first try. It all took about 10 seconds," Lillian recalled in a 2010 interview at her Florida home.

She also recounted the time on that visit when she watched Peggy lead a big stallion through his training paces with a short leash. "The stallion reared up on its back legs, towering over Peg, and Peg pulled him right back down and under control with one firm jerk. It was an amazing show of strength. Peg was very strong."

Danea Johnson, a patient of Peg Ryen's who became a good friend and shared her enthusiasm for Arabian horses and saw her at various horse shows, said Peggy "could lift that trailer, and hitch it. I mean that woman amazed me. I didn't believe it, what she could do. I mean she'd take those big, huge bags of feed and throw those things up there."

Doug Ryen's sister, Cindy Settle, described her brother as "big and strong," adding, "He wasn't a tough guy, but he was tough. He could take care of himself."

CHAPTER EIGHT

The Canyon Corral Bar

The Canyon Corral Bar was located about a mile and a half down from the Ryen house at the intersection of Peyton Road and Carbon Canyon Road. It was a neighborhood establishment frequented mostly by horse people who knew each other, at least by sight, if not by name. Children often accompanied their parents to dinner there, just as the Ryen family had done on various occasions. There was a dance floor that did not get much use. Business was brisk on Friday and Saturday nights when the band started playing at 9 p.m. On Saturday night, June 4, some fifty to sixty patrons filled both the bar and restaurant areas.

Earlier that night, three young men entered the bar around 8:30 p.m. No one in the bar had ever seen any of them before. Instead of cowboy garb, they wore T-shirts, jeans and tennis shoes. Two of the men had military-type haircuts and one had brown hair that hung below his ears. Stenciled on the back of his T-shirt were the words, "May the Force be with you." They ordered one round of beers and asked their waitress, Kathy Royals, if there was any place to shoot pool in the area. She mentioned two places and they left just as the band was getting ready to come on. One of the places Royals mentioned was the La Vida Hot Springs Bar in Brea, about six miles away. One of the men told her he had heard of it and she gave them directions. Apparently that is where they went next. A waitress there, Mary Risi, told San Bernardino Sheriff's Detective Phil Dana three days after the murders were discovered that she remembered serving three young, white men the night of the Ryen/Hughes murders, June 4. Her description of the men was similar to those already given to sheriff's deputies and detectives by various people at the Canyon Corral Bar.

About three hours after they had left the Canyon Corral Bar, the three men surprised everyone who had seen them the first time by returning for another round of beers. But this time, two of the men were noticeably inebriated or strung out on drugs as they staggered to a table near the bar. The man with the long brown hair could not keep his head up, resting it flat down on the table after Royals again took their orders. The manager of the bar, Shirley Killian, approached the table and asked one of the men sitting with him if his friend was taking a nap. He said his friend was "very tired." This interchange got the man to raise his head and turn the back of his head to the bar manager. Killian then told the bartender to cut them off.

Two of the men—whom one bar patron would later describe as "a couple of young loud mouths"—then began harassing three women at the bar. Killian made no notice of this, but did stop one of the men about fifteen minutes later as he attempted to leave the bar with an open bottle of beer. She got the bottle from him without incident. About a minute later she went out into the parking lot to see if the men had left. She only saw two of them; the third man had remained in the bar. One was leaning up against a small red car and the other was standing next to a light-colored vehicle trying to coax the other man to get into the larger light-colored vehicle. Killian told detectives that the vehicle was "larger than the average car, could have been a pickup, could have been something else." What it could have been was the Ryens' station wagon.

Two things had prompted sheriff's deputies and detectives to interview Killian and others at the bar on the night on June 4. One was the discovery of the second bloody shirt not far from the bar on June 7, and the second was a phone call the sheriff's office received on June 6 from Pam Smith, a regular bar patron. When Smith heard initial reports that police were looking for three men in connection with the Ryen/Hughes murders, she reported the three strange men she had seen the night of the murders at the Canyon Corral Bar.

A number of oddities surfaced about the way sheriff's investigators handled the information about the three white men seen at the Canyon Corral Bar the night of the murders. Although they would interview the bar manager, the bartender, two waitresses, the bouncer and two or three regular bar patrons, none of the investigators asked any of these people to do a composite sketch of the three men. Nor would investigators show any of the subjects interviewed any photo arrays for purposes of identification. Detective Phil Dana said he did not ask the waitress at La Vida Bar to do a drawing, when he interviewed her on June 8, because he did not view the men as suspects. He said this despite knowing that a couple had reported on June 6 seeing three or four white men driving a white station wagon away from the Ryens' house around midnight the night of the murders.

Based on official police reports, investigators made no attempt to find out who else was in the bar that night. If they would have contacted Lance Stark, a regular patron of the bar, they would have learned of two of the men being rude and abusive to three women at the bar. The women, in turn, would have told them that two of the men had blood splatter on their clothes and skin and that one of the men had on coveralls that were heavily blood splattered.

CHAPTER NINE

A Prime Suspect

Two *days after the news media reported* that a bloody tan T-shirt had been found on Peyton Road below the Ryens' house, Diana Roper, believing her live-in boyfriend, Lee Furrow, had very likely been involved in the Ryen/Hughes murders, called her father, Bill Kellison, for advice. Roper had come across the coveralls Furrow had changed out of when he briefly returned to Roper's home in Mentrone pre-dawn on June 5. The coveralls, left on the floor on a walk-in bedroom closet, were heavily splattered with blood and had horse hair on the lower leg area. When Bill Kellison saw the coveralls, he called the Yucaipa Substation of the San Bernardino County Sheriff's Department to report the bloody coveralls in his daughter's possession.

San Bernardino County Sheriff Deputy Rick Eckley, the property manager at the substation, was dispatched to Roper's home in Mentrone, which is forty-five miles east of Chino Hills. Once he saw the bloody coveralls, Eckley called his supervisor, Sergeant Mike Stodelle, to come out and take a look at them. To get a better view, they spread the coveralls over the hood the police car. They then bagged the coveralls and Eckley took them back with him to the Yucaipa Substation.

Before Eckley left, Roper told him she had additional information she wanted to relay about Furrow and her suspicions of his involvement in the Chino Hills murders but that she wanted to speak directly with a homicide detective about those matters. (What Roper wanted to tell homicide was that when Furrow arrived in the early morning hours of June 5 he was no longer wearing the tan T-shirt and jeans she had laid out for him to wear to the US Music Festival they attended separately on June 4. Further, she remembered the T-shirt was a Fruit-of-the-Loom, medium size with a pocket in front because she had recently bought it for Furrow at a K-Mart. Roper's description of the T-shirt perfectly matched the blood-stained tan T-shirt deputies found near the Canyon Corral Bar two days after the murders were discovered.)

Once back at the station, Eckley made a written report, stating that the coveralls were "heavily splattered" with blood and that Diana Roper "suspects that the bloody coveralls are from the Chino murders and has further information regarding that incident and/or possible suspects." His report said that Roper wanted to be contacted by homicide about that information.

Eckley then contacted his superior, Sergeant Greg Benge, who instructed him to forward his report to Sergeant Arthur, the chief investigating officer in the homicide division.

The next day, June 10, 1983, Sergeant Benge informed Arthur about the contents of the deputy's report.

Neither Arthur nor any other detective would make any attempt to recover the coveralls despite Eckley making several further attempts to contact the homicide division in June and July 1983 regarding the coveralls. None of his telephone calls were returned.

A few days after turning over the blood-stained coveralls to Eckley, Roper learned from news reports that a hatchet had been involved in the Chino Hill murders. This prompted her to check Furrow's tools hanging on nails in the wash room. When she saw that except for his hatchet, all his tools were there, she called Eckley and reported that discovery to him.

Roper's sister, Karee Kellison, was also at Roper's house when Furrow returned pre-dawn on June 5. When a deputy interviewed her after Roper turned in the bloody coveralls, she was "too terrified" of Furrow to say what she had seen that night. If she had not been so fearful of Furrow, she would have confirmed what Roper told Deputy Eckley about Furrow returning in coveralls. She had also seen something that night that her sister had not:

When she heard a car pull up that night she looked outside and saw Furrow and a woman get out of a station wagon. She said there was insufficient light to identify the other occupants of the car.

Roper had good reason to suspect Eugene Leland "Lee" Furrow as a violent murderer. Furrow had already been convicted in the 1974 murder of Mary Sue Kitts. He admitted strangling the seventeen-year-old girl, hacking her up and throwing her body parts into the Friant-Kern Canal with stones tied to them. Kitts's body parts were never found. Furrow turned state's witness and testified against Clarence Ray Allen, the leader of the Allen Gang, who Furrow testified had ordered the murder of Kitts. Allen received a life sentence. In return for testifying against Allen at the Kitts's murder trial, the prosecution allowed Furrow to plead guilty to second-degree murder, for which he served four and a half years in prison. He was released on June 12, 1982, just a little less than a year before the Ryen/Hughes murders. The afternoon of the Chino Hills murders, Furrow had gone to the county jail to post bail for a friend, Michael Darnell, who was being released after spending the night in jail.

No homicide detective would contact Roper. Eleven months after she turned in the bloody coveralls, Roper heard on the news that the little boy who survived the attack had originally said that his attackers were three white men. This prompted Roper to call her father and set up an interview with a homicide detective at the Yucaipa Substation on May 16. During this interview, Roper told Detective James Stalanker about Lee Furrow returning to her home in Mentrone pre-dawn on June 5, 1983, dressed in coveralls that he left in a heap on the floor of a bedroom closet. When she looked at the coveralls a day or two later she saw Arabian horse hair on the legs of the coveralls and blood caked all over them, particularly on the front zipper.

Roper also told Stalanker that after it came out in the news that a hatchet had been one of the murder weapons, she had checked and found that Furrow's hatchet was missing from the back porch where he kept his tools hung on nails. Except for the hatchet, all of his other tools were still there. She also told Stalanaker that Furrow's hatchet had an "orange" handle, just as did the hatchet recovered near the crime scene by Sergeant Rick Roper the day the murders were discovered.

She told Stalanker that what convinced her Furrow was involved in the Chino Hills murders was when she heard about police finding a bloody tan T-shirt that was linked to the crime. She told him Furrow had been wearing a tan T-shirt with a pocket in front the day he attended the country music festival, but the shirt was now missing.

All of this information about Furrow prompted Stalanker to attempt to set up an interview with Furrow. When Furrow's attorney, Chuck Mason, called Stalanker the next day to ask why the detective wanted to see his client, Stalanaker told him it was based on information Roper had provided about Furrow's possible involvement in the Chino Hills murders and, in particular, the bloody coveralls she said belonged to Furrow.

Shortly after Roper turned over the coveralls in June of 1983, Roper told Furrow about that. He was angry, but what was done was done. After two years of living with Roper, he was moving out anyway to live with his new wife, Debbie Glasgow. Furrow simply denied leaving the coveralls there and Roper told him she knew otherwise and so did her younger sister who had seen him come home in the coveralls the night of the Chino Hills murders.

What had no doubt surprised Furrow, who as an ex-con who had pled guilty to second-degree murder could expect police scrutiny, was that it had taken the sheriff's department this long to seek to question him about the coveralls. Just when he thought they never would, his attorney told him he was wanted for questioning about the coveralls.

Furrow, now quite agitated, drove over to see Roper. Roper thought Furrow might kill her on the spot if she knew that she had spoken with a detective the day before, so she played dumb, telling Furrow the cops were probably just getting around to investigating the coveralls she had given eleven months earlier.

As soon as Furrow left, an angry Roper called Stalanaker on the phone, telling him, "That was really a bad spot to be put in, when I was promised that never…" Stalanaker cut her off to say that he had only promised her that her name would not "be in any newspapers, dear."

Later on during the phone call, after Stalanaker had agreed not to let Furrow know that Roper had spoken with him the day before, Roper asked Stalanaker if the coveralls had ever been tested in the lab. When he said they had not, Roper said, "Jesus!"

STALANKER: I'LL BE HONEST WITH YOU. THEY WERE DESTROYED SIX MONTHS LATER.
ROPER: WERE THEY REALLY?
STALANKER: YEAH.
ROPER: AND THEY NEVER LABBED THE BLOOD OR NOTHING?
STALANKER: NO.
ROPER: OH, MAN.

Detective Stalanaker and Sergeant Arthur interviewed Furrow on May 17, 1984 at the homicide office. Stalanaker had told Furrow's attorney that the purpose of interviewing his client was to clear him as a suspect in the Chino Hills murders. Furrow came without his lawyer.

Stalanaker began the interview at 5:33 p.m. by telling Furrow he wanted to question him concerning statements Diana Roper had made about him leaving bloody coveralls in the closet shortly after the Chino Hills murders. Stalanaker's first substantive question was if Roper had "an axe to grind with you."

FURROW: OH, YEAH, DEFINITELY.
STALANAKER: WHAT WOULD THAT BE?
FURROW: I RAN OFF AND MARRIED HER BEST GIRLFRIEND (LAUGHS).
STALANAKER: AND WHO IS THAT?
FURROW: DEBBIE.
STALANAKER: PARDON ME.
FURROW: GLASGOW—DEBBIE GLASGOW.

STALANAKER: OKAY. THAT'S DIANA'S BEST GIRLFRIEND?

FURROW: IT WAS (LAUGHS).

STALANAKER: WHERE IS DEBBIE NOW?

FURROW: SHE'S, UH, IN SAN DIEGO AND WE'RE BROKE UP AND
SHE'S, UH, WITH ONE OF MY BEST FRIENDS (LAUGHS).

Furrow told the detectives that the night of the US Festival he called Roper collect from the festival grounds around midnight or 12:30 a.m., asking her to come pick him and Debbie Glasgow up. When Roper refused, Furrow and Glasgow hitchhiked back to Roper's house in Mentrone, arriving there around 1 p.m. Furrow said he had stopped at the house just long enough to pick up his brother's jacket and then he and Glasgow left on his motorcycle for San Diego. It took them about two hours to get there, so he estimated their arrival time at 3 p.m.

Neither detective attempted to quiz Furrow about the significant time differences between his account and what Roper had told Stalanaker. Roper had said she had been home for more than an hour before Furrow called her about a ride around 1:40 a.m. and that Furrow and Glasgow did not arrive for at least an hour after that.

At one point, Stalanaker asked Furrow, "Did you hear, at all, anything about the Cooper murders"? Furrow said he heard about them in San Diego.

Stalanaker wanted to know if Roper said anything about "Cooper to you" when Furrow returned to Mentrone two weeks later and Roper had told him she had turned in his bloody coveralls.

"Well, I don't know, you know, she didn't say, you know, anything. She just said that that she'd given them [the coveralls] for that reason, you know. Cause' she thought maybe they, on their way, escaping or whatever, stopped at our house, you know, our little house in Mentrone, and dropped those pants off, you know. Uh, I don't know what, you know, what she was trying to, you know, say at the time, you know," Furrow answered.

The answer was preposterous, but it generated no follow-up questions. They had apparently heard enough and their job of "clearing" Furrow—whom Stalanker listed in his report as "Furrows"—was working out well.

Stalanaker now wanted to know what was Roper's problem.

STALANAKER: WHAT IS, IS DIANA DOING, SELLING DRUGS AND
STUFF OR WAS SHE JUST SCREWED UP OR...(INAUDIBLE)
FURROW: I DON'T KNOW IF SHE HAS, SHE HAS A NEW BOYFRIEND
[KENNETH KOON]—I HEAR HE'S IN JAIL. YOU KNOW, UH, SHE USED
TO BE OUT PARTYING AND STUFF ALL THE TIME. I JUST KIND OF
STAY AWAY FROM HER CAUSE', YOU KNOW, I'VE GOT A GIRLFRIEND
NOW THAT THEY DON'T GET ALONG AND SHE'S [ROPER] CAUSED A
LOT OF PROBLEMS IN OUR, OUR RELATIONSHIP ALREADY AND, YOU
KNOW, I JUST TRY TO STAY AWAY FROM HER.

Sergeant Arthur now weighed in, asking Furrow about his murdering Mary Sue Kitts in1974. "I haven't murdered anybody—I had a second degree murder," he said, saying that was all behind him, he had paid for that crime, and he did not want to talk about it. They could read the transcripts from the trial if they wanted to know more about it.

Arthur asked him if he would take a polygraph about whether he had any involvement in the Chino Hills murders, if the coveralls that Roper turned in were his, and if the coveralls had blood on them. Furrow said he would "be glad to."

As they were discussing the logistics of the polygraph, Arthur said, "I don't know that a polygraph will be needed." Stalanaker said, "I don't either." Twenty-two minutes after it had begun, the only police contact with Eugene Lee Furrow in connection with the Chino Hills murders was over.

Furrow would not be subjected to a polygraph and neither Stalanaker nor Arthur would ever interview Roper again. Kevin Cooper, he of "the Cooper murders," was their man.

CHAPTER TEN

Mistakes Happen

K<i>evin Cooper,</i> a twenty-five-old habitual criminal who had grown up in Pittsburgh, Pennsylvania, arrived at the California Institute for Men at Chino on April 29, 1983. The prison houses a high-security reception center where every adult male convicted of a felony in Southern California is sent for evaluation and eventual placement within the state's vast prison system.

Cooper was admitted under the name David Trautman. He had been arrested in connection with a home burglary in Los Angeles in January of 1983. At the police station, he had displayed the driver's license of David Anthony Trautman. L.A. police subsequently linked him to another Hollywood burglary and learned through a search of the National Crime Information Center that Cooper was using the name Trautman as an alias. Nonetheless, the L.A. District Attorney's Office charged him under the Trautman name.

On March 21, 1983, using the alias David Trautman, Cooper pled guilty to two counts of first-degree burglary on the stipulation that the judge impose the middle sentence—four years—on each count and order that the sentences run concurrently. The judge accepted the plea bargain and set the sentencing for April 19. He did this despite being informed during the hearing by Cooper's court-appointed attorney of the possibility of pending charges against Cooper in Pennsylvania. Cooper's case was assigned that day to deputy probation officer, Joan Etzkorn, to conduct a pre-sentencing investigation.

The next day, the California Governor's Office mailed a Pennsylvania warrant for Cooper's extradition to the Los Angeles Police Department.

Although Etzkorn notated on a worksheet that "Kevin Cooper" is an alias for David Trautman—information she later admitted she got directly from Cooper—she ran only Trautman's criminal history in California and with the FBI and found no prior arrests. She could have rectified that error by checking with the investigative police officer who had noted in his supplemental report that Cooper was an escapee from a Pennsylvania mental hospital.

At Cooper's sentencing on April 19, the judge upheld the plea bargain agreement.

The following day, Los Angeles police returned the un-served Pennsylvania warrant for Cooper's extradition to the governor's office in Sacramento. The attached report stated that not serving the warrant while Cooper was in custody in Los Angeles is in accord with "normal practice and appears reasonable when compared with existing alternatives." In other words, as far as Los Angeles authorities were concerned, Cooper's crimes in Los Angeles took precedence over the far more serious charges pending against him in Pennsylvania.

Three days later, an investigator from the Allegheny County District Attorney's Office in Pennsylvania phoned the processing center's records office at CIM to inform personnel there that Pennsylvania would issue a warrant for Cooper's extradition. As promised, on May 18 a detainer clerk at CIM's reception center received a packet of information from Pennsylvania authorities that informed them that David Trautman is actually Kevin Cooper and that Cooper is a high escape risk. The packet contained bench warrants and detainers for Cooper. In a letter dated, May 18, 1983, CIM prison officials acknowledged receipt of the warrants. The purpose of sending the warrants was to request Cooper's extradition to Pennsylvania to stand trial on the kidnapping, rape, auto theft, and escape charges pending against him there. The information about Cooper from Pennsylvania would not enter his file until the day he escaped.

In the midst of these communications from Pennsylvania to CIM, Trautman's classification was under review at the CIM reception center while his file still contained no references to the charges pending against him in Pennsylvania. As it turned out, he would be designated for transfer to a minimum-security prison camp in Susanville in Northern California. On May 24, when the reception center at CIM found out Susanville had no vacancies, Cooper was designated for the minimum-security section of CIM, where he took up lodging on June 1. The next day, he fled.

Five hours before Cooper escaped at 3 p.m., CIM had one final chance to save itself from committing its most colossal blunder since it opened in 1941. The persistent investigator from Allegheny County phoned the records officer at the CIM reception center for a status update on of Pennsylvania's warrants to extradite Cooper. The records officer responded by requesting that Cooper's file be pulled at the minimum-security unit at CIM, but the file was not sent over. Several hours later, alerted by now to Cooper's escape, prison officials opened his file and found the warrants from Pennsylvania loose in it. How the warrants got there late in the day of Cooper's escape was never explained.

Knowing now that Cooper was a potentially dangerous escapee, scores of prison personnel searched the surrounding area for Cooper until 11 p.m. before giving up. In what turned out to be a major public relations fiasco for CIM, Cooper's escape would not be publicized until after the Ryen/Hughes murders.

It would be fair to say that the massive cuts in state spending caused by the passage of Proposition 13 in 1978 had left probation and prison officials unable to administer their most basic functions properly. The same could be said of fire departments, public libraries and public school systems throughout the state. California's vaunted public school system plummeted from the top ten in the nation to forty-eighth place in a few years. Proposition 13, which capped real estate taxes at one percent of assessed value and limited any future property assessments to a maximum of two percent a year, resulted in a fifty-seven percent decline in state revenue from the state's primary funding source.

In the five years since Proposition 13 took effect, as Southern California's prison population continued to increase, Los Angeles County cut its probation officers from four-thousand-four hundred to three-thousand-two hundred, causing caseloads for its probation officers to spike from one-hundred-fifty to more than three-hundred. As deputy probation officer Etzkorn prepared to make her pre-sentencing recommendations concerning Cooper, she had fifteen other cases to write up in seven work days, according to an article in the *Los Angeles Times*, "giving her little more than three hours for each report."

By 1983 at CIM, there were 4,310 inmates crammed into a prison built with a capacity of housing 2,634 men. Without enough cells, prisoners slept in day rooms, classrooms and a gym. The minimum-security section had dormitories built to house 976 men, but when Cooper was assigned there it held 1,740 prisoners. When Cooper escaped on June 2, 1983, he was the fourteenth inmate to walk away from the minimum-security section of CIM that year. He would not be the last. In 1986, the *Los Angeles Times* reported the ninth escape from CIM since Cooper's in 1983.

Overcrowding in California prisons proved to be an intractable problem well into the 21st century. In August of 2009, as the state was grappling with a $24 billion budget deficit, a three-judge panel of the Ninth Circuit Court of Appeals ordered the largest prison reduction ever imposed on a state when it ruled that California must reduce its prison population from 150,000 to 110,000 by 2011. In a harshly critical 184 page order, the judges wrote that the overcrowding was a violation of the Eight Amendment of the Constitution, which prohibits cruel and unusual punishment.

The State of California appealed the court order to the U.S. Supreme Court, but on May 23, 2011, the U.S. Supreme Court reaffirmed the Ninth's order, giving the state two years to reduce prison overcrowding by 46,000 prisoners. Gov. Jerry Brown's response was to propose reassigning tens of thousands of inmates convicted of non-violent crimes to serve their sentences in county jails.

"County jail expansion does not solve the underlying problems," said Professor Ruth Wilson Gilmore, the author of *Golden Gulag*, a book about how politics and economic forces produced California's prison boom. "We know that public safety is a direct outcome of public education, affordable housing and living-wage jobs. These are goals we can achieve now if we take this opportunity to shrink prisons and jails. Building bigger [county] jails to ease prison numbers is the same as rearranging the deck chairs on the *Titanic:* wasting the same dollars in different directions."

CHAPTER ELEVEN

The Escape

C*lad in brown jacket*, blue jeans and well-worn tennis shoes, his hair in flat, tight braids, Kevin Cooper climbed through a hole in the prison's short fence and walked away from the minimum-security section of the prison across an open field.

Cooper had been running away since age seven. This was no different—same problem, different place. He wanted out, and if the opportunity came along, he would take it.

As he was jogging away on Edison Avenue, the main road fronting the prison complex, he saw a pickup truck coming toward him being driven by Lieutenant Cornelius Shephard, a CIM correctional officer, who was just coming to work. To try to throw him off, Cooper waved. Shephard slammed on his brakes and put the pickup in reverse. Cooper ran in between some houses and made his way to a nearby lumber yard. Shephard used a phone at a nearby private residence to alert the prison of the escape. A full-scale search for Cooper began in minutes.

At the lumber yard, Cooper walked in like a customer and went to the back of the lot where he climbed a twenty-five-foot-high stack of lumber and laid down until he felt sure no one had noticed him. From this perch, he could see traffic on Edison Avenue, including police cars and CIM vehicles driving around looking for him. He ate an orange he had brought with him and smoked some Kool cigarettes as he spent the next five or six hours waiting for all the customers and employees to leave the lumber yard at closing time. At dusk he hopped a fence to another lumber yard and got into the cab of an eighteen-wheel truck loaded with lumber. After dark he made his way to a highway, walking through fields that parallel Edison Avenue. After crossing the highway, he fell into a muddy drainage ditch that soaked his clothes and shoes.

He did not know the area and did not know where he was going. Other than getting as far away from CIM as possible without being detected, he had no particular destination in mind. Because it was chilly, he kept the jacket on, crossed a state highway and soon found himself in a neighborhood.

He climbed up a steep dirt hill and came to a large open, fenced field. He could smell horses. They sensed him too and made noises, snorting and trotting away from him with their ears pinned. He waited until they got quiet. It was so foggy he could barely see. As he walked up the steep fence line, he fell numerous times, and then began clinging to the fence as he walked up. Arriving at Old English Road, he saw a light on outside a house and noticed that the garage door was not completely shut. He pulled the garage door open, but it was too dark to see anything inside. He flicked his cigarette lighter on and looked in to see a golf cart, some stereo components, a refrigerator and a doorway leading to the main house.

Hungry and thirsty, his first priority was the refrigerator. There he found some cold bottles of beer. In a workshop extension of the garage, he sat down and drank a beer, smoked another Kool, and thought things over for awhile. Back in the garage, he found a flashlight. Because his clothes were wet and caked in mud, he got a ladder and climbed up to check the shelves to try to find some clothes to change into. He found a pair of yellow tennis shoes and some old rags. He took off his shoes and socks, rolled up his pant legs and dried off, then put the yellow tennis shoes on his bare feet. They fit. It was time for another beer and a smoke in the workshop as he considered his next move.

Working under the assumption that the house was occupied, he decided to case the outside of the house by walking around it and looking in all the windows. He saw no sign of activity. To him the house looked vacant, but he was not sure about that. He decided then to try the door from the garage to the main house. It was unlocked. He cracked it open and stuck his head in but could not see anything. He let himself in. No lights were on and the drapes were pulled shut. He walked to the kitchen and then through the rest of the one-level house. At the front door, he turned the lock and the door swung open. This startled him. He closed the door and made his way back to the garage. He smoked another cigarette and mulled over his options. He decided to find out if anyone was home by going out to the front door and knocking on it. If someone were to answer the door, his plan was to ask "if Joe Blow lived there." But no one did, so he let himself in the front door.

With a flashlight, he now walked through all the rooms of the house. He saw that one bedroom was furnished and the other three were empty. One of the empty bedrooms contained only a headboard attached to a wall. Inside the furnished bedroom, the closets were full of clothes and the bathroom adjacent to it was stocked with towels and toiletries. Returning to the kitchen, he made a sandwich and turned on the radio, checking with various stations to see if there was anything about his escape on the news. There was not. Although some one-hundred-fifty personnel from the California Institute for Men had spent hours looking for Cooper, his escape would not be reported by prison officials until two days after the Ryen/Hughes murders were discovered.

In the living room, he turned on the TV after moving it to the floor and turning down the brightness and contrast dials. He just missed the late news so he turned off the TV and replaced it on its stand.

Back in the kitchen, he had another sandwich. He went to the furnished bedroom and sat on the bed and smoked a Kool, then put it out in an ashtray in the living room. From a phone in the living room, he called a woman friend, Yolanda Jackson, in Los Angeles, and they talked for two hours, the call ending at 2:07 a.m. on Friday, June 3, 1983. He asked her to come and get him but she refused, telling him to turn himself in. In fact, he did not know where he was or how to direct her to him.

That night, three miles from CIM, and still wearing his prison-issued jeans and shirt, he laid down on the bedcover on the bed in the furnished bedroom with his feet on the floor and quickly fell asleep. He slept soundly, not awakening until it was light outside. When he did awake, he felt a strong sense of vulnerability, realizing he could have been seen in bed from outside the bedroom window. To make sure no one has entered the house while he was asleep, he walked through every room in the house again.

Before calling his former girlfriend in Pittsburgh, Pennsylvania, he used a coffee machine in the kitchen to make himself a cup of coffee. His calmness belied the predicament he was in. He told his former girlfriend, Diane Williams, that a new law in California led to his early release from prison, but he had no funds and asked her to try to put together some money to wire to him once he found a place to live. He also asked her to call his mother for money, something she was reluctant to do because his mother did not like her.

Cooper knew he needed to buy some time: He felt if he could avoid detection for two more days, the authorities would assume he had fled to Los Angles or some other place and quit looking for him in the Chino area. All of his subsequent actions were designed to further his escape.

He spent most of Friday re-braiding his long hair into cornrows to change his appearance, a process that took him hours to accomplish.

He stayed most of Friday in the living room. From time to time, he turned on the TV and radio to find out if his escape had been reported to the news media, but heard no mention of it. The front window provided him with a view of one ranch house about four-hundred yards below. Standing back five feet from the window so as not to be seen from the outside, he was able to see people working with horses in the fields outside that house. The ranch he was seeing belonged to Larry Lease, a part-owner of the vacant house Cooper was in.

With a steak knife from a kitchen drawer, he let out the hem of two pair of pants that he found in the furnished bedroom closet. He put his dirty prison clothes and tennis shoes in a white plastic bag, intending to take the bag with him and dispose of it elsewhere.

During the day he smoked the last of the Kools he had and now began rolling his own cigarettes, using loose tobacco issued free at CIM. He carefully collected the tobacco from the butts of the hand-rolled cigarette and placed it in a small box he kept in a closet, out of sight, in case someone were to enter the house.

In the afternoon he opened a bottle of chilled Mogen David wine, but found the taste "nasty" and spat it out, refilling the bottle with tap water and placing it back in the refrigerator. He contented himself with Pepsi and lemonade.

To make himself less vulnerable while he slept, he decided he would sleep on the floor of the closet of the bedroom with the attached headboard in it and pull the closet's sliding doors shut. Earlier in the day he moved blankets and pillows into the closet. That night, he washed his underwear, socks and T-shirt in the bathroom sink of the furnished bedroom and then hung the items out to dry in the closet of the empty bedroom.

After listening to the late news, he went to sleep nude in the closet with a green blanket wrapped around him. During the night he had a wet dream, depositing semen on the green blanket.

On Saturday morning about 10, he was about to take a bath in the tub in the bathroom off the furnished bedroom. He cracked the window in the bathroom open so he could hear if anyone was driving up while he was in the shower. After starting the water running, he heard a car drive up the driveway. He turned the water off and ran down the hall to peek out the living room window and saw a blue car come to a stop in the driveway. He ran back to the bathroom, closed the door and put his underwear and socks on. He cracked open the bathroom door a minute or two later and saw a woman leaving through the front door. He returned to the living room and heard a car door open and the car's engine start up. He watched as the car drove away. He sighed in relief, but now knew it was no longer safe for him to stay in this house. He considered leaving as soon as he could get dressed, but decided it would be too risky to leave in daylight. His plan was to wait until dark to make his exit. He knew from approaching the house on Thursday night that it would be pitch black outside once it grew dark.

Displaying the nerves of a house burglar, which he was, he returned to the bathroom to take a bath, but found the water lukewarm. He took his clothes, a towel and a bar of soap to the other bathroom. He turned on the shower, stepped on the shower sill with a bare foot and tested the water's temperature by sticking his hand in, but the water there was tepid too. He ended up taking a sponge bath in the sink of the bathroom off the furnished bedroom where the water was warm.

After washing up, he shaved off his half beard and mustache. Those changes, plus earlier re-braiding his hair into cornrows, significantly altered his appearance, but he remained the lone black person in Chino Hills.

He spent Saturday afternoon watching TV, listening to the radio—still no news of his escape—and watching the driveway to see if anyone else was coming up to the house. For the hyper-active Cooper, sitting around the house was excruciating. He could not wait for darkness to fall. Then, once again, he could flee.

CHAPTER TWELVE

Cooper on The Run

At 8 p.m. on June 4, 1983, Kevin Cooper made his last call from the hideout house below the Ryens' house, phoning Diane Williams in Pittsburgh. She had not arranged for any money, but they talked until 8:37 p.m. By now he could see that it was dark outside. The sun set that night at 7:59 p.m. His plan was to exit by the same route he approached the house. Knowing he would be going down steep hillsides and having to cross a creek, he returned to the furnished bedroom and took his socks off and changed back into his prison clothes and tennis shoes, placing his newly acquired clean clothes—four pair of pants and four or five shirts—in a green shoulder bag with yellow straps and handles.

"At dark, I go out the same way I came in, falling almost all the way down the dirt hill I'd climbed up two nights before. The hill is very steep and muddy and my shoes have no traction."

When he got to the creek, he waded into water that was thigh high. Once across the creek, he took off his prison jacket, pants and shoes, dried his legs and feet off with the jacket, put his socks back on and changed back into the clean clothes taken from the furnished bedroom—a pair of Army pants, a white shirt and the yellow tennis shoes. He put his jacket, pants and shoes in a white plastic bag and made his way through a field that runs parallel to Old English Road.

He arrived at a busy intersection on Peyton Road near a fire station, carrying the two bags. Standing at the intersection, he asked a man in a convertible stopped at a red light which way was Mexico. The man pointed in the correct direction and drove off. Cooper walked to the freeway with no other plan than to take the first hitchhike ride he could get and go wherever that took him. He put his thumb out and started trying to hitch-hike. Eventually, a white couple in a customized yellow van with wide tires and side pipes picked him up.

"I didn't care where they were going—wherever the van went. My mindset was I'm free. I'm experiencing life. I'm going," Cooper said.

He sat on an ottoman centered behind the two front seats and rode with them for about an hour and a half, deep into Southern California. They pulled over at an off ramp and let him out.

Unable to catch another ride, he began walking down the shoulder of the freeway until a middle-aged white man in a small four-door K-Car picked him up and drove him the rest of the way to the border, dropping him off at a bus station in San Ysidro. From the bus station, he could see the ramp that goes across the border into Mexico. With no money for a room, he walked around for awhile before returning to spend the night in the waiting room of the bus station.

He was not sure if a passport or what documentation was needed to enter Mexico, so he asked some tourists at the border the next morning about that. They told him there was no identification requirement. In a shopping district on the U.S. side of the border, he snatched a purse from a woman and made his way to the border. He crossed without incident, went to a taxi stand and had the driver take him to Tijuana. Inside the woman's purse were $10 or $15 in bills and a bag of quarters totaling $105. He paid the cabbie and went directly to Woolworth's for breakfast.

After breakfast, he went shopping for some essentials, buying tooth-paste, hair grease, soap, body lotion, and a washrag. He also bought an orange Chevy Blazer baseball cap and a pair of soft-soled black shoes. Afterwards, he stole a watch from a sidewalk vendor.

At 4:30 p.m. he checked into the Enva Hotel in downtown Tijuana under the alias Angel Jackson, listing Yolanda Jackson's address in Los Angeles as his own. He paid the $6 required for his room in advance with quarters. The clerk, Petra Carrillo, logged his time of arrival and his name in the registry book.

The next afternoon, he placed a collect call to Diane Williams in Pittsburgh, who informed him he was being accused "of killing a family in a funny part of California." At this point, he was not actually being accused of the murders, but simply being identified as one of three recent escapees—two from CIM and one from a nearby youth detention camp—who were wanted for questioning in connection with the incredibly brutal Ryen/Hughes murders. That night he would see his mug shot on TV in a Tijuana bar.

While in Tijuana, Cooper read in the June 7 San Diego edition of the *Los Angeles Times* that David Trautman, the alias he was known by at the California Institute for Men, was wanted for questioning in connection with the Chino Hills murders. When he read the next day's edition, he saw that both Trautman and Kevin Cooper were suspects. Later that morning, he boarded a bus for the port city of Ensenada, in Baja California, Mexico, about seventy miles to the south.

CHAPTER THIRTEEN

Manhunt

Two days after the discovery of the murders, two employees of Roger Lang, one of the owners of the vacant house just below the Ryens' house, searched the house and discovered bedding on the floor of the closet of an empty bedroom that contained only an attached headboard. They also noticed a hatchet sheath and a green button that appeared to have blood on it lying on the floor. They immediately alerted authorities. When fingerprints were lifted, several of them were a match for Kevin Cooper, a recent escapee from the nearby prison in Chino. Within minutes of the print match, an all-points bulletin was issued for Cooper's arrest in conjunction with his escape. A San Bernardino Sheriff's spokesman said Cooper was also being sought for questioning in the Chino Hills murders, although there was no evidence linking him to the slayings.

Over the next two days, this would change radically. On June 9, Sheriff Floyd Tidwell called a late afternoon news conference to announce that earlier that day warrants for the arrest of prison escapee Kevin Cooper had been issued for the murders of Doug and Peggy Ryen, their daughter Jessica, and Chris Hughes, and the attempted murder of Josh Ryen. Tidwell said his investigators believed that Cooper "was the only one involved."

"We have evidence in our possession that places Kevin Cooper at the crime scene and other evidence that gives us cause to believe that Kevin Cooper was responsible for the murders," the sheriff stated.

Tidwell said the crime scene included the vacant house below the Ryens' house, where Cooper's fingerprints were detected, along with bloodstains and clothing, implying the bloodstains and clothing implicated Cooper.

From that day on, the full power and authority of the San Bernardino County Sheriff's Department locked in on Cooper as the lone assailant. The largest manhunt in California history was launched. Seventy sheriff's deputies would be assigned to pursue the alleged ax murderer.

To further tie Cooper to the murders, a sheriff's spokesperson told reporters that Cooper had called a girlfriend from a telephone in the Ryens' house. This was a blatant misrepresentation and so easily disprove that it would never be alleged again. But for the time, it served its purpose of making the news media believe Cooper was obviously guilty.

Sergeant Billy Arthur of the San Bernardino Sheriff's Department would lead the investigation. Early on he adopted the hypothesis that Cooper was some sort of crazed, super-predator whose motive for the killings was theft of the Ryens' station wagon to aid his escape.

Back in Pittsburgh, Cooper's adoptive mother, Esther Cooper, appealed to her son to give himself up.

Newspapers and television stations throughout Southern California would show Cooper's mug shot, a somewhat menacing photo of him in full Afro, and a picture of a 1977 white Buick station wagon in every news cycle.

Five days after the discovery of the murders, California Governor George Deukmejian, buying into the lone-assailant theory, invoked a seldom-used state law to announce a $10,000 reward "for information leading to the conviction of the killer."

Hundreds of leads poured in from citizens claiming to have seen Cooper as well as the Ryens' white station wagon in Mexico and in various locales in Southern California, particularly the Long Beach area.

The search for Cooper would dominate the local news cycles. As weeks began to pass by, the best explanation for not nabbing Cooper that a San Bernardino County Sheriff's Department spokesperson could come up with was that "Cooper is a very average looking guy."

San Bernardino County Sheriff's Deputy Steve Morgan advanced another theory—an utter fabrication—about why Cooper had not been apprehended on June 28, telling the news media about reports from Long Beach that various citizens there had reported seeing Cooper in the area dressed as a woman, adding, "Cooper is known to have associated with transvestites and homosexuals in the past, and it is on that basis that the theory [that he may be dressed as woman] is proposed." Morgan termed Cooper "a homosexual with a history of making friends with transvestites."

Based on the assumption that Cooper was hiding out in Long Beach at the home of a transvestite, detectives for San Bernardino had thirty-year-old Jeffrey Elmore arrested. Sheriff's spokesperson Captain Schuyler informed the media that Elmore did not know Cooper, but it was known that Cooper was a homosexual who associated with transvestites and that the search for him would remain concentrated in the Long Beach area.

As Cooper continued to elude capture, the pressure on the sheriff's department mounted from the local citizens—many now newly armed for self-protection—and the news media to apprehend Cooper. Whether out of frustration, vindictiveness or just plain meanness, various sheriff's department officials portrayed Cooper as a demented, maniacal killer with Houdini-like powers for escape, claiming he had escaped more than ten times from prisons and mental hospitals in Pennsylvania. (As an adult, he had escaped once while on a job-release program while serving a sentence in a minimum-security prison in Pennsylvania and once from a state mental facility where he had been sent for a pre-sentencing evaluation.)

Demonizing Cooper was a crucial strategy the sheriff's department adopted the day Cooper's fingerprints were found in the vacant house below the Ryens' house. The more Sheriff Floyd Tidwell and his subordinates could make Cooper appear to be capable of perpetrating the horrendous murders, the more easily they could get around the inconvenient fact of how implausible it was that one person could have wielded three separate weapons and overpowered two very fit adults and three children, hacking and stabbing four of them to death in a few minutes.

The manhunt caught its first major break at 8 a.m. on June 11 when a man out walking his dog in a church parking lot in Long Beach spotted the Ryens' well-publicized white station wagon. Dust prints on the hood of the car indicated someone had recently closed it. Thinking they might catch whoever parked the car in the lot and believing that the car had been driven in the Long Beach area for the past two or three days, according to what Captain Phillip Schuyler would tell a reporter from the *Daily Report* that afternoon, sheriff's deputies staked out the car and waited. The sheriff's department would soon bungle that opportunity, abandoning the stakeout at 3 p.m. after news of the finding of the station wagon was broadcast on local TV and radio stations. Captain Schuyler said the media got the news of the car "prematurely."

As days quickly turned into weeks and weeks into nearly two months, it became more and more obvious the fugitive would have to catch himself.

CHAPTER FOURTEEN

Cooper Aboard
the Illa Tika

S *hortly after arriving in Ensenada on June 9*, Cooper met Owen Handy, a thirty-five-year-old, disabled ex-Marine from Eureka, California, whose thirty-two-foot sailboat—the *Illa Tika*—was in dry dock there. Handy approached Cooper and asked him if he wanted some work painting his boat. Cooper, still using the alias Angel Jackson and claiming he was an artist from Philadelphia, agreed to sign on for food and a place to sleep on Handy's rickety, wooden sailboat. On board with Handy were his Costa Rican wife, Angelica, and the couple's five-year-old daughter, Karol Vanessa.

Cooper and Owen Handy spent the next two days painting the boat and prepping it for sea. They also smoked some of Handy's marijuana. As Cooper was collecting his belongings to leave, Handy asked him if he wanted to sail with them to Costa Rica and Panama to pick up a ton of marijuana to sell in Humboldt County. Eureka, where Handy was from, is the county seat of Humboldt County, which is located on the far North Coast, two-hundred miles north of San Francisco.

Before they could set sail, a report of a hurricane was broadcast, putting off the trip to Costa Rica and Panama until the fall months. Cooper still had about $70 in cash, most of it in quarters. To help pay part of his keep, he gave Angelica $40 for grocery money and paid $5 to a man Handy owed.

The *Illa Tika* set sail for San Francisco on June 13 with Handy promising Cooper he would teach him how to navigate and sail. Once under sail in rough seas, Cooper got seasick and began vomiting violently, spitting out overboard the bridge plate of his upper and lower front teeth. During the two-week long sail, Cooper remained seasick until Handy docked the *Illa Tika* at Cat Harbor, a small, rocky island about twenty-two miles southwest of Los Angeles. En route, Cooper tossed overboard his prison clothes and tennis shoes.

On a radio aboard the sailboat, the Handys and Cooper heard several mentions of the authorities looking for the suspected Chino Hills ax-murderer Kevin Cooper in Long Beach.

After two days at Cat Harbor, Handy again set sail for San Francisco, but rough seas forced him to turn around. This time they docked at Pelican Cove, a tranquil inlet on the northeast side of rugged Santa Cruz Island, about twenty-five miles offshore from Santa Barbara, California. It was now early July.

By this time, Cooper had established enough rapport with the Handys for them to leave him alone on the sailboat while they went to Santa Barbara—Handy to collect his $600 disability check and Angelica and her young daughter to shop.

On the beach at Pelican Cove, Cooper found a blue bag that contained cosmetics, two pair of sun glasses, and a small knife with a string attached it. He began wearing the knife around his neck.

On July 28, Cooper befriended a recently married couple who were docked on a sailboat near the *Illa Tika*. "I met them arguing," Cooper said in an interview. "Domestic violence. I broke it up. Smoked weed with them. Hung out with them a lot that day and night." Cooper gave the couple a guided tour of the island and baked cookies for them. Cooper and Kim Englehart, a thirty-six-year-old special effects worker from North Hollywood, spent the afternoon "drinking and smoking weed," according to Cooper.

Englehart and his twenty-six-year-old wife, Deborah Englehart, invited Cooper and the Handy family over for a fish cookout that evening. After a late dinner, the Handys returned to their boat. Kim Englehart eventually passed out. "He [Kim Englehart] went to sleep and when he woke up we [Deborah Englehart and I] were fucking and all hell broke loose," Cooper said in an interview. "He jumped on her, not me." (Santa Barbara Sheriff's Department photos of Deborah Englehart taken on July 30 would confirm her right eye was swollen and dark.)

Kim Englehart would call the U.S. Coast Guard at 4 a.m. on Saturday, July 30, and report that his wife had been raped by a black man at knifepoint. The Coast Guard enlisted the assistance of the Santa Barbara Sheriff's department to make the arrest. As the Coast Guard cutter approached the *Illa Tika* that morning, Cooper tossed the knife away and dove overboard, swam about thirty yards to a rubber dinghy and began furiously rowing it toward shore. He got within two-hundred yards of Santa Cruz Island before Santa Barbara deputies overtook him in a motorized dinghy just before 9 a.m.

Cooper told the deputies he was Angel Jackson. It did not dawn on them that they had just captured the most wanted fugitive in California. Later that afternoon, when Deborah Englehart saw a wanted poster for Kevin Cooper in the Santa Barbara Sheriff's Office, she told authorities, "My God, that's the man who raped me." Deputies soon fingerprinted Cooper and confirmed his identity.

Handy would tell authorities that Cooper was sea sick for most of the two weeks they sailed and he spent most of his time below deck "sketching and sleeping on a mattress." Handy said he stored three rifles and two handguns under that mattress.

San Bernardino County Sheriff's detectives, including lead detective Sergeant Billy Arthur, drove to the Santa Barbara County Jail early the next afternoon and brought Cooper back to San Bernardino in handcuffs chained around his stomach and leg irons. A newspaper account said Cooper "looked subdued as he walked quietly to the awaiting sheriff's car."

CHAPTER FIFTEEN

Kevin Cooper

As a barefoot *Kevin Cooper* was escorted back to San Bernardino in chains and leg irons, his enigmatic life had finally reached the point of no more escapes. It had been a long time coming, but coming all the same.

Kevin Cooper did not find out he was adopted until he was eleven or twelve years old during one of his juvenile court proceedings. His birth name was Richard Goodman. He was born in Pittsburgh, Pennsylvania on January 8, 1958. At two months of age his mother placed him in an orphanage. Four months later Melvin and Esther Cooper, parents of a four-year-old daughter, adopted him, changing his name to Kevin Cooper.

The Coopers lived in Pittsburgh's largest black neighborhood, Homewood-Brushton in the city's East End, an area devastated by rioting following the assassination of Dr. Martin Luther King Jr. in April of 1968. Gang warfare and the crack epidemic soon followed.

Melvin Cooper was a captain on the Pittsburgh Fire Department and a disciplinarian. In an interview conducted in 2009, Cooper said that from age five on his adoptive father began enforcing his rules with a thick leather belt he would ominously remove from his uniform.

"My father was always trying to prove something about what a big man he was." Cooper said. "He couldn't get in the military and he couldn't get on the police force, so he became a fireman. He was stern. Sometimes after he beat me I would run away. I'd ended up in juvenile court when I was twelve and I ran away again. When I find myself in a situation I don't like, I run. It is ingrained in me."

Cooper's first juvenile arrest occurred at age seven. Numerous others would follow for such infractions of theft and breaking and entering. A school evaluation done while he was in fifth grade revealed he had an average I.Q. but suffered from attention deficit disorder. The evaluation stated, "[Kevin] has a short attention span, impatience, immaturity and is hyperactive." It neglected to diagnose that he was dyslexic. He was transferred to an alternative school for children who do not respond well to regular classroom instruction. Here his academic performance improved for the next two years, but he continued to end up in juvenile detention for various infractions. At age thirteen, in the process of making his escape from a juvenile facility in a stolen vehicle, he was severely injured in a car accident on August 11, 1971.

He sustained multiple facial fractures, concussions, and a brain injury known as CSF Rhino rhea (nasal leakage of cerebral fluids, indicating rupture of the membranes around the brain). All of his front teeth were knocked out.

Hospital notes from his twenty-seven-day stay show that he was agitated, combative, and uncooperative. To the staff, these symptoms indicated traumatic brain injury of moderate to marked severity. To stabilize Cooper's head injuries, doctors surgically placed wires and splints from his head to his shoulders. These would remain in place for three months after his release and then be removed surgically at the hospital.

The brain injuries continued to alter Cooper's behavior throughout his teenage years. He dropped out of high school and was in and out of the juvenile system for running away from home and for breaking into unoccupied dwellings. Once he was convicted of stealing his adoptive father's credit cards.

In 1976, at age fifteen, Cooper was charged with popping the transmission of a car in an attempt to steal it and with resisting arrest. The juvenile court judge ordered him to report to a counselor once a week.

By mid-1977 he was serving a one-to-two year sentence in the state prison for first-time adult offenders at Greensburg, Pennsylvania for burglarizing a home. According to records at the Pennsylvania State Bureau of Correction, he escaped while on a work detail outside the prison.

Recaptured, he was sent to a state maximum security prison in Huntingdon. Paroled eleven months later, he would be arrested and convicted twice again for burglary and served added time for parole violations in connection with those convictions. When he was released in 1982, he was placed on ten years' probation.

In June of 1982, he was arrested after his girlfriend, Diane Williams, swore out a complaint charging him with assault and making "terroristic threats." Those charges were dropped the next day when Williams refused to press the charges and instead drove him home. His last arrest in Pennsylvania—for a string of burglaries—occurred in the summer of 1982.

As he was awaiting trial for those burglaries, a court-appointed psychiatrist assigned Cooper on August 26 to Mayview State Hospital, a minimum-security, state mental facility, for mental evaluation. Mayview, located in a suburban Bridgeville, about thirty-five miles from Pittsburgh, is known for its "easy time." Activities include berry-picking, basketball, bowling, therapy, and counseling.

A competency hearing in September found Cooper to be "mentally incompetent to stand trial" due to his experiencing suicidal "auditory delusions."

While at Mayview, Cooper stole the driver's license of another inmate, David Anthony Trautman. On the evening of October 8, 1982, Cooper escaped by climbing out a window in the facility's bowling alley. He followed railroad tracks to nearby Upper St. Clair and stopped at a house with cars in the driveway. When he could not jump start either car, he broke into the house to try to find car keys, but did not succeed. While he was in the house, a seventeen-year-old girl who was a friend of the family that owned the house drove up out front, parked her car and went to knock on the front door. Cooper opened the door and told her that her friend was upstairs. As she entered the home, Cooper took control of her by hitting her in the face with a camera he was in the process of stealing. Grabbing the back of her hair, he walked her back to her car and forced her into the front passenger side of her car and made her crouch on the floor with her face pointing down. He then drove to Pittsburgh, where he abandoned the girl in a secluded city park, and took off in her car.

The girl reported to Pittsburgh police that she had been kidnapped and her car stolen, but also that she had been raped. Pittsburgh authorities issued warrants for Cooper's arrest on all three charges plus escaping from custody.

Cooper went to New York City for a couple of weeks, and then traveled by bus to Las Vegas where he spent two weeks. There he began a relationship with a woman who lived in Hollywood, California, and he returned to Hollywood and moved in with her. She became pregnant and later in 1983, after the Chino Hills murders, she had his son. For awhile Cooper tried a job in telemarketing, but switched to selling marijuana, and then reverted to doing burglaries, breaking into homes and businesses. His conviction for two burglaries in Los Angeles landed him at the California Institute for Men.

CHAPTER SIXTEEN

Presumed Guilty

As *Kevin Cooper arrived* at the San Bernardino County Jail on Sunday night July 31, 1983, a phalanx of newspaper photographers and television cameras recorded his long-awaited return. A crowd estimated at sixty people, some who had brought young children with them, had formed at the back gate of the jail. They "rushed the fence and began to jeer and taunt the mass murder suspect," a reporter for the *San Bernardino Sun* wrote the next day.

"An angry crowd jeered the manacled and barefoot mass-murder suspect," a United Press International dispatch reported. "'Gas chamber, gas chamber,' screamed some members of the crowd as Cooper stared straight ahead, expressionless."

"I think they should do the same thing to him as he did to them," UPI quoted another man as yelling out.

Earlier that Sunday, an all-day benefit concert to raise money to help pay for Josh Ryen's medical bills was held at Chino Downs, with about twenty bands donating their time. One of the band members brought an enthusiastic cheer from the crowd of several hundred when he said about Cooper's arrest, "We're just glad they caught that sucker." A news account the next day stated that the "crowd expressed considerable hostility toward Cooper and many expressed the wish that he would receive swift and severe punishment. Few of the suggestions involved the judicial process."

One man told the reporter, "That way we could save the taxpayers the hundreds of thousands of dollars it will take to try him and the thousands it will take to feed him while he's in prison."

Public hostility toward him was so intense that San Bernardino County District Attorney Dennis Kottmeier knew better than to even attempt to hold Cooper's arraignment on August 1 at the Municipal Courthouse, opting instead for the security of the county jail. "We can't afford to make any mistakes or have any problems at this point," Detective Chico Rosales told the news media in explaining why the arraignment would not be open to the public. "At this point, he can't be placed anywhere with the general population."

Rosales said the sheriff's department had received "dozens" of calls that day expressing anger at Cooper. He said there were no threats per se, but that people said such things as, "I hope he gets the gas chamber, I hope he gets the max."

Cooper's arraignment on four counts of first-degree murder and one count of first-degree attempted murder was held that afternoon in the lineup room of the county jail. One newspaper account again depicted Cooper as "calm" and "expressionless."

In the news media accounts there was a striking incredulity to Cooper's calm and expressionless demeanor. The subtext was how could such a demon be so composed? Not one reporter, columnist or commentator thought to deduce that Cooper was calm and expressionless because he knew he had nothing to do with the Ryen/Hughes murders, that the charges against him were baseless and would soon be disproved.

Sentiment against Cooper ran deep with the Ryens' neighbors on Old English Road in Chino Hills. Tom Dalisio told a *Daily News* reporter the day Cooper was brought back to San Bernardino that "I sometimes fantasize what I'd do to him. I wondered if I would climb that fence and tear him apart?"

Once Sheriff Tidwell identified Cooper as the lone assailant in the Chino Hills murders, the California Institute for Men at Chino came under fierce public attack. A Chino Hills neighborhood group quickly formed to demand timely notice from CIM in the event of future escapes. "Maybe the Ryens would have had their door locked if they knew Kevin Cooper had escaped from CIM," Peggy Koob, the president of the group told a reporter. She said her group also now opposed any expansion of

CIM, words that would soon be heeded: Plans to expand CIM to house an additional eight-hundred inmates were scuttled nine days after the murders were discovered. Phil Guthrie, a spokesperson for the State Department of Corrections, said, "The thing that tipped the deliberation [about the expansion] was the escape."

In commenting upon the negative fallout from Cooper's escape, the newly appointed director of the California Department of Corrections, George F. Denton, said, "In terms of consequences, it is probably the most disastrous thing that's happened to any [prison] system in a long time."

The California Legislature acted seven days after the warrants for Cooper's arrest were issued to endorse adding $500,000 to the state budget to enclose the minimum-security section of CIM with a sixteen-foot-high fence with razor wiring on top. (In September, when $500,000 proved insufficient for a fence that high, the legislature authorized construction of a twelve-foot-high fence and installation of a warning system to alert area residents to sound when a prisoner escapes. Only CIM, of the state's twelve prisons, was designated for the warning system.)

On July 5, 1983, the *Fontana Herald News* ran a headline that left no doubt about Cooper's guilt: "Chino killer still sought month later."

Cooper's prison escape soon spurred the organization of an ad hoc group calling itself "Citizens Opposed to the Prison." Its sole goal was to fight a planned maximum-security prison in the San Bernardino County town of Adelanto in the high desert. In a campaign to get signatures on a petition opposing the proposed prison, the group ran advertisements in two local newspapers and set up a booth at the San Bernardino State Fair in late August of 1983 that resembled a jail cell. To further attract attention, an old wanted poster of Cooper was displayed under a sign reading, "Do you want this man to be your neighbor?"

The campaign netted some seven-thousand signatures opposing the construction of any new jails in San Bernardino County. The group traveled to Sacramento to present the signatures to Governor Deukmejian.

The treasurer of the group was Nadia Katz, the wife of San Bernardino County Superior Court Judge Joseph Katz. She told a reporter that day that over five-thousand voters signed the petition. When the reporter asked her if she thought it might be unfair to display a wanted poster for a person who had not yet gone to trial, Katz said she did not think that was "particularly prejudicial."

"The point of the poster was to show residents what kind of people would be in the maximum-security prison planned for Adelanto. We weren't really prejudging him. The idea was if he was convicted, he might be sent here. Besides, I don't think the newspapers are in a position to criticize anyone for prejudging Kevin Cooper," Katz shot back.

The next day, a Sunday, an editorial in the *San Bernardino Sun* took sharp exception to Katz's comments:

ONE WOULD THINK FAMILIES OF JUDICIAL OFFICERS WOULD BE SENSITIVE TO THE REQUIREMENTS OF THE LAW'S DUE PROCESS.

PART OF THAT PROCESS INVOLVES THE PRESUMPTION THAT A PERSON IS FREE FROM GUILT OF A PRESUMED OFFENSE UNTIL THE EVIDENCE HAS BEEN WEIGHED AND HE HAS BEEN CONVICTED.

IF THE SCORN FOR COOPER CAN SO THOROUGHLY PERMEATE THE PUBLIC THAT THE WIFE OF A SUPERIOR COURT JUDGE CAN SEE NO HARM IN THE "WANTED POSTERS," WE ARE DRIFTING DANGEROUSLY CLOSE TO A MOB MENTALITY.

If hate mail could kill, Cooper would have been dead soon after he arrived at the San Bernardino County Jail. All of the mail in his file at the Orrick law office in San Francisco, except for one letter from *San Bernardino Sun* staff writer Ramon Coronado asking him if he wanted him to tell his side of the story, was virulently racist.

Racist hate mail was one thing, but Cooper's life was far more at risk in his maximum-security cell inside the San Bernardino County Jail. As every prisoner in every prison in the United States knows only too well, no one incarcerated is truly safe. Cooper, a black man accused of ax-murdering four whites and slashing the throat of a defenseless eight-year-old boy, was particularly vulnerable to reprisal from both inmates and guards. They only needed the opportunity.

At 7:30 p.m. on September 12 the opportunity presented itself. David Cota, an eighteen-year-old convicted murderer, lurked in the shower awaiting his chance to avenge his race. While Cooper stood with his back to his cell's door, changing his clothes for a session with his attorney, his cell door was electronically opened and Cota charged in to assault him. If Cota had a shiv or was more adept at hand-to-hand combat, Cooper would have been dead in an instant. Cooper fought him off, tumbling with Cota outside his cell, calling for help. The other two white inmates in the unit made noises to cover Cooper's plea for help. A guard, hearing the commotion, soon arrived and broke up the fight.

His public defender, David Negus, told reporters the next day that if Cooper "had been housed with black inmates I don't think this would have happened."

Cooper and three white inmates were the only prisoners housed in the jail's maximum-security unit at the time of the assault, said Lt. Ross Moore, who was in charge of the jail when Cooper was assaulted.

Moore made no attempt to account for where the escort guard happened to be or who electronically opened the door to Cooper's cell. Nor did he try to explain how it could be possible that more than one inmate at a time could be out of his cell when jail rules in the maximum-security unit prohibited that.

Cota had been recently convicted of murder and was awaiting a hearing in Superior Court for allegedly detonating a small hand-made explosive in the jail earlier in the year.

Captain Philip Schuyler, a spokesperson for the San Bernardino Sheriff's Department, said Cota was out of his cell and hiding in a shower. "He was not taking a shower. We're not sure how he got there. He should not have been out there."

Cooper sustained scratches to his head and shoulder and was treated by a jail nurse. Moore said he did not believe Cota was injured.

Instead of removing Cota and the other two white inmates from the maximum-security unit or placing a guard outside Cooper's cell to protect him, Cooper was sent to the "Captain's Hole," an isolation cell without hot water, TV or phone access. A front page headline in a local newspaper the next day read, "Cooper isolated for his protection following assault."

Cooper's first foray outside the jail occurred at his arraignment on August 11, 1983 at the West Valley Municipal Courthouse in Ontario. Security was tight as Cooper was escorted through a tunnel running between the courthouse and jail. A front page article in the *Daily Report* said "Deputies and marshals, all wearing bullet-proof vests and some equipped with walkie-talkies, were stationed in the courtroom, the hall and outside the courthouse."

The newspaper article stated there were no demonstrators present, but reported that "bumper stickers reading 'Fry Kevin Cooper' have been printed."

Once again, Cooper's demeanor was spotlighted: "Cooper sat quietly at the counsel table through the entire proceeding." The newspaper quoted his attorney, David Negus, describing him as "calm."

At the arraignment, Cooper entered a plea of not guilty to the four murders and the attempted murder. Outside the courthouse about ten demonstrators "waved Confederate flags and shouted racial slurs about Cooper, who is black. One demonstrator held a toy monkey in the air with a sign draped around its neck that read, 'Hang Kevin the Ape.'"

Prior to Cooper's preliminary hearing, Channel 7, KABC in Los Angeles, ran an ad in *TV Guide* about an upcoming program entitled, "Profile of a Murderer," based on interviews conducted with Owen and Angelica Handy about their two months living on their boat with Cooper. The show never aired.

By the time Cooper's preliminary hearing got underway on November 9, 1983 there were demonstrators outside the courthouse carrying signs that read, "Fry the Nigger," Kill the African Troglodyte," and other racial epithets.

All pretense of presuming Cooper's innocence was discarded when Bill and Mary Ann Hughes, the parents of victim Christopher Hughes, filed a $10 million wrongful death suit in Los Angeles County Superior Court on January 25, 1984. Named in the thirty-one-page filing were Kevin Cooper, the State of California; Los Angeles County; City of Los Angeles.; California Institution for Men; and Mayview State Hospital in Pennsylvania. John Q. Adams, the attorney representing the Hughes family, said the couple would in addition seek compensation for "other damages" to be determined at trial.

In the suit, the Hughes alleged that "Cooper mutilated [Chris's] body by inflicting a minimum of twenty-five stab and chop wounds." Moreover, the suit asserted that Cooper killed for the "purpose of causing [the parents] to suffer great mental and emotional anguish and physical distress."

A Culture of Corruption

With ten sheriff's substations, four jails, and more than one-thousand sheriff's deputies, the San Bernardino County Sheriff's Department is a fiefdom, with its own rules, unto itself.

The sheriff's department that Sheriff Floyd Tidwell took over in 1983 unabashedly represented the "good ol' boy" network. Tidwell's predecessor, Sheriff Frank Bland, controlled a secret fund known as "county bread" that was funded by the cash the sheriff's office confiscated in making drug busts or other type of arrests. On a monthly basis, Bland doled out checks in $100 and $200 increments to four or five high-ranking underlings to spread around as they saw fit. The *San Bernardino Sun* reported in 1983 that a good deal of this money routinely ended up paying for sheriff's department parties and booze. By the time the scandal hit, Bland had already announced his retirement and the appointment of Tidwell to serve out the remainder of his term.

The retiring sheriff handpicking his successor and stepping down early in an election year was a custom that dated back to the 1950s and it virtually guaranteed no outside candidate for the sheriff's office could win election. It was a custom Tidwell would honor when he retired eight years later and so would his successors. Current sheriff, Rod Hoops, was appointed to complete the term of Sheriff Gary Penrod.

"This is the ultimate good ol' boy network in full operation," wrote Steven Williams, the opinion page editor of the *Victorville*

Daily, about the long-standing appointment practice operating in the sheriff's office. "Interlopers—people outside the system who oppose the anointed one to seek the office—have not been successful in San Bernardino County in the last fifty-four years."

Although Tidwell had spent his entire thirty-year career in the San Bernardino Sheriff's Department, he was a virtual unknown to the majority of the county's voters, despite his personal flamboyance for sporting turquoise jewelry and cowboy boots. The Chino Hills murders were about to change all that for good or ill. How he handled the highest-profile case in San Bernardino County history would make or break the tobacco-spittin' "cowboy sheriff" who would use the murders to cement the rattlesnake-tough image he cultivated.

Once Tidwell announced to the news media that Kevin Cooper was the lone perpetrator of the Ryen/Hughes murders four days after the bodies were discovered, he entered a *mano a mano* battle with the fugitive. Any evidence that supported Cooper's innocence would be systematically ignored and crucial pieces of it destroyed by his underlings.

Tidwell possessed an overwhelming sense of entitlement, seeing himself immune to, if not above, the law. Early on in his eight-year reign as sheriff he began raiding the sheriff's department property division to steal confiscated firearms and continued to do so until his retirement in 1991. It would not be until June of 2003, when sheriff's detectives served search warrants on Tidwell's two sons, Boone and Steven Tidwell, in connection with a scheme to enrich their bail bond businesses that Tidwell's gun theft would come to light.

Detectives, searching for evidence to link Tidwell's sons to an elaborate bail-solicitation ring they had established at the county jails, found fourteen stolen guns at Boone Tidwell's home and ten at Steven's home. Both men informed detectives their father had given them the guns while they had served as deputy sheriffs in San Bernardino County. "Guess what, those guns were given to me by Floyd Tidwell, so you might want to talk to him sometime. You know how we get those, don't you?" Steven Tidwell is quoted as saying in a police report in June of 2003 when deputies found the pilfered guns in his house.

Former Sheriff Tidwell had reason to feel entitled. Before a search warrant could be issued for his house in the high desert, someone in the sheriff's office tipped him off, giving him the time he needed to prepare for the search. Mike Cardwell, a former deputy chief in the sheriff's department who retired in 2003, "has been particularly galled by the lack of an investigation into who leaked the search warrant to Tidwell. He advocated convening a grand jury, granting Tidwell immunity and ordering him to tell who tipped him off or face another criminal charge," according to an article in the *San Bernardino Sun*:

IT'S NECESSARY TO INVESTIGATE, CARDWELL ARGUED, BE-
CAUSE ALERTING TIDWELL TO THE SEARCH WARRANT ELIMINATED
INVESTIGATORS' CHANCES TO SURPRISE THE EX-SHERIFF, GIVING
TIDWELL AMPLE TIME TO TAKE PRE-EMPTIVE ACTION. "THE CASE
MIGHT HAVE BEEN ABLE TO TAKE A WHOLE DIFFERENT TURN,"
CARDWELL SAID. "THERE'S NO TELLING WHAT WE COULD HAVE
FOUND." CARDWELL BELIEVES THE LEAK WAS MADE AT A SENIOR
ADMINISTRATIVE LEVEL BECAUSE FEW PEOPLE KNEW DETECTIVES
PLANNED TO SERVE TIDWELL WITH THE SEARCH WARRANT.

Cardwell said that detectives were still writing their affidavit, a requirement to obtain the warrant, when they informed their supervisor of their intentions. "The supervisor then informed someone on a senior level because getting a search warrant on the former sheriff's residence could be touchy. We don't think it took long for whoever tipped off Floyd," Cardwell told the *Sun*.

Deputy District Attorney Cheryl Kersey said convening a grand jury and offering Tidwell immunity to divulge who tipped him off about the search warrant would be futile. "Quite frankly, I don't think

[Tidwell will] ever tell us," she said because Tidwell would only face a contempt charge, a misdemeanor, and would unlikely face prison time.

A more candid answer might have been to simply say what D.A. Michael Ramos said about ferreting out who leaked word of the search warrant to Tidwell: "We need to move on. We need to move forward."

The San Bernardino County D.A.'s Office was in no hurry to prosecute the retired sheriff even after investigators discovered he had stolen at least 523 guns from the county's property room. When challenged about the delay in the case, San Bernardino Assistant D.A. Bill Lee said by way of explanation, "the case got stuck in the system."

D.A. Ramos termed Tidwell's massive theft as "several errors in judgment."

Some newspapers reported that investigators suspected the thefts were as high as eight-hundred to one-thousand guns.

Eleven months later, in May of 2004, Tidwell turned over eighty-nine of the stolen guns—valued at $25,000—before plea bargaining to four felony counts of concealing stolen property and agreeing to pay a $10,000 fine. Part of the plea bargain worked out before Superior Court Judge J. Michael Welch, over the strenuous objections of Assistant D.A. Kersey, would allow Tidwell to avoid prison if he cooperated with the ongoing search for more than four-hundred of the still missing guns and have the felonies reduced to misdemeanors.

In arguing against the reduction of the crimes to misdemeanors, Kersey told the judge that Tidwell "had been uncooperative, had sought to capitalize on his stature and had pursued special treatment from current Sheriff Gary Penrod," the *Los Angeles Times* reported.

Tidwell's attorney told the judge that as a convicted felon, the former sheriff would be barred from retaining his personal arsenal of guns, guns he needed to protect himself and his family from criminals he had "put away." The attorney said sending Tidwell to prison would be like "sending Colonel Sanders to a chicken coop."

A letter to the editor in the *Riverside Press Enterprise* took on the unusually generous plea bargain, "Floyd Tidwell's prosecution features too much bargain and not enough plea."

Sun staff writer Paul Oberjuerge reported that investigators told him that several sheriff deputies who worked in the property division knew Tidwell was "raiding the property room" all along, adding "but who was going to stop him? The man was armed."

Oberjuerge quoted investigators who paraphrased Sergeant Gary Eisenbiesz as saying, "[Tidwell] used to go through the [property] division, as if shopping, to take his pick of weapons."

The weapons Tidwell was taking home were mostly firearms confiscated by the sheriff's department used in crimes or taken away from citizens for being unregistered. Many should have been returned to their original owners or, in the case of banned firearms, destroyed upon receipt. One of the guns Tidwell did turn in was a .30 caliber fully automatic M2 carbine that is banned under both California and federal law. A few of the guns he gave to his sons were also contraband under the state's assault-weapon ban. One was a Sites Spectra machine gun pistol and the other an Inter Dynamic KG-99 machine gun pistol.

In early November of 2004, Judge Welch, after Tidwell turned in about thirty-five more guns in the intervening months, reduced Tidwell's felonies to misdemeanors, fined him $10,000, and placed him on three-years' of unsupervised probation. Was Tidwell remorseful?

"I'm not guilty of anything, dang it," he is quoted in the *Los Angeles Times* following his sentencing. "I've turned in every gun I had. The others have either been destroyed or distributed, and I gave a list of those [distributed guns] to the sheriff's department, and they said they'd contact those people. What else can I do?" The truth was that at least over four-hundred guns Tidwell had stolen remained unaccounted for.

Swept under the rug throughout the entire year-and-a-half investigation into Tidwell's thefts was the fact that he had admittedly given many of the guns to deputies and volunteer deputies and had turned each of them into felons for accepting the contraband. In the process, he corrupted them and turned the sheriff's department into a privileged club, creating a culture that could easily lead to many sorts of abuses, including framing a black man for a crime three white men committed.

Under Tidwell, the San Bernardino Sheriff's Department became a law into itself. If it was common knowledge within the department that the sheriff was stealing the place blind, what might his minions do? One of them—the acting head of the crime lab—would follow suit in a major way and be more responsible for setting the framing of Kevin Cooper on its path that any other deputy.

CHAPTER EIGHTEEN

The Battle for Josh

S*hortly after Joshua Douglas Ryen was born* in Santa Ana on
September 5, 1974, the Ryens moved into their new home on Old
English Road in Chino Hills.

With Doug and Peggy now not only working at Dr. Howell's clinic but
also living in a house just above her, the opportunities for friction between
the laid-back Ryens and the set-in-her-ways grandmother were about to
be tested to the hilt.

The relationship between Doug and his mother-in-law, and for that
matter between Peggy and her mother, was already a fraught one. Dr.
Howell was a very accomplished, successful chiropractor who was used to
getting her way. She was not one to hide her disapproval and was stinting
with praise.

In a letter to her half sister, Lillian Shaffer, Peggy wrote about the
tension between Doug and her mother at her mother's clinic. "Doug is
working hard—at working with Mom. You can imagine how hard she is
to work with. They do very well ninety-nine percent of the time and then
they have to have a summit meeting and yell and scream at each other and
then all's well. Doug's practice is growing steadily. He's got such a great
personality and everyone loves him. He's the kind of guy who never meets
a stranger. I know you'd like him."

Lillian knew from years of experience of her own how difficult relating
to her mother was. In a 2010 interview, Lillian said there was never a time
in her life when she felt her mother's acceptance, approval, or love.

In a subsequent letter to Lillian Shaffer, Peggy returned to the subject of her mother. "Mom's ready for either a nervous breakdown or heart attack soon. She's finally talking to us again—a little."

Over time, Dr. Howell grew to deeply resent Doug. As she approached her mid-sixties, she began cutting her hours back at the clinic. By now, Peggy only worked at the clinic on Wednesday. When Doug opted to make that his day off, Dr. Howell seethed but said nothing.

In the summer of 1979, while Lillian Shaffer and her eight children were visiting the Ryens in Chino Hills, her mother took her aside and asked her to inform Doug and Peggy that she wanted them to move out of her clinic and start their own. "Doug came down to the park where I was with the kids and I told him what Mom had asked me to do," Lillian said. "Doug wasn't at all surprised. He laughed and said that sounds just like her." The next year, the Ryens opened their own clinic in Santa Ana.

Soon after that, Dr. Howell put her Chino Hills home on the market and moved to Temecula, seeing patients both at her Santa Ana office and her ranch house. The breach between her and Doug and Peggy would continue to fester. Lillian said in an interview that Peggy had told her a year before she was murdered that her mother had not spoken to her or Doug in over a year.

In September of 1982, just eight months before their murders, Doug and Peggy had their wills redrafted to remove Mary Howell as the legal guardian of their children. Their new wills stipulated that in the event of their deaths or incapacitations, Doug's oldest brother, Dick Ryen, would be the guardian for Jessica and Josh. Dick Ryen operated a successful book distribution business in New Jersey. He and his wife, Sally, had three children. Two had already left home but they had a son who was still a teenager when the new wills were finalized.

As soon as Josh was released from the Loma Linda University Hospital on June 18, Dick and Sally Ryen accompanied him back to their home in Oradell, New Jersey, an upscale New York City suburb. Mary Howell had spent all thirteen days Josh was hospitalized sitting at his side. At the time of his release to Dick and Sally Ryen, she seemed resigned to the dictates of the Ryens' will. Privately, however, she was appalled at losing guardianship of Josh. Just before Josh departed for New Jersey, his grandmother, according to Lorna M. Forbes, a psychiatrist Dr. Howell would hire to help her overturn the custody stipulation in the Ryens' wills, took him aside and said, "Hey, Josh, let's you and me have a secret. You are my boy. Nothing is going to take you away from me. You have to go with Dick, but not for long." She soon hired a Los Angeles attorney and filed suit in San Bernardino Superior Court, contesting the custody issue of her daughter and son-in-law's wills.

The closed hearings before Judge Philip Schaefer lasted four days in mid-September, offering something of a bizarre twist to the tragedy of the murders. Josh did not appear at the hearing, but the judge heard testimony from eleven witnesses, including Dick Ryen, Mary Howell, Dr. Lorna Forbes, the psychiatrist Dr. Howell hired to treat Josh, a psychologist hired by Dick Ryen, and the attorney who drafted Doug and Peggy Ryens' wills. From that testimony the judge deduced that Josh preferred to live with his grandmother. "His preferences were articulated through other witnesses," the judge told reporters after rendering his decision. "He [Josh] had an ongoing relationship with her since his birth. He feels very close, familiar and comfortable with her. There was no controversy about what his preference was."

Judge Schaefer ruled that Dr. Howell, then sixty-nine-years-old, would have custody of Josh through the school year and that his uncle would have custody during school vacations. "The court followed the law of what is the best interest of the child," the judge said. "In the short term, his best interests are served by living with his grandmother, and in the long term, his best interests are served by living with the Ryen family." The judge, without explaining why this was in Josh's best long-term interests, also named Dr. Howell the administrator of Josh's estate.

"Richard Ryen felt very strongly that he had an obligation to the parents to carry through on their wishes," his attorney George W. Young told reporters after the decision was handed down. Cindy Settle, Doug Ryen's sister, said her brother spent over $25,000 in legal fees to uphold Doug and Peggy's wills.

Dick Ryen's attorney told reporters, "The ruling is in our favor and in effect we won." Young could not have been further off in that assessment. None of the Ryens would ever see Josh again. Neither would Peggy's half-sister, Lillian Shaffer.

"My mother absolutely brainwashed Josh against all of his relatives on both sides, Lillian said. "Josh thinks we are all a bunch of monsters. I've invited Josh to family reunions every year, but he never responds. We all love him dearly and want to be a part of his life."

"Dr. Mary Howell was a wicked witch," Cindy Settle said. "Neither Doug nor Peggy wanted her to have custody of their children. They moved up north [to Olympia] to get away from Mary. During the custody battle, Mary Howell committed to allowing Josh to visit his Ryen relatives in Iowa and New Jersey, but after winning custody she refused to let Josh see any of them again. All the birthday cards and presents the Ryen relatives sent Josh in Temecula, Mary boxed up and sent back to them. She wrote on the outside, 'My son does not need these things.'"

By the time summer vacation came around in 1984, Dr. Howell was well along in her quest to not just be Josh's guardian during the school year but to adopt him outright as her own child. She wanted to circumvent the Superior Court decision of joint custody by going directly to the California Department of Adoptions.

As part of this application process, Dr. Howell once again retained the services of Dr. Lorna Forbes. A specialist in treating children who have survived the murder of a family member, Dr. Forbes had begun counseling Josh in October of 1983 just after he returned from living with his uncle's family in New Jersey. The psychiatrist submitted an eleven-page letter, dated June 6, 1985, to the Department of Adoptions.

The letter was an out-and-out attack on Josh's parents. It depicted Mary Howell as the central nurturer to Josh throughout his life, contend-ing that the bond she had with him was stronger than he had with either parent. On the concluding page, Dr. Forbes wrote, "...it was clear [prior to his parents' deaths] that the boy felt left out and rejected by his parents, and had, because of the lack of nurturance by his alcoholic father, and obsessively preoccupied mother, experienced his grandmother acting as a psychological parent."

The letter also dredged up many grudges Dr. Howell harbored for Doug. She saw him as a wanton philanderer and a chronic drunk. Dr. Forbes quotes Dr. Howell saying about Doug, "He didn't like working too much. He wanted to be a country gentleman."

To further support that Dr. Howell was Josh's main nurturer, Dr. Forbes stated, "Joshua's pregnancy was not wanted" and that both parents favored his sister Jessica at his expense. "There was thus, every reason to believe that the bonding, i.e., parent-child relationship was not a strong one…he [Josh] experienced most of his nurturing from his grandmother."

Dr. Forbes wrote that Josh did not like living in New Jersey, quoting him as saying, "It's house-to-house with no room to play. Grandma has a big ranch. I wish I were living with my grandma. I have told them [his uncle and aunt in New Jersey] that I want to live with my grandma."

Peggy would also take her lumps from Dr. Forbes. "It is evident that Joshua is deeply tied to his grandmother. His mother was so involved with horses that he was emotionally neglected."

In her second to last paragraph, Dr. Forbes warned the Department of Adoptions that if Josh were forced to live away from his grandmother "he would see this as punishment, and could become suicidal." Earlier she had advanced the theory that Josh, because he survived while his parents, sister and best friend were all brutally murdered, felt "survivor's guilt."

"In my many years of consulting with adoption agencies I have come to have a vast experience. All of that only serves to make me feel strongly committed to facilitating his being adopted by 'psychological mother,' Mary Howell," the letter concluded.

The Department of Adoptions agreed.

The image of Doug and Peggy Ryen that Dr. Howell conveyed to Dr. Forbes was at complete odds with the impressions the couple created among their closest friends and neighbors. Rob and Pam Hess, photographers who travel eleven months a year throughout the United States to Arabian horse shows, met the Ryens in 1976. They stayed a couple of times a year at the

Ryens' house when they were in Southern California. Their last visit had
been in April of 1983, two months before the Ryens and Chris Hughes
were murdered. In May, Pam Hess had spoken with Peggy by phone.

In an interview at their studio in Olympia, Washington on May 31,
1984, defense investigator Ron Forbush asked Pam Hess to describe the
Ryen family. "Well I can't think of anyone who put their children first as
much as they did," she said. "Peg lived for her children. And as a result I
know that she drove two hours a day to see that they went to Montessori
school and she was very emphatic about their education."

Mrs. Hess said Jessica and Josh were extremely polite. "It was always
'Mr. and Mrs. Hess,' and 'thank you very much.'"

She said Doug "also tried to spend as much time as possible with the
children on his days off...They were quite a close family."

Toward the end of the thirty-five-minute interview, Pam Hess told
Forbush, "...there were no two individuals that we were more fond of than
Doug and Peg, because they were always concerned about us as individuals.
And where a lot of our clients and friends would take us out to dinner, they
understood what it's like to be on the road and Peg would always cook our
very, very favorites and, you know, make it quite a festive occasion for us.
We miss them dearly."

An article in the Ontario *Daily Report* on June 7, 1983, headlined "Ryens Characterized as Jolly and Good-Natured," quotes Josh Ryen's Montessori teacher Alma Wiesner saying, "They were the best kind of people.
They were always there for anything when you needed them." Wiesner said
Peggy Ryen was "avidly interested" in her children's progress at school and
interrupted her day at a horse show recently to join Josh and Jessica at a
school carnival.

Pearl Larson, the secretary of the Arabian Horse Breeding Association, said, "What a shame for such a lovely, nice young couple. The world
needs more people like them. They were always jolly and good-natured.
They were very good sports." She said the Ryens fit right into the Arabian
horse community, "Where the job of breeding Arabians is paramount, and
victory in horse shows is 'nice' but only secondary."

CHAPTER NINETEEN

The Players

For indigent defendants such as Kevin Cooper, the State of California funds a Public Defender's Office in each county. David Negus, who had joined the San Bernardino County Public Defender Office after graduating from the UCLA Law School in 1974, volunteered to represent the reviled defendant. In an interview in 2010, he ingeniously said about the district attorney's rationale for taking the case, "Kottmeier tried the case because he is an egoist. He wanted it for the same reason I did: More publicity than any case in San Bernardino County in the thirty years I was in the county."

By the time Negus was assigned the Cooper case, he had been involved in about one-hundred-twenty jury trials, but only ten of those were murder cases.

If one were to search the Internet for renowned public defenders one would find there is not one mentioned. As Clarence Darrow stated over a hundred years ago and is still valid today, "…the courts are not instruments of justice. When your case gets into court it will make little difference whether you are guilty or innocent, but it's better if you have a smart lawyer. And you cannot have a smart lawyer unless you have money. First and last it's a question of money…We have no system for doing justice, not the slightest in the world."

Darrow said that if the courts were organized to promote justice "the people would elect somebody to defend all these criminals, somebody as smart as the prosecutor—and give him as many detectives and as many assistants to help, and pay as much money to defend you."

There is something of the absent-minded professor about Negus. His intelligence is obvious, but his lack of flare and conviction is even more so. He comes off more as a theorist than an advocate, as one who prides himself on knowing the law rather than being a champion of it.

"[Negus is] the most hard-working defense attorney I ever came across," said District Attorney Kottmeier in an interview, adding, that "being prepared was his strong suit." He said Negus also possessed "a photographic memory."

"The disadvantage for him was he did not have a trial attorney's ability to highlight the information he should have to the jury," Kottmeier said, explaining that Negus was oblivious to where he stood in the courtroom and did not use the inflection of his voice to verbally impart important "information in an effective manner."

Ron Forbush, the lone private investigator Negus hired to assist him in Cooper's defense, said Negus was "brilliant," but the one word that would best describe him was "eccentric." He said the second word would be "disheveled." Asked his impression of Negus's appearance, Cooper said "...his clothes needed to be ironed. He was rumpled, and maybe every once in a while his shirttail hung out. But that's him."

Among themselves, the jurors referred to Negus as "Columbo," after the tousled detective played by Peter Falk during the 1970s.

Forbush, after a long career as a homicide detective for the San Bernardino County Sheriff's Department, followed by five years as a real estate agent, had just set up his own private investigative firm when Negus invited him to assist in Cooper's defense. As a detective, Forbush had investigated hundreds of murders, but this would be his first on the defense side. Hired in 1962 by then Captain Floyd Tidwell, Forbush retired in 1977 as commander of homicide. Along the way he hired Billy Arthur.

Although both Negus and Forbush grew fond of Kevin Cooper—and he of them, Cooper referring to Forbush as "Uncle Ron"—neither will take a position on his guilt or innocence. Asked in 2010 if he thought Cooper were innocent, Negus said, "That's a question I'm afraid we'll never know the answer to." In an interview he gave the Ontario *Daily Bulletin* in 2004, Negus delivered a more lackluster response when asked if he thought

Cooper had killed the Ryens and Chris Hughes: "Obviously, if it wasn't Kevin, then it was a tremendous coincidence that Kevin was hiding out next door. But coincidences happen."

Forbush, in a separate 2010 interview, said he found Cooper "very personable" and said he was "not a bullshitter," but demurred on the question of innocence. "Kevin certainly had the opportunity being so close to the Ryen house."

The prosecution was headed by San Bernardino County District Attorney Dennis Kottmeier, who assigned the most publicized case in county history to himself. His intention was to make this prosecution the signature achievement of his career, just as Vincent Bugliosi had done in the Manson case. But unlike Bugliosi, who had both a sense of fair play about a prosecutor's role and a working rapport with the accused cult leader he prosecuted, Kottmeier had neither.

Kottmeier was appointed district attorney in 1981 when his predecessor stepped down to open the way for him. He had joined the district attorney's office in 1969 and had been promoted to chief deputy district attorney ten years later.

With his dark beard and no mustache, Kottmeier presented a severe visage; something of the avenger palpably lurks behind his intensity and assuredness. Whereas Negus viewed the case before him and the law itself in shades of gray, the district attorney worked without ambiguity. He was convinced in his bone marrow that Cooper—and Cooper alone—was guilty.

Asked his impression of Kottmeier, Negus said, "Dennis is a nut. A Mennonite. Very religious. He thinks he's Abe Lincoln. He made a horror movie in high school, a cult classic. A grandstander. Not bad as a trial lawyer, with a high conviction rate. He thinks he is an orator. He's a stuffed shirt and acts that way in court."

In response to written questions submitted to him, Cooper wrote: "Kottmeier appeared to be a racist, not only in his appearance, but in his actions as well. That beard with no mustache was right out of the 19th century."

Assistant D.A. John Kochis served as co-counsel to Kottmeier. Kochis, a clean-cut, earnest young prosecutor—a former altar boy—provided a much-needed balance to the theatrical prosecutor in terms of courtroom style, but he was no less driven to send Cooper to the gas chamber.

Sergeant Billy Arthur, the lead detective, sat at the prosecution table throughout the trial. Both the D.A. and Arthur had staff on site at their disposal. In addition, in a spirit of collegiality, the San Diego D.A.'s Office extended the use of its courthouse facilities and staff to Kottmeier. A California deputy attorney general in the San Diego office was assigned to provide advice to the prosecution.

Superior Court Judge Richard Clyde Garner, who out of earshot was referred to as "King Richard," would preside at Cooper's trial. A 1957 graduate of the University of San Francisco's Law School, Garner was a former assistant district attorney in the San Bernardino County D.A.'s Office until he was appointed a municipal judge in Ontario in 1965. Five years later, at age 45, he was elected to the Superior Court of San Bernardino County.

Both Negus and Kottmeier had extensive experience with the judge, although Kottmeier had not appeared before him since becoming district attorney three years earlier. From his experience with Judge Garner, Negus said he knew the judge to be "a very religious, opinionated man, with a quick temper." "His [Judge Garner's] bailiff used to say when I made him [Judge Garner] red in the face he wasn't that dangerous, but when he got white look out," Negus said. "In the little world of Ontario Superior Court, I had lots of trials with him. He is not a pro-defense judge." Nor did Negus have much regard for the judge's intelligence, saying in specific reference to Judge Garner that "superior court judges are not necessarily the most brilliant people in our profession."

CHAPTER TWENTY

Trial Preparation

Although Kevin Cooper was arrested on July 29, 1983, his trial for the murders of Doug and Peggy Ryen, their ten-year-old daughter, Jessica, eleven-year-old Chris Hughes, and the attempted murder of eight-year-old Josh Ryen would not begin until October 23, 1984.

In an early pre-trial session, Judge Garner had encouraged Negus to bring in co-counsel to assist him in his trial preparation and trial presentation. Negus had declined the offer, saying he preferred to go it alone, telling the judge he did not work that well with other attorneys at his side. This decision, perhaps more than any other, would hamstring the defense and lead perforce to Cooper's conviction.

"If Negus did not work well with other attorneys at his side, he shouldn't have taken such a case. The judge should have admonished him. This is a case where he not only needed a second seat but a supportive staff," said Richard Melick, a retired defense attorney with forty years of trial experience in the Boston area.

Not having co-counsel at his side doomed Cooper's defense from the outset. In August of 1983, when the prosecution turned over several thousand pages of discovery—various police logs, police reports, witness interviews, crime lab, and medical examiner reports connected to the crime—Negus asked Municipal Court Judge David C. Merriam for a continuance to go through them prior to the preliminary hearing and to postpone the preliminary hearing until the last week of October. When the judge refused to grant the continuance and set September 23, 1983 as the date for the preliminary hearing, Negus should have brought on co-counsel and numerous paralegals to at least go through and notate the discovery.

When questioned why he did not bring on paralegals to go through the discovery, Negus said, "I do better if I know the material myself, so I know the evidence. My experience with paralegals has not been positive." So why not bring in another attorney to go over the discovery? "I chose not to."

"Several thousand pages of discovery immediately says that he [Negus] needs help in the form of many attorneys and paralegals," Melick said. "There is a huge amount of sifting, cataloging, developing leads for further discover, etc.

"He requested a continuance of less than three months, which was far less than he needed, and at the end of whatever period there should be a status conference, not a preliminary hearing. Status to determine how his preparation was proceeding and when he would be ready for trial."

Knowing what is in the discovery is crucial to pre-trial planning for any defense attorney. The discovery would have generated numerous leads for Negus and his investigator to explore and would have indicated what witnesses to interview in preparation for both the preliminary hearing and trial.

Instead, Negus simply set the discovery aside and pursued what he considered to be a better use of his time. From the arraignment, Negus knew the prosecution would introduce into evidence a drop of blood alleg-edly recovered at the crime scene as coming from Cooper, as well as other blood and serum evidence from the hideout house and the Ryens' station wagon that tended to link Cooper to the murders. As a result, Negus said, "I spent all of my time boning up on serology and didn't get around to reading the discovery until early in 1984."

"Setting the discovery aside was a major mistake because there were de-positions to be noticed, summaries of the transcripts to be written, requests for production of documents to be drafted, newly discovered witnesses to be pursued," Melick said. "By not reading the discovery, he has simply and totally ignored a fountain of information from which he should have com-menced his own discovery."

As a result of not reading the discovery, Negus did not learn of the coveralls belonging to convicted murderer Lee Furrow that were turned in by Diana Roper until after Deputy Rick Eckley had destroyed them. The coveralls were, without a doubt, the single most important piece of exculpatory evidence the defense could have used to turn the prosecution's case against Cooper on its head. If blood from any of the murder victims was on them, the case against Cooper would have collapsed. Lee Furrow and his accomplices, not Kevin Cooper, would have gone on trial for the Chino Hills massacre. Cooper would have pled guilty to escaping from prison, and then most likely extradited to Pennsylvania and been long forgotten.

It would not be until Diana Roper called Negus on May 17, 1984 that he found out that she had turned over to the sheriff's substation in Yucaipa the bloody coveralls she believed were connected to the Chino Hills murders. Negus, ever-wary of crank calls, put her off by telling her to call his investigator, which she did.

Ron Forbush interviewed her the next evening for one hour at her home in Mentrone. What had prompted Roper to call Negus and then Forbush was homicide Detective Jim Stalanaker informing her that day before that the coveralls she had turned in had been destroyed and never sent to the lab for testing. Roper and her father had gone to see Detective Stalanaker after hearing on the news that the little boy who survived the slaughter had originally said three white men were the attackers. Roper wanted to find out why the sheriff's department had never followed up on investigating Furrow about the coveralls.

Before answering any of Forbush's questions, Roper asked him if talking to him would expose her because going public with what she had to say about the coveralls "could cost me my life." Forbush told her he would do his best to keep her name from the media but that she might be called as a witness and that would be publicized.

"If this fits together, I will testify. I will, you know, no ifs, ands, or buts about it," she said, adding a moment later, "If these people [Furrow and associates] are guilty, if it all ties in, I will be more than glad to testify and so will other people that saw certain things…It's only right."

Forbush was leery of her immediately, asking her if she had any history of mental illness or treatment for mental illness. She answered, "No, no." He also asked her if she had any arrests. She said none as an adult.

The story she told the former detective turned investigator had some surreal elements to it, but in various particulars it tied into the Ryen/Hughes murders in remarkable ways.

Roper, then twenty-seven years old, said that on the day of the Chino Hills murders she had attended the US Music Festival with her sister, Karee Kellison, Debbie Glasgow, who had a thing for Furrow, and Becky Darnell, the wife of Michael Darnell, whom Furrow picked up at the jail that afternoon. The festival was held at Glen Helen Amphitheater, thirty miles northeast of Chino Hills and twenty-four miles northwest of Mentrone.

At some point during the afternoon, Roper said Glasgow bought her a Coke and spiked it with LSD that turned her into a "zombie" for the next ten hours at the festival.

Roper never saw Furrow at the country music show, but her sister did. Near the end of the festival, around 11:30 p.m., Roper was stable enough to drive and she left with her sister. Glasgow had joined up with Furrow by then. Around 1:40 a.m. Furrow called Roper and asked him to come pick him and Glasgow up at the festival grounds. Roper refused.

Furrow and Glasgow arrived at Roper's house in Mentrone less than an hour later, but Furrow only stayed long enough to change out of the coveralls he had on and pick up a gun at the house. He and Glasgow left on his Harley Davidson motorcycle. After that night, Furrow no longer stayed at Roper's house. By this time he had secretly married Glasgow in Arizona.

Two or three days later the odor emanating from the coveralls on the floor of the walk-in closet in the master bedroom caused Roper to pick them up. "There was blood all over the butt, back, everywhere and mostly where the zipper was," she told Forbush. "There was like gray and white horse hair on the inside legs of them." Roper thought the horse hair was from an Arabian horse.

Roper related how she had called her father, Bill Kellison, and asked him to come take a look at the coveralls. Her father saw the blood and horse hair and called the sheriff's department. A deputy picked up the coveralls that afternoon. She never heard another thing about the coveralls and no one from homicide ever contacted her.

Roper told Forbush that Furrow "is a very strange person" and had murdered a young girl at the behest of gang leader Clarence Ray Allen. She said Furrow always carried a large buck knife and he still had that.

As Forbush's skepticism was mounting, Roper told him she had given Furrow a tan T-shirt with a pocket in front and that his hatchet was missing from the back porch but his other tools were still there. She said she had told the sheriff's office about the tan T-shirt and the missing hatchet, then said, "The bloody coveralls is the main thing. There's no ifs, ands, or buts about them."

She said Furrow had been on "acid" at the music festival.

Roper told Forbush how astounded she was when Detective Stalanaker informed her that the coveralls she had turned in had been destroyed in December of 1983 without ever being tested at the lab. She quotes herself saying to Stalnaker, "I says you mean to tell me that them coveralls that were covered with the blood and hair and sweat were not labbed two days after a Chino massacre? Whether it was rabbit blood, dog blood, human blood, when it's that close to a massacre and they weren't sure who'd done it, you automatically would take them and labbed them, just in case."

At the end of the interview, Forbush asked her if she would accept a subpoena to testify for the defense at Cooper's trial. "No problem," she said.

In an interview in Ontario in 2010, Forbush said he considered Roper "a whack job," and neither he nor Negus "gave much credence to her claim about the bloody coveralls." Negus confirmed that in a 2011 telephone interview, saying that after he listened to Forbush's interview of her that he "thought she was nuts. A meth nut." Negus never took the time to interview Roper himself.

Asked what he thought about Roper identifying the exact tan T-shirt that was found not far from the Canyon Corral Bar, he said, "I don't recall her doing that." Asked why the combination of Roper identifying the tan T-shirt along with the bloody coveralls turned in did not make her the defense's star witness at trial, he said, "If you want to try the case differently

than I did, be my guest. But I think she would not be a good witness."
Pressed for a reason why she would not have made a good witness, Negus
said, "I truly don't remember it very well. Perhaps based on the phone call
to me or what Ron told me about her. We were very leery...You don't want
to be made to look silly by putting on bad witnesses."

CHAPTER TWENTY-ONE

Change of Venue

Local pre-trial publicity, tinged with ugly racial overtones, had been so overwhelmingly negative against Kevin Cooper since he was identified by Sheriff Tidwell as the lone assailant on June 9, 1983, that San Bernardino County Superior Court Judge Richard Garner granted the defense's change of venue motion, the first in the history of San Bernardino County. Public Defender David Negus's change of venue motion had requested the trial be moved to Sacramento, Oakland, or downtown Los Angeles. Each of those venues had significant enough black populations to afford his client the opportunity of having something approximating a jury of his peers. In granting the defense motion, Judge Garner denied the defense request for any of those venues, opting to hold the trial in San Diego.

Judge Garner's reasoning for not wanting to move the trial to either of the Northern California courtrooms had plausibility: Oakland was just over four-hundred miles away and Sacramento was another eighty miles past that. The judge did not want to impose such travel distances on the families and friends of the victims, or on most of the witnesses who would be coming from San Bernardino County. In addition, both of those venues would sharply escalate the county's own expenses in prosecuting Cooper.

Judge Garner had no such grounds in denying the venue change to downtown Los Angeles, just forty-two miles due west of Ontario. In fact, if he had the concerns of the families and friends of the victims in mind,

Los Angeles was by far his best option. His explanation for turning down Los Angeles was that the courtrooms there were "too busy." In addition, the prosecution had refused to stipulate to moving the trial to Los Angeles.

In announcing the change of venue to San Diego, which is one-hundred-fifteen miles southwest of Ontario, he suited his own preferences and convenience. He owned a condo in San Diego where he could stay throughout the trial and expense his lodging per diem back to San Bernardino County.

When Judge Garner chose San Diego, Negus thought at least he meant the jury pool would be drawn from city residents. When jury summons were sent to both county and city residents, Negus reinstated his change of venue motion at a pre-trial session in Superior Court in San Diego on September 11, 1984, just prior to jury selection.

Negus had various points to argue: Because Kevin Cooper is black and the victims were white, he would have a better chance of getting a jury of his peers in Sacramento, Oakland or downtown Los Angeles; Cooper is from out of state while people in San Diego County have close ties to San Bernardino County; the grandmother of Josh Ryen lives on the county line; people connected with the case live in North San Diego County; North San Diego County and San Bernardino County are similar in geography, racial makeup, and the occupation of their residents.

To bolster his argument for a change of venue away from San Diego, Negus had conducted an extensive study of pre-trial publicity in San Diego County. He said the *Los Angeles Times* San Diego edition had a circulation of 40,000 to 50,000 households and that the newspaper had published sixty-seven articles about the case; the *San Diego Tribune* published forty articles, the *San Diego Union* forty-five, averaging about two articles a month since the murders.

Of those articles in the San Diego newspapers, only three included references to the defense side of the case, Negus said, adding that all of the TV and radio coverage was from a prosecution perspective.

"The article in the *Tribune* last Friday only stated the prosecution point of view, the prosecution's evidence," Negus told the court. "It also mentioned charges being brought in Santa Barbara [rape], even though Mr. Cooper has not been tried on those charges and the Santa Barbara district attorney was 'at least equivocal' as to even trying him on those unsubstantiated charges." Negus said the article stated the rape charge "without suggesting there is a considerable amount of information regarding the falsity of those charges."

As a result of such newspaper reporting, Negus said, potential jurors are getting "the notion that Mr. Cooper is a dangerous individual and we will not be given a chance in the course of this trial to disprove those charges."

To Negus, the entire reason for moving the trial out of San Bernardino County applied equally to San Diego County because both counties share the same sort of political climate and basic demographics. "Mr. Cooper has become a symbol of what people don't like about having prisons in their communities," Negus said. "The symbol is as strong in San Diego as it was in San Bernardino. The assumption behind the symbol is that Mr. Cooper is guilty."

The argument Negus made for the change of venue was grounded and persuasive.

Judge Garner denied the motion.

Based on that decision, Negus had every right to request a sequestered jury, but opted not to. "I felt that a sequestered jury would not be a happy jury," Negus said.

Jury selection commenced. Three-hundred potential jurors had been summoned from San Diego County. Jury selection would take over a month. After questioning one-hundred-twenty-six of them, a jury of nine whites, two blacks, and one Hispanic was impaneled.

Most prosecutors and defense attorneys believe jury selection is such a crucial factor in the outcome of a high-profile case that they routinely retain jury consultants to assist them during the process. For the indigent Kevin Cooper, no such luxury was sought.

At the O.J. Simpson murder trial in 1995, where both the defense and prosecution used jury consultants, it took nearly two months to pick the jury. Despite the fact that the racial composition of the initial jury pool was forty percent white, twenty-eight percent black, seventeen percent Hispanic, and fifteen percent Asian, Simpson's jury ended up with nine blacks, one Hispanic and just two whites. Although the murders Simpson was on trial for occurred in upscale, predominantly white Sana Monica, the prosecutors chose to file the case in downtown Los Angeles. Vincent Bugliosi, the prosecutor at the Charles Manson trial, said that mistake "dwarfed anything the prosecution did" in losing the case.

CHAPTER TWENTY-TWO

The Prosecution's Opening Statements

The importance of opening statements is often overlooked. Books have been written about the greatest closing arguments. Clarence Darrow's plea to spare the lives of Leopold and Loeb is on this list, but no book records any of the famed advocate's opening statements. In his 2001 book entitled *Winning Your Trial in Opening Statement*, P.C. Bobb cites a University of Chicago Law School study that showed an eighty percent correlation between the ultimate verdict and the verdict jurors would have rendered following an opening statement. Put another way, eight out of ten cases tried before a jury are decided before one piece of evidence has been introduced.

There are a number of reasons for the significance of opening statements, but a main one is that this is the time that jurors are freshest and most interested in the case. Their minds are uncluttered and open to information. In the days that follow, the jury will sit through numbing direct and cross-examination of experts and witnesses and try to fit that information in with what they were told by the prosecution and defense attorneys in their openings. If they are not given a clear story of the case from the opening, jurors are left to provide their own story. For the prosecution and defense attorney, this is their opportunity to tell that story and their last chance to speak directly to the jury until closing argument at the end of the trial.

A trial, in essence, is a contest between competing story lines. A good trial lawyer is like the narrator in the play *Our Town* by Thornton Wilder. Through his calm, sympathetic command of the scene about to unfold, he becomes the audience's guide and trusted friend. He conveys an omniscience and empathy for the characters he is about to introduce that is spellbinding. No matter how unfortunate or upsetting the facts may be, the narrator will see the audience through to the other side, to a brighter day where goodness and righteousness prevail once again.

A good trial lawyer knows the defendant is not the only one on trial. During opening statements, jurors will be formulating their opinions of opposing counsel during the hour or so each side takes to address the jury. They will be assessing each attorney's demeanor, competence, likability, and, above all, credibility. As they old saying goes, you never get a second chance to make a first impression.

What the prosecutor and the defense attorney say in opening statements is not evidence. Evidence will come only from the witness stand and exhibits entered during the course of the trial.

Because the prosecution has the burden of proof, it goes first. The burden is to prove the state's case beyond a reasonable doubt. The prosecutor's job is to let the jury know what evidence the state has and what this evidence is supposed to prove.

Opening statements are supposed to be devoid of argument and limited to the facts, but neither of these two caveats seemed to be of much concern to Kottmeier as he addressed the jury. He would repeatedly step out of bounds during his opening, not because he did not know better, but because he seemed more than anything else to want to overcome the inherent weakness of his case against Cooper with his zeal for Cooper's conviction.

Despite the bravado that characterized Kottmeier's courtroom demeanor, the case he had mounted against Cooper was based entirely on circumstantial evidence. Other than young Josh Ryen, there were no eyewitnesses to the murders. The prosecution had no witnesses—no girlfriends, acquaintances or even jailhouse snitches—who would say that Cooper confessed his crimes to them.

Other than one highly questionable drop of blood that the prosecution alleged linked Cooper to the crime scene, the only other bits of evidence were equally dubious. One consisted of sole impressions the prosecution falsely contended were left by a tennis shoe only available in state institutions such as CIM. One impression was found on a bed sheet, and the other on a Jacuzzi cover just outside the master bedroom. Neither impression had been observed or marked by detectives or crime lab technicians in their original casing of the Ryens' house. The other piece of evidence concerned a roll-your-own cigarette butt the prosecution alleged Cooper had smoked and left in the Ryens' station wagon that was recovered in Long Beach a week after the murders.

Except for those highly suspicious links to Cooper, the most remarkable thing about the crime scene was its utter lack of evidence connecting the defendant to it. Not one hair of his or any other black person was found in the Ryen home or grounds. It would be virtually impossible for an assailant committing the frenzied murders not to have shed numerous hair fibers during the attack.

Kottmeier began his opening statement by describing Chino Hills as "the perfect place to raise a family," so secure residents could leave their doors unlocked and the keys in their vehicles, despite the fact they lived less than three miles from the California Institute for Men.

"Little could they know that on April the 29th, 1983, a prisoner was being admitted to the Chino (sic) Institution (sic) for Men that would have deadly consequences when it (sic) crossed their path about a month later," the prosecutor said.

This prisoner was Kevin Cooper, a "felon" who was using the alias of David Anthony Trautman. Kottmeier did not reveal that Cooper had been convicted of two run-of-the-mill burglaries in Los Angeles.

Kottmeier detailed how Cooper had escaped from CIM on the afternoon of June 2, wearing prison clothing that included Pro-Keds Dude tennis shoes that were only supplied to institutions and were not available for retail purchase. His only reference to Cooper's hair was to misrepresent to the jury that he had worn it in a "modified Afro" when he escaped. The truth was Cooper had spent hours fixing into flat braids the day before he escaped.

During his opening, Kottmeier advanced numerous false assumptions he had made about Cooper. It did not seem to matter to him that he did not have the evidence to back up his claims. Horrendous murders had been committed and Cooper had been the perpetrator, the facts be damned. One example was he had Cooper sleeping in a vacant bedroom closet the first night, a move Cooper did not make until his second night. Cooper's first night was spent in a bed in a furnished bedroom. He also said Cooper had taken a hatchet he found near the fireplace in the hideout house into the closet with him at night, something Kottmeier had no way of knowing and had no basis for claiming.

Another wild assumption Kottmeier advanced was that "Kevin Cooper was surprised after he left the Ryen house and left the hideout when he found that the Ryen car had the keys in the ignition."

This last claim was counterintuitive on two levels. As an experienced car thief, Cooper would have checked the car and the truck for keys before entering the Ryen house. If the keys were in either vehicle, he would have no need to enter the house. As an escaped convict, the last thing he would have wanted to do was to kill the Ryens and Chris Hughes and set off the largest manhunt in California history.

Kottmeier also advanced the bizarre notion that after committing the murders that Cooper had the calmness of mind to return to the hideout house and take a shower, change clothes, and then return to the Ryen house to drive off in the station wagon.

Although Kottmeier fancies himself something of an orator, the conclusion to his opening statement was so abrupt—that Kevin Cooper has caused the people of Chino Hills to lose "their sense of security"—that Judge Garner asked him, "Have you concluded, counsel"?

CHAPTER TWENTY-THREE

The Defense's Opening Statement

There is in D.A. Kottmeier, as he stood in the well of the courtroom just feet from the jury box during his opening statement, a bravado that conveys the notion that the case against Cooper was a slam dunk, when, in fact, it was anything but. The defense would have innumerable opportunities throughout the trial to derail the story Kottmeier told, but Public Defender David Negus's best opportunity to turn the case against Cooper around was to make a spirited, logical opening statement that ripped apart the flimsy circumstantial evidence case the prosecution had just presented.

Not only could Negus skewer the numerous false assumptions Kottmeier had just presented, but he could go into great detail about the stunning lack of real evidence linking Cooper to the murders.

A murder trial is a battle between opposing counsel, not a debate among well-meaning colleagues who sit on separate sides of the courtroom aisle. Johnny Cochran did not get O.J. Simpson off by making a friend of Marcia Clark. He won an acquittal for Simpson by exposing Detective Mark Fuhrman's deep-rooted racism and making it possible for the jury to believe that police were capable of planting evidence at a crime scene to bring down an uppity black man.

In many ways, Negus faced the same challenge that confronted Cochran. Negus's theory of the case was that because the investigators had so befouled the crime scene that they covered their tracks by pinning the murders on a convenient scapegoat who happened to be a black prison escapee who had holed up in a house just below the Ryens' hilltop home. In allowing over seventy different people, including sheriff's department brass, detectives, and deputies, personnel from the district attorney's office, neighbors and media, to traipse through the Ryens' home and property in the first two days, the investigators had compromised the integrity of the crime scene. Detectives and deputies had even been allowed to eat in the Ryens' sunken living room and use a hall bathroom in the house. In their haste to dismantle the crime scene on the second day after the murders were discovered, the investigators had forfeited their ability to connect anyone other than Cooper to the horrendous crimes. Once the investigators had seized on Cooper as the most likely suspect, they methodically ignored leads and evidence that implicated others. They even went so far as to destroy evidence that could possibly exculpate Cooper.

All this Negus knew going in.

As Negus stood to begin his opening statement, it became clear immediately that the case befogged him. Instead of coming out firing, he began by asking the jurors "to relax and try to be comfortable." He then told them he would be neither as brief nor as dramatic as the district attorney had been in his opening. In short, his first sally to the jurors was to dull their appetite for the spectacle of a vigorous defense they expected and were open to then more than they ever would be again in the course of the four-month long trial.

In their opening statements, great defense lawyers shoot down the prosecution's narrative. Instead of taking on Kottmeier, Negus proceeded as though he were presiding at a night-school seminar for first-semester law students. Instead of being compelled to listen to what he had to say, the jurors were now released to evaluate the public defender before them.

What they saw was what they could have taken for a rumpled professor, embodying the odd combination of aloofness and politeness.

While Kottmeier saw himself as an avenger, Negus saw himself as a theorist trying to solve an inexplicable puzzle. The oddest thing about Negus's opening statement was that he seemed to be operating in a parallel universe from Kottmeier. Rather than making Cooper's innocence his top priority, and countering the charges Kottmeier had hurled at his client,

Negus focused on how the sheriff's department had botched the crime scene and investigation. Negus wanted to put the investigation on trial, but the only one on trial was Kevin Cooper.

In the second paragraph of his opening, Negus said:

THE REASON THAT MY PRESENTATION IS GOING TO DIFFER IS BECAUSE THE PRIMARY EMPHASIS OF WHAT I HAVE TO SAY TO YOU DEALS WITH THE QUESTION: HOW DO WE KNOW WHAT HAPPENED DURING THIS PARTICULAR CRIME, THAT IS, NOT THE CONCLUSIONS, BUT THE EVI-DENCE THAT LEADS PEOPLE TO MAKE CONCLUSIONS. THAT PARTICULAR ISSUE IS NOWHERE AS DRAMATIC AS A RECONSTRUCTION OF THE CRIME WHICH TAKES PLACE AFTER WE'VE GONE THROUGH THAT PARTICULAR PROCESS. I'M AFRAID THAT WHAT THE EVIDENCE IS GOING TO SHOW IS NOTHING SO DEFINITIVE AS WHAT MR. KOTTMEIER WOULD SUGGEST TO YOU.

If Negus's first two paragraphs had not anesthetized the jurors, his third paragraph would do the job when he said, "On the one hand, there is the suspicion based upon certain evidence that Kevin Cooper did the crime. I'm not going to be able to prove to you that he didn't, that he is innocent; I'm not going to be able to prove that beyond a reasonable doubt at all."

"To say that he was not going to prove that his client did not perform the crime was to give the case away," former trial attorney Richard Melick said. "This is catastrophic. I am surprised that the judge didn't call an in-chambers conference and suggest that counsel might want to rephrase his words and then instruct opposing counsel not to mention to the jury that such had been said."

Although he could not prove that his client was innocent, Negus told the jury that there is other evidence in the case "that points in the other direction." He then mentioned the fact that when young Josh Ryen first arrived at Loma Linda University Hospital he had communicated in the emergency room to two different people that three white males were his attackers. This was the first bit of new information the jury had heard from Negus, but he did not expound on it and give it the heft it deserved. Rather than name the people and describe the circumstances of Josh's communication, he reverted to his lament about "probably never know(ing)" whether it was his client or the three, white males who committed the crimes at the Ryen home because "the sheriff's office of my county was overwhelmed by the complexity of the task they had before them and they botched the investigation, making it impossible for us to ever know exactly what happened or whether Josh's initial statement in the operating room was correct."

"Again, he gives the case away. Rather than saying he will probably never know whether it was his client or the other three men, he needs to be continually promoting his client's innocence," Melick said.

Instead of underlining the importance of Josh's initial communications, Negus, in effect, was undermining it by calling the accuracy of his communications into question.

If there was other evidence that pointed away from his client, the jury would have to wait to hear it. Negus now began a tutorial on the Chino Hills area and the California Institute for Men, finishing the latter by acknowledging his client had escaped from that prison on the afternoon of June 2, 1983. He then for reasons only he knew, recounted in detail Cooper's escape route and his ending up at the vacant Lease house, covering the same ground Kottmeier had gone over.

Negus finally got back on track by naming the two people who separately questioned Josh in the ER and learned from him that his attackers were three white males.

Negus expanded on the multiple-perpetrator notion by mentioning a June 14 hospital interview of Josh conducted by Detective Hector O'Campo. To protect Josh's interests, the hospital assigned Dr. Jerry Hoyle, a staff psychologist, to sit in on the interview. Dr. Hoyle made two pages of notes during the ninety-minute interview, notes which Negus said referenced Josh discussing multiple attackers at least five times. Dr. Hoyle quotes Josh stating, "They did this" and "They chased us."

During Josh's thirteen-day stay at Loma Linda University Hospital, he twice had occasion to see a picture of the fugitive sought for the deaths of his family and Chris Hughes on the television set in his room and said Cooper was not involved. Negus would only reference one of them.

Negus told the jurors that at two pre-trial hearings Detective O'Campo had denied under oath discussing the crime or the crime scene with Josh until the June 14 interview. Negus, without saying so directly, was inferring that O'Campo was willing to perjure himself because of his own bias against Cooper as the perpetrator. "O'Campo has strong opinions about who is responsible; he has told various witnesses that he knows Kevin Cooper did the crime," Negus stated.

Instead of saying that he believed O'Campo had perjured himself as part of his bias against Cooper, Negus said, "O'Campo was dishonest about not discussing the crime with Josh prior to June 14th." To support this claim, Negus said hospital nurse Linda Headley "remembered that on June 6 O'Campo interviewing Josh and Josh describing three Mexicans. Also Dr. Howell remembers O'Campo interviewing Josh on either June 6th or June 7th and describing three Mexicans."

Negus said that despite Sergeant Arthur instructing O'Campo to tape record the June 14 interview, he failed to do that. Later O'Campo typed up a report and threw away his notes from the interview. In his report, O'Campo wrote that Josh had never seen his attacker. Dr. Hoyle's notes, on the other hand, quote Josh referring to his attackers as "they" numerous times. "O'Campo will deny any references to Josh saying 'they.'"

O'Campo, Negus said, was not alone in his pre-judgment of Cooper. "Once formal charges were filed against Kevin Cooper on June 9th, the San Bernardino County Sheriff's Department dropped most of its investigation into other possible suspects and did not pursue them again until after they found out Forbush [the defense investigator] had been looking into them."

When Negus finally got around to bringing up other potential perpetrators and evidence that pointed at them he referenced the information in terms of showing how shoddy the police investigation was rather than to highlight the probable existence of other perpetrators.

"In the immediate aftermath of discovering the murders, when all the police had to go on was what Josh had communicated, police searched the area around the Ryen house and interviewed neighbors," Negus said. "They went to the Canyon Corral Bar and found out that three, young, white men—all strangers—had been there twice the night of the murders." Negus should have dwelled on these three men. The fact that they had returned to the bar around midnight and were perceived to be extremely drunk or high on drugs made them subjects of interest, but Negus said nothing about this.

He went from mentioning the three strange men to telling the jurors that deputies had found a blood-stained towel and a blood-stained tan T-shirt on Peyton Road, the only road leading away from the Ryen house that goes down to the Canyon Corral Bar. Instead of making the obvious connection of the blood-stained items to the men in the nearby bar, Negus reverted to form by saying that investigators did not get around to showing the bloody T-shirt to anyone at the bar until eleven months later and never asked anyone at the bar to help the police do a composite drawing of the three men. If the police investigation had been on trial, Negus would have been backing a winning strategy.

When next he came to mentioning the coveralls turned in by Diana Roper—the strongest piece of actual evidence that would point away from his client as the attacker—Negus almost apologized for bringing up the subject. "I suppose another example of the type of evidence that shows how the sheriff's office investigated this particular crime is a piece of evidence that could well have no significance whatsoever in the case. But it was a pair of blood-splattered coveralls that were found by a young woman in Yucaipa, which is probably thirty-five miles or so east of Chino in San Bernardino County...She found these blood-splattered coveralls and she felt on June the 10th, 1983, that they were connected to the Ryen homicides."

He then explained that when the deputy who collected the coveralls attempted to alert homicide about this potential new evidence, "homicide wasn't interested. They were out scouring Southern California with a gigantic task force trying to find Kevin Cooper, and they essentially ignored the young deputy. So he logged them into evidence, kept them for six months and threw them in a Dempsey Dumpster, and for all we know, they are no more, at least are no more as far as this particular case is concerned."

The blood-spattered coveralls should have been the linchpin of Negus's opening statement, not evidence "that could well have no significance whatsoever in the case," as Negus told the jury. In addition to being blood-splattered, the coveralls Diana Roper turned in also had horse hair matted to them from the knee down. Most importantly, the coveralls belonged to Roper's then live-in boyfriend, Lee Furrow, a man convicted a few years earlier of murdering a seventeen-year-old girl, cutting her body into parts, and dumping her body parts into a canal to stop her from testifying against gang leader Clarence Ray Allen.

But Negus made no reference to Furrow or Allen and the jury would never hear their names at Kevin Cooper's trial. By ignoring the most powerful evidence the defense had its disposal—the statements of Diana Roper about Lee Furrow—Negus showed he did not grasp the case. The sloppy investigation of the crime scene and the sheriff's office fixation on making Kevin Cooper a scapegoat for this incompetence rendered Negus impotent as an advocate. While he understood the sheriff's office motive for going after an escaped felon, he did not understand how the tragedy at the Ryen home went down. The case simply befuddled him. Without Roper to put it all together for him, Negus never developed an alternative scenario to show the jury that Cooper was, in fact, a scapegoat.

Without an alternative scenario to advance to the jury, Negus was left to mine the many ways the investigators mishandled the crime scene. In great detail, he described how the Sheriff's Crime Lab dispatched two young, inexperienced lab technicians to process the very complicated crime scene at the Ryens' house late in the afternoon of the day the bodies were discovered. "Rather than undertaking a systematic and thorough collection and preservation of evidence, they acted in a very random, undisciplined and basically just inexperienced manner," Negus said.

A proper processing of the crime scene, Negus said, could have answered many questions even in the absence of an eyewitness. Processed carefully and systematically, the crime scene could have divulged the various positions of the victims and their assailants during the course of the attack. "In a crime scene where there are multiple victims, it is necessary that one be able to distinguish whose blood is at a certain place in the room," Negus said. "There are very easy techniques for doing this, but it is necessary to collect adequate numbers of samples and preserve them so that the work can be done."

The next afternoon around 2 p.m., two more experienced criminalists from the Crime Lab, Craig Ogino and Daniel Gregonis, arrived at the crime scene. Negus said that Gregonis wanted to take one-hundred or more blood samples from the walls to reconstruct what had happened, but by the time he and Ogino arrived the decision had already been made to tear down the crime scene and cart it off for storage at a warehouse. Negus did not inform the jury that this decision to strike the crime scene had been ordered by Kevin Cooper's prosecutor, District Attorney Kottmeier.

When Ogino and Gregonis informed Sergeant Karl Swanlund, who was in charge of dismantling the crime scene, that they wanted to hold the crime scene together for another day or longer so they could analyze the physical evidence to try to interpret the blood splatter patterns and try to discover evidence that had not been collected the day before, Swanlund refused. Gregonis "tried to appeal by going up the chain of command and asked Bill Baird, the acting director of the Crime Lab, to intervene…" Baird refused and ordered Ogino and Gregonis to assist in dismantling the crime scene.

By June 7, the walls, the closet doors, the bed and all the furnishings in the master bedroom had been transported to a warehouse. The warehouse, however, was poorly air-conditioned and temperatures inside reached over 120 degrees, "wiping out the blood constituents very early," Negus said.

He next told the jury that beginning on June 9 the investigation "zeroed in on Kevin Cooper and neglected to follow up leads and evidence that pointed in a direction other than Mr. Cooper." Negus said he was not claiming "a deliberate frame-up of an innocent man," but working on the "mistaken conviction that Mr. Cooper was the sole perpetrator, a bias set in that distorted the investigation."

Although the assertion was true, Negus did not give it the specifics it needed to be understood by the jury.

There was no narrative to Negus's opening statement. He had not written his opening down on paper and had not rehearsed it in front of anyone. As a result, he was not telling the jurors a story that had any cohesion to it, but was going on and on in different, competing directions as ideas or theories seemed to pop into his head. By the time he took up the critical subject of the murder weapons involved, he had gone on for more than an hour and was nowhere near wrapping up.

"The absence of a clear, compelling narrative in Negus's opening statement was a problem from the start. Negus did not offer a concise set of events of the murder which would show Cooper not guilty and others who were. He didn't provide a road map for the jury," Melick said. "And second, an hour is too long. The jury cannot be alert for that time on one topic. I am surprised the judge permitted it."

Of the many oddities about this case, the number of weapons used during the attack offered the most clear, logical evidence that more than one assailant was involved in the massacre. It did not stand to reason that one perpetrator would wield a hatchet, a knife and an ice pick. In fact, Dr. Root, the medical examiner who performed the autopsies on the victims, had testified during Negus's cross-examination at the preliminary hearing that he "had to concede that the wounds which he saw on the victims came from at least two different types of knives." Root testified that he felt this way because he could not "imagine one knife which could have, would have been able to inflict the whole range of stab wounds that he had before him."

Negus was really onto something now. This gave him the opportunity to say that if it was a stretch to believe that one perpetrator used three separate weapons, it begged credibility to posit four weapons being deployed. But Negus did not take this opportunity. He moved on to say that Dr. Root, after conferring with D.A. Kottmeier during a break in the hearing, returned to the stand to retract what he had just said about there being two knives involved, that one knife could have done all the various stab wounds inflicted. Negus said Kottmeier had shown Dr. Root a photograph of some knives that the medical examiner had previously rejected as resembling the knife. The jury had no foundation for understanding what Negus was telling them about the knife photos. It would have served him far better to wait to bring this up on cross-examination when Dr. Root took the stand to testify for the prosecution.

Negus would wind down with some random points:

• There was a detective who twice lied under oath at pre-trial hearings about not being in the bedroom where Cooper slept at the hideout house, the same bedroom where a hatchet sheath was found;

• If the original lab analysis of the lone blood drop from the Ryen home linking Cooper to the crime is correct, the blood did not come from Cooper;

• Seventy-five people traipsed through the crime scene, trampling and obliterating important evidence;

• The keys to the Ryens' truck were in it and no money or valuables were taken;

• The crime scene was corrupted. All the brass of the San Bernardino Sheriff Department were congregated in the Ryen living room where footprints and blood were leading from and some of the investigators were even sitting on the stairs where the shoeprints were found;

• There were traces of blood found in both bathrooms, indicating there were two people involved. Even the police used the bathrooms prior to it being processed for evidence;

• Most of the evidence that would have enabled us to objectively and rationally assess the crime scene has been lost to us.

Negus concluded his opening as he had begun it by saying, "So, unfortunately, I can't be Perry Mason. I don't think at the end of this case that we will really know who committed the crime. Thank you."

Asked what he thought about Negus telling the jury they would not know who committed the crime by the end of the case, Melick said, "It was his job to identify the perpetrator(s) for the jury during the course of the trial, but he gave up. Sad."

CHAPTER TWENTY-FOUR

Junk Science

The *evidentiary case* the San Bernardino County Sheriff's Department mounted against Kevin Cooper underscored the pervasive flaw in most forensic work conducted by county and city law enforcement jurisdictions across the United States. As was true in San Bernardino County, about eighty percent of forensic lab technicians are affiliated with police or prosecution agencies. Even though their lab jobs will have them performing highly scientific testing of such forensic material as blood, saliva, shoe prints, and even analyzing tobacco—all of which along with Luminol testing was performed in the Cooper case—none of the lab employees are scientists in any sense. What they are is what their titles say they are: deputy sheriffs. As such they went through the same basic training any other potential deputy sheriff experiences before being assigned a badge and a gun.

In making crime lab personnel part of law enforcement, an inherent conflict of interest is built right into the investigative process.

During Cooper's trial, Public Defender Negus highlighted this problem during his cross-examination of David Stockwell, a crime lab criminalist. When Negus asked him about the conflict of interest in his being both a criminalist and a deputy sheriff, Stockwell responded that his interpretation of evidence tended to favor the prosecution's side of the case, admitting that where one or more conclusions could be drawn "he favors" the prosecution.

"It is quite common to find laboratory facilities and personnel who are, for all intents and purposes, an arm of the prosecution," according to James Starrs, a professor of law and forensic science at George Washington

University in Washington, D.C. "They analyze material submitted, on all but rare occasions, solely by the prosecution. They testify almost exclusively on behalf of the prosecution...As a result, their impartiality is replaced by a viewpoint colored brightly with prosecutorial bias."

In *Tainting Evidence: Inside the Scandal at the FBI Crime Lab* by John F. Kelly and Phillip K. Wearne, the authors write about the lack of impartiality in law-enforcement run crime labs: "The potential conflict of loyalties and interests are obvious. Scientists are expected to retain a critical sense, to follow nothing but reason, to maintain an open mind. We expect the results, the science, to bear witness in court unencumbered by any other consideration. Complete impartiality may be an aspirational ideal, but what chance is there of coming anywhere near this ideal if the police or the FBI pay your wages"?

William Thompson, professor of criminalistics at University of Irvine in California, describes the culture of such law-enforcement run crime labs as "often inimical to good scientific practice. The reward system, promotion, incentives...in the end your paycheck is based on successful prosecutions, not good science."

Lab technicians such as Daniel Gregonis are called "criminalists" instead of forensic scientists because they are not scientists, simply lab technicians assigned to do forensic analysis. Gregonis, as is typical of lab technicians across the country, did not have to establish any degree of competence in forensic science to be hired. Nor did he have to obtain any sort of certification or licensing to get the job. Not even peer review was required.

Dr. David A. Stoney, the former executive director of McCrone Research Institute in Chicago, the largest independent research organization in the world dedicated to teaching microcopy and microanalysis, says the absence of certification for criminalists removes the possibility of official sanction—one cannot be removed from a professional organization that does not exist. "There is, in many ways, no forensic science profession as such. What are the entry requirements? Employment and function. One joins the profession when one is hired by a crime lab and one begins to write reports and testify in court."

Jurors, like the public at large, basically continue to believe that expert testimony, particularly when it comes to forensics, is reliable and trustworthy. As Kelly and Wearne wrote in *Tainting Evidence*, "Together or apart, the words 'forensic' and 'scientific' are today commonly used as everyday adjectives that imply definitive, detailed and comprehensively argued." The vast majority of jurors has scant or no scientific training and knows next to nothing about the forensics of blood typing, fingerprints, bite marks, hair analysis, or shoe prints. Popular television shows such as "CSI" burnish the image of crime labs and give them a credibility that is hard to erode even when an entire crime lab, such as the one in Houston, Texas, was shut down in 2003 for routinely falsifying evidence against defendants. The Houston Crime Lab had been corrupt for years before a local television station, KHOU-TV, hired forensic scientist William Thompson to examine eight DNA cases processed by the Houston Police Department to prove it. ""The criminal justice system in Houston is completely dysfunctional," Professor Thompson said.

An Adam Liptak column in The *New York Times* on March 11, 2003, carried the headline, "Worst Crime Lab in the Country—Or Is Houston Typical." In the column, Liptak wrote:

LEGAL EXPERTS SAY THE LABORATORY IS THE WORST IN THE COUN-TRY, BUT TROUBLES THERE ARE ALSO SEEN IN OTHER CRIME LABORA-TORIES. STANDARDS ARE OFTEN LAX OR NONEXISTENT, TECHNICIANS ARE POORLY TRAINED AND DEFENSE LAWYERS OFTEN HAVE NO MONEY TO HIRE THEIR OWN EXPERTS. QUESTIONS ABOUT THE WORK OF LABO-RATORIES AND THEIR TECHNICIANS IN OKLAHOMA CITY, MONTANA AND WASHINGTON STATE AND ELSEWHERE HAVE LED TO SIMILAR REVIEWS. BUT THE POSSIBLE PROBLEMS IN HOUSTON ARE MUCH GREATER. MORE DEFENDANTS FROM HARRIS COUNTY, OF WHICH HOUSTON IS A PART, HAVE BEEN EXECUTED THAN FROM ANY OTHER COUNTY IN THE COUNTRY...

THE AUDIT OF THE HOUSTON LABORATORY, COMPLETED IN DECEMBER, FOUND THAT TECHNICIANS HAD MISINTERPRETED DATA, WERE POORLY TRAINED AND KEPT SHODDY RECORDS. IN MOST CASES, THEY USED UP

ALL AVAILABLE EVIDENCE, BARRING DEFENSE EXPERTS FROM REFUTING
OR VERIFYING THEIR RESULTS. EVEN THE LABORATORY'S BUILDING
WAS A MESS, WITH A LEAKY ROOF HAVING CONTAMINATED EVIDENCE.

David Dow, a University of Houston law professor who represents death row inmates in capital appeals, said there were two different problems in the crime lab: "scientific incompetence and corruption. That's a deadly combination. Once you have corruption, there is no reason to think that this is limited to DNA cases or cases where there is scientific evidence of any sort."

To explore the question of how widespread the prosecution's use of tainted evidence in getting convictions, *USA Today* and the Gannett News Service did a national survey in 1994 by mining legal and media databases. The survey found eighty-five instances since 1974 of prosecutors knowingly and unknowingly using tainted evidence to convict innocent defendants or to free the guilty. The survey also found that during that same twenty-year period, forty-eight defendants who had been given the death penalty had been set free after their convictions were determined to be based on fabricated evidence or because exonerating or exculpatory evidence had been withheld by the prosecution.

In commenting on the *USA Today*/Gannett survey, Ray Taylor, a San Antonio-based attorney and forensic pathology expert, said, "The public perception is that faking science is rare. The truth is it happens all the time."

CHAPTER TWENTY-FIVE

Pro-Keds Dude

he prosecution's evidentiary case against Cooper essentially consisted of three shoeprints; a drop of blood collected at the Ryens' house; a cigarette butt and some tobacco in the Ryens' stolen station wagon, a hatchet sheath, a button from a prison jacket, and Luminol tests. Each, in turn, will be looked at, but to the jury, the most significant pieces of evidence that tied Cooper to the murders were the shoeprints, particularly a bloody one on a sheet in the Ryens' master bedroom, and a very small drop of blood collected from a hallway wall near the Ryens' living room.

Following opening statements, the first thing the prosecution wanted to establish was that Cooper was wearing a new pair of special prison-issue Pro-Keds Dude tennis shoes when he escaped from prison, while he was in the vacant house and while he was on his murder rampage at the Ryens' house. One was found in the dust on the floor inside the vacant house; one was a bloody print on a crumpled sheet in the Ryens' master bedroom; the other was on a Jacuzzi cover outside the Ryens' master bedroom.

Each of the prints has a suspicious provenance, but the bloody one on the sheet is the most questionable and the most incriminating to Cooper. During Cooper's trial, only Deputy Gail Duffy would testify to having seen the bloody shoeprint while the heavily blood-soaked crumpled sheet was still in the Ryens' bedroom. He would do this despite having given sworn testimony at Cooper's preliminary hearing that he had not seen the print in the master bedroom.

When Crime Lab Deputies David Stockwell and Pat Schecter picked up the crumpled sheet about six hours after the murders were discovered on June 5, neither had, as they folded and packaged the sheet for processing at the crime lab, noticed the bloody print on it. At Cooper's trial, Deputy Stockwell testified that sometime later while he was in the crime lab, he could not recall exactly when, he decided to refold the sheet to match the way it had been crumpled on the floor of the master bedroom. He stated that the refolding connected the separated parts of a bloody shoeprint.

Acting lab manager William Baird had already requisitioned a couple of pairs of Pro-Keds Dude shoes from the California Institute for Men and had them on hand at the crime lab when Stockwell "discovered" the bloody shoeprint. One pair Baird had was new and the other used; both were in Cooper's approximate size. Baird proceeded to match that shoeprint, the one on the Jacuzzi cover and the one in the vacant house to a Pro-Keds Dude.

To use the Pro-Keds to tie Cooper to the murders, the prosecution presented testimony that the shoe was a special-issue shoe that its manufacturer, Stride Rite, only makes for institutions and does not sell at any retail stores or outlets. During pre-trial hearings held months before the trial would begin, the prosecution began asserting the notion that Pro-Keds were made specifically for institutional use and were not available for purchase by the public. When CIM Warden Midge Carroll read about this claim in the newspaper, she knew it was false but just to be sure she made inquiries with various prison staff. Her staff confirmed that all the shoes issued at the prison were common, ordinary shoes that were available for purchase at retail outlets in California and through catalog sales. Warden Carroll then promptly called one of the two lead detectives on the case—either Sergeant Arthur or Detective Gary Woods—and so advised him. This call did not produce the result she thought it would. As pre-trial hearings continued, the prosecution continued to reference the special prison-issue tennis shoes. Warden Carroll made several more phone calls to homicide in an attempt to set the record straight, but none of these calls were returned.

Despite Warden Carroll's having informed one of the two lead detectives on the case that Pro-Keds were not "special issue" tennis shoes, i.e., manufactured solely for institutional use, Assistant D.A. John Kochis put the prison's supervisor of recreation on the stand to testify exactly to the contrary. Louis Arjo stated that Pro-Keds "are a state contract issue."

To put the shoes on Cooper's feet, the prosecution would use James Taylor, an inmate at CIM, to testify that he issued a new pair of Pro-Keds Dude shoes to Cooper shortly before his escape. Inmates frequently testify against fellow prisoners in order to gain something down the road in return. "I've never met James Taylor," Cooper said in an interview. "Dude thought I was from San Diego because that's where he's from. He never gave me nothing."

Due to a callous on Cooper's foot that caused him to limp, the prison staff at the reception center gave him permission slip, called a "chrono," to exchange the hard-soled, prison-issued brogans he was wearing for either tennis shoes or soft-soled shoes. "I gave Sidney Mason a chrono that said I could get a softer-soled shoe. Mason was an escort guard at the reception center," Cooper said. The tennis shoes Cooper did get were a pair of used, well-worn P.F. Flyers. These shoes, unlike Pro-Keds Dude shoes that have red and blue stripes on the sides, had no stripes. Their sole pattern has no diamond shape.

Before Taylor took the stand, with the media and the jury out of the room, Kochis told the judge that Taylor did not want any camera coverage of his testimony because TVs "are available in state prisons and he feels that it may jeopardize his safety if his face and name are broadcast throughout the state prisons as a witness for the prosecution." The judge agreed to bar the use of still or video cameras during Taylor's testimony.

Kochis then told the court that Taylor also did want it known that he was now incarcerated at Susanville. The subtext of what Kochis was saying about not identifying Susanville was that Taylor was a snitch who was sent off to Susanville for his own protection, protection he now needed because if it became known that he testified against Cooper every inmate in every prison in California would now view him as a snitch, including those at Susanville.

Negus said he had a problem with agreeing to that stipulation in advance even though he was not sure he would ask Taylor about his incarceration at Susanville, but then added that the character of the various prisons is a factor that could affect the witness's bias. He told the judge he wanted to keep that option open.

Judge Garner said it sounded reasonable to him to withhold from the media and the public at large where Taylor is incarcerated. He told Negus if he wanted to ask Taylor about Susanville that he do that in chambers, out of the presence of the jury and the media. Negus said he did not care about the media being excluded, but if he decided to raise it, it would be "because I think the jurors should know."

The judge suggested an impromptu hearing "to see if there is any special bias or prejudice that might come out of the simple location where he is located."

Negus said he was not opposed to such a hearing, adding that his offer of proof for showing bias "is that not all institutions are created equal, and as far as the Northern California institutions that one can be sent to for discipline, Susanville is the lightest and the most easiest time of the ones that you can be sent to as opposed to San Quentin, Folsom, Soledad, Tracy—the other Northern California institutions."

The bias that Negus wanted the judge to consider and allow the jury to weigh as it heard Taylor's testimony was that by taking Taylor out of medium security at CIM and favoring him with much easier time to serve in minimum-security Susanville that the D.A.'s office had co-opted or bought Taylor's testimony.

Snitch testimony, as every judge, prosecutor and defense attorney knows, is extremely unreliable. In Taylor's case, his cooperation with the prosecution got him transferred out of the medium-security section at CIM to the minimum-security only prison at Susanville. This was a major benefit for an inmate with three felonies who had recently accumulated a fourth at CIM for marijuana possession. (On March 11, 1985, less than a month after Cooper was found guilty, D.A. Kottmeier wrote a letter to Daniel McCarthy of the California Department of Corrections requesting that Taylor be given a reduction in his sentence. Kottmeier's letter stated,

"Mr. Taylor's testimony [that he had given Cooper a pair of Pro-Keds Dude tennis shoes] was of critical importance both at the preliminary hearing and at [Cooper's] jury trial.")

For the case against Cooper, Taylor was of critical importance. The fact was Taylor was the only witness the prosecution had who would testify that Cooper had a pair of black Pro-Keds Dude high tops.

Taylor's treatment at CIM also indicated that he was a snitch. Although he had three felony convictions dating from 1976, his most recent for grand theft in 1980, he was serving his time in the minimum-security part of the prison. He had also wormed his way into the cushy job of handing out and collecting equipment in recreation, one of the most coveted and perk-laden jobs in the prison. Even when Taylor was busted for marijuana possession in 1983 and pled guilty to that felony, he retained his equipment job. The new felony did cause him to be moved to the medium-security level of the prison, but not for long.

One of the perks Taylor had in the equipment room was access to a television set. He was watching TV the day Sheriff Tidwell identified Kevin Cooper as the lone perpetrator of the Chino Hills murders, June 9, 1983. Later that afternoon, two sheriff's deputies came to CIM to Photostat the soles of various tennis shoes available at the prison. There was a particular interest in the Pro-Keds shoe. Taylor, who was made aware of this interest by Al Hill, another supervisor in recreation, subsequently approached Arjo to tell him he had given Cooper a pair of Pro-Keds three or four days before he escaped.

During Negus's extensive cross-examination of Taylor he never got around to asking him where he was incarcerated or how he came to be transferred to Susanville. Thus the jury never had any inkling of the potential bias attached to Taylor's testimony. Negus did allude to Taylor being a snitch by asking him about an inmate named Ronnie Edwards who got busted for marijuana possession several hours after Taylor was caught with the contraband. Taylor denied ratting out Edwards. Negus did not call Edwards as a rebuttal witness. The jurors were left to sort out the truth on their own. At the end of his time on the witness stand, Taylor's assertion that he had given Cooper a pair of Pro-Keds was intact.

The prosecution's next goal was to convince the jury that Pro-Keds Dude is a special-contract shoe only available to state institutions such as CIM. To establish this critical point, the prosecution called Michael Newberry. As the general merchandising manager for the Pro-Keds division of Stride Rite, Newberry had the aura of an unimpeachable source. Who, better than he, would know about the sales and distribution of Pro-Keds? He testified that Stride Rite has a contract with the State of California to provide Pro-Keds to various institutions, including CIM. Newberry stated that Pro-Keds are not sold anywhere in California on a retail basis, nor are they sold across the counter on a retail basis in any state in the United States.

What his testimony amounted to was that if a sole impression of a Pro-Keds shoe was found at the Ryen crime scene, there was an overwhelming likelihood that it came from an inmate at CIM, and certainly not from any member of the general public.

On cross-examination, Newberry estimated that prior to being sworn in as a witness for the prosecution, he had ten phone conversations with Sergeant Billy Arthur and Detective Gary Woods and that he had two or three contacts with William Baird, the acting head of the San Bernardino County Sheriff's Department Crime Lab. (Baird admitted during his cross-examination by Negus that he might have told Newberry that the sheriff's department wanted his testimony so the prosecution could "shut down certain defenses.")

A number of inferences could be made from this unusually high number of contacts Newberry had with Arthur, Woods and Baird, but Negus did not pursue the matter. He did get Newberry to testify that Stride Rite had sold no Pro-Keds to CIM in 1982 or 1983. This fact alone would undermine the prosecution's claim that the Pro-Keds issued to Cooper were new, but Negus did not develop that likelihood.

From the preliminary hearing through other pre-trial hearings, Negus knew that the prosecution was claiming that Pro-Keds were a special prison issue shoe and what the implications of that meant for his client.

In terms of all the evidence the prosecution would introduce at trial, the Pro-Keds Dude being a prison issue shoe was arguably the most damning the jury had to consider.

Had Negus taken the time to research the claim that Pro-Keds were "a prison-issue shoe" by calling Stride Rite to check it out, he would have learned that the Pro-Keds Dude brand sold to institutions is the same shoe that Stride Rite sold to retail stores in New York, Atlanta and Chicago and to smaller chains and individual stores, including those on the West Coast, through its catalog sales department. In short, there was nothing "special issue" about the shoe and individual stores in California could order it through the Stride Rite catalog.

If Negus had known the facts about Pro-Keds Dude sales and distribution, he could have impeached Newberry during his cross-examination for so blatantly misrepresenting that Pro-Keds Dude was a special shoe sold only to institutions.

CHAPTER TWENTY-SIX

A-41

The second major piece of evidence the prosecution presented to the jury was a blood sample that acting crime lab manager William Baird ordered collected on June 6. The sample was a small, single drop of blood at the far end of a hallway wall outside the Ryens' master bedroom, near the living room, a few inches above the hallway carpeting. Luminol tests found no traces of blood on the carpet below it. In some respects, considering its location, it had all the trappings of a throw-down gun.

Deputy David Stockwell, who had been a crime lab technician for eleven months and had never worked a crime scene with multiple murder victims, testified at trial that his collection procedure "was to gouge the wall and remove plasterboard of the wall where the bloodstains were." He described the blood drop as "a trailing one and there were several droplets beneath it which looked to be consistent with the large drop of blood. I believe I took them all." Stockwell put the scrapes in a metal pill box, labeled "A-41," and turned it over to Daniel Gregonis, a criminalist in the crime lab for testing.

Gregonis, who had a Bachelor of Science degree in criminalistics, was the crime lab's blood expert. Still in his mid-twenties, he had been hired as a sheriff's deputy to work in the San Bernardino County Sheriff's Department Crime Lab after graduating from the Metropolitan State College in Denver, Colorado, five years earlier. Accurately typing the myriad characteristics or markers of blood is an advanced and highly specialized science. Laboratories that specialize in this practice are headed by scientists with advanced degrees in medicine, pathology, biology, and/or biochemistry.

Gregonis had no such background and no one else in the sheriff's lab did either. What he had learned about blood typing was elementary, through the trial-and-error, hit-and-miss learning curve of on-the-job experience. All humans and many other primates can be typed for the ABO blood group. There are four principal types: A, B, AB, and O. There are two antigens and two antibodies that are mostly responsible for the ABO types. In most cases, the specific combination of these four components determines an individual's blood type. While Gregonis had become proficient in typing blood into the four ABO groups, the more sophisticated testing of the blood's enzymes and serum proteins remained beyond his skill level and scientific knowledge. For good reason, he approached these advance typing diagnoses with less than full confidence and was not above skirting normal and accepted lab procedures to cobble together his results.

When Gregonis received the A-41 sample on June 7, he was in no hurry to begin testing it. He waited five days, until June 12, to even test it to determine if the sample was human blood. He found that it was and it had an ABO of A. This was three days after warrants for Cooper's arrest had been issued by the San Bernardino County Sheriff's Department and also after Cooper's genetic profile had arrived at the crime lab, courtesy of the Pittsburgh, Pennsylvania Police Department.

With this profile, Gregonis now knew that Cooper's ABO was A and his genetic profile contained an extremely rare identifier, an enzyme known as peptidase A 2-1, a phenotype that essentially only occurs among ten percent of blacks. If Gregonis could match Cooper's genetic profile to the genetic profile of A-41, the sheriff's department would have, albeit only one, a serological link to Cooper at the crime scene.

Gregonis delayed the most sensitive and discriminating tests of A-41 until he had a vial of Cooper's blood that was withdrawn from Cooper in the crime lab on August 1, two days after his arrest.

On August 2, Gregonis ran tests taken from Cooper's vial of blood. He got accurate readings on most of the markers, but incorrectly identified one of Cooper's serological markers, his EAP type, calling it a "B." Then, instead of running a blind test of A-41 and Cooper's blood sample as lab testing protocol called for, Gregonis placed a sample of Cooper's blood on the

same testing plate with A-41 and reported that the blood characteristics of
A-41 matched those of Cooper's blood, including the EAP reading of B.
In his zeal to match Cooper's genetic profile to A-41, Gregonis got trapped
by his own misreading of Cooper's EAP into miscalling the EAP of A-41
to match it. (In pre-trial testimony, Gregonis denied under oath that he
had tested Cooper's blood on the same plate as he tested A-41. At trial,
under cross-examination, he admitted that he only blind tested A-41 until
he had the vial of Cooper's blood in the lab in early August, now admitting
he misrepresented himself at the pre-trial hearing.) Elated by his findings,
Gregonis called D.A. Kottmeier and informed him that day. Kottmeier
and Assistant D.A. Kochis drove to the lab and went over the results with
Gregonis. The next day Kochis called Public Defender David Negus to
inform him the prosecution now had serological confirmation that Cooper
had been at the crime scene.

Negus, for his part, was unaware any testing of A-41 was taking place.
Although the testing Gregonis was performing on A-41 would consume
most of what little remained of an extremely small sample to begin with,
Gregonis had not alerted him, thus preempting Negus from having his
expert do any independent testing on A-41 while a sufficient quantity of it
was still available.

At Negus's behest, Edward Blake, a serology expert the defense retained, called Gregonis to inform him he wanted to be involved in any
further testing of A-41 that Gregonis performed in the crime lab. Gregonis
agreed to send Blake some Polaroid photos of A-41 for him to review. In
mid-August, Blake informed Gregonis that he was prepared to proceed
with the testing of A-41, but Gregonis put him off, telling him he wanted
to conduct some additional testing on Cooper's blood before doing any
more A-41 testing.

Beginning on October 3, Gregonis and Blake met for three days at the
crime lab. What remained of the A-41 sample was in a small pill box that
had been stored in the lab's freezer. To do the testing, the plaster chips in
the pill box were placed in a test tube and a solution was added to dissolve
the blood off the chips. There was enough blood in the solution to run a
transferrin test. Transferrin is a plasma protein that transports iron through

the blood to the liver, spleen, and bone marrow. Running that test used up most of the solution, leaving, according to Gregonis, "only a little bit of solution." What remained was insufficient to get valid results on another plasma protein known as haptoglobin.

At this point, both Gregonis and Blake considered the A-41 sample exhausted. By the time these last two tests were completed, a very small amount of A-41 remained in solution form. Gregonis placed what was left of it in a vial and placed it in the lab's freezer. He then discarded all chips used in the solution.

On several different occasions afterwards, Gregonis would testify at pre-trial hearings that after October 5 all the blood in the pill box containing A-41 had been consumed during analysis. A photo taken in the lab of A-41 on July 11, 1984 showed that all that remained of it were white speckles, flakes of plaster scraped from a wall near the Ryens' living room.

Gregonis, though, was far from finished with testing A-41. In early July of 1984, just two months before Cooper would plead not guilty to all capital charges, Gregonis would "just out of curiosity (sic) sake" open the pill box and see "a very small quantity of blood remaining." Gregonis and Blake tested that blood in October, but the results were inconclusive.

In August, Blake independently tested a known sample of Cooper's blood and found that A-41 could not have come from him because Cooper's EAP was actually not B, but the much rarer rB, an acid phosphatase type.

By now aware that Blake had read Cooper's EAP as an rB, Gregonis went to consult with Dr. Brian Wraxall on October 17 at his Serological Research Institute in Richmond, California, a private lab he established in 1978. Wraxall, the chief forensic serologist at his institute, was the inventor of numerous serology tests, including the EAP test. Because Gregonis knew there was not enough of the A-41 sample remaining to test, he brought along the plate he had used in doing the haptoglogin test on A-41 back in early October. Wraxall ran an isoelectric focusing test for EAP to determine if A-41 was either a B, as Gregonis had called it, or an rB, but Wraxall's test was inconclusive. Wraxall told him that the plate, by then, was too degraded to make any determination.

Somewhere along the line, most likely some time after striking out at Dr. Wraxall's lab and as the opening of Kevin Cooper's trial approached, Gregonis altered his lab notes from early August of 1983 to comport with Cooper's actual EAP. His notes now reflected that both A-41 and Cooper's blood had an EAP of rB rather than B.

Under cross-examination at Cooper's trial, Negus asked Gregonis when he first changed his mind about Cooper being not a B but an rB. His first response was to say he made the change after self-educating himself to learn how to see "what an rB looks like on my system." In reality, he would soon admit he changed his mind in August of 1984 either after Assistant D.A. Kochis called him to inform him Cooper was rB or after he phoned some experts and learned from them how to read rB on his system.

NEGUS: DID YOU CHANGE YOUR MIND ABOUT A-41 AFTER YOU LEARNED THAT IF YOUR ORIGINAL CALL WAS ACCURATE, A-41 COULDN'T HAVE COME FROM MR. COOPER?

GREGONIS: NOT IMMEDIATELY, NO. BUT IT WAS AFTER. YES.

NEGUS: PRIOR TO YOUR LEARNING THAT IF YOUR ORIGINAL CALL ABOUT A-41 WAS CORRECT, THEN IT COULDN'T HAVE COME FROM MR. COOPER, HOW MANY TIMES DID YOU TESTIFY UNDER OATH THAT A-41 WAS A B AND NOTHING ELSE BUT A B?

GREGONIS: IT'S PROBABLY ABOUT THREE TIMES.

Under further questioning, Negus forced Gregonis to admit to numerous other mistakes he had made in his handling of the tests of A-41 and other blood samples. Gregonis's work on the victims' blood was typical. He said by the time he got around to testing their blood samples, their blood had degraded too much to provide results much beyond their ABO blood types. He said he did not do some of the standard serology tests simply because those tests were not part of his routine at the time. When Negus asked him if everything that serologists knew how to do to keep samples from degrading were not done in this case, Gregonis responded, "That is correct. It's being done at the current time."

Negus pressed him, "But it wasn't done from the beginning"?

"That is correct, yes, not with all the samples," Gregonis said.

During the next series of questions, Gregonis said he had not attempted to do those tests which would use the least amount of sample for the maximum amount of information. Asked specifically about his testing of A-41, Gregonis admitted to two instances where he had been wasteful. He also said his photos of his test results for A-41 were not discernible and that no other serologist could check his work.

Question by question, Negus exposed Gregonis for the inexperienced, inadequately trained lab technician he was. By the time Negus posed his final question about A-41, asking Gregonis "if the accuracy of our knowledge of A-41 depended on the accuracy of your perceptions," Gregonis's status as an expert witness was in full retreat when he quietly answered, "That is true, yes."

CHAPTER TWENTY-SEVEN

Cigarettes and Tobacco

While hiding out in the vacant house, Cooper, once he ran out of the Kools he had with him, rolled his own cigarettes using a prison-issue tobacco known as Role-Rite. The deputies who inspected the vacant house collected the cigarette butts Cooper had left behind, but did not process all of them into evidence. They also brought in some loose tobacco that was in a small, white box in the closet of the bedroom, but did not measure or weigh it. Deputies also subsequently recovered and took into evidence a hand-rolled cigarette butt from Cooper's own car that had been impounded in Los Angeles after he was convicted of burglary and sent to California Institute for Men.

The Ryen's white station wagon would be found in the parking lot at St. Anthony's Catholic Church just north of downtown Long Beach on June 11, six days after the murders were discovered. Long Beach is forty-five miles northwest of Chino Hills. Deputies reported that the car's rear door was unlocked and that dust prints on the hood indicated it had recently been shut. A description of the stolen car had been widely publicized in the media.

The deputies' initial visual inspection of the station wagon made note of its contents, as did a second inventory of the car's interior when deputies impounded it and processed it for evidence. Neither of these detailed reports indicated the presence of cigarette butts or loose tobacco in the car. A later inventory report—handwritten, undated, unsigned—would include both.

This report detailed finding loose tobacco, consistent with Role-Rite, in the station wagon. "Consistent with" is one of those expressions criminalists like to use when they are unable to assert certainty about a piece of evidence. In regards to this loose tobacco, it could well have been dropped there by Doug Ryen, who sometimes smoked a pipe when he drove. When Negus cross-examined the criminalist who analyzed the tobacco evidence from the station wagon, Deputy Craig Ogino admitted there was "a slight difference" between the loose tobacco in the station wagon and the Roll-Rite tobacco issued by the California Institute for Men. In other words, the loose tobacco in the car in no way incriminated Cooper.

Considering that Cooper was alleged to have fled alone in the station wagon, the loose tobacco's location, on the floor between the front passenger seat and the front passenger door, was puzzling, and so were the locations of the two cigarette butts.

The rolled butt was in the passenger side seat, pressed into the crevice by the vertical and horizontal portions of the seat. The Viceroy was under the passenger seat. The location of both the rolled butt and the Viceroy butt suggested someone sitting in the passenger seat had deposited them. The blood evidence in the car also supported the notion that someone had sat in the passenger seat. When Luminol testing of the car was conducted the day after it was found, a positive reaction for blood was detected from the passenger compartment, seat and floorboard. There was also blood on the lower portion of the driver's door, the driver's headrest, and in the back seat area as well. Blood in three separate areas of the station wagon would support the eyewitness testimony of Mr. and Mrs. Leonard, who reported seeing three or four white men driving rapidly away from the direction of the Ryens' house around midnight the night of the assault at the Ryens' house.

CHAPTER TWENTY-EIGHT

Hatchet Sheath and Button

Within hours of discovering the murders, a citizen found a bloody hatchet beside the road leading away from the Ryens' house. By then detectives knew that one of the murder weapons was a hatchet. The next day, at the request of Larry Lease, one of the owners of the vacant house where Cooper hid out, two detectives thoroughly searched the house below the Ryen house, purportedly looking for possible suspects. At this time the sheriff's department did not know that Cooper had hid out there for two days. The detectives found the house to be unoccupied and did not report finding any evidence.

The next day, Roger Lang, a joint owner of the hideout house, asked two ranch employees of his to go to the vacant house "to see if anything was out of place, or missing." Richard Sibbitt said Lang specifically asked him to see if the hatchet was missing, mentioning to him that his wife often stored it in a kitchen drawer. When Sibbitt did not see the hatchet by the fireplace, where he testified he had seen it less than two weeks ago when he helped ranch manger Kathy Bilbia move out, he checked the kitchen drawers but found no hatchet. He and Perry Burcham then walked through the rest of the house. In an empty bedroom, Burcham opened the closet doors and saw bedding on the floor. Over by the headboard, Sibbitt saw a hatchet sheath on the floor. He told Burcham not to touch anything and the two went up the Ryens' house to report their findings to Deputy Bobby Phillips.

Phillips alerted Sergeant Karl Swanlund, who was in charge of the Ryen crime scene, and the two of them entered the vacant house. They saw the bedding in the closet, the hatchet sheath near the headboard, and also a green button with what appeared to be blood on it on the floor near the sheath. Both items were in plain view in the bedroom that had no furnishings other than a built-in headboard. Swanlund called in the crime lab technicians to process the vacant house. Cooper's fingerprints were in abundance throughout the house. Two days later, warrants for Cooper's arrest were issued.

Detective Steve Moran, who conducted the first search of the vacant house with Detective Bob Hall the day after the murders were discovered, would disavow ever entering the bedroom where the sheath and button were subsequently found by Sibbitt and Burcham. At pre-trial hearings, Moran would testify two times under oath that neither he nor Detective Hall had bothered to look into that room. This disclaimer would prove false about a year later when three of his fingerprints were lifted from inside the closet door of the empty bedroom, just feet away from where the sheath and button were found. To David Negus, and later to Cooper's appellate attorneys, Detective Moran's lying about never searching the bedroom was highly suggestive that both the hatchet sheath and the button were planted in the bedroom to incriminate Cooper.

The blood-stained green button was similar to buttons sewn on jackets issued at the California Institute for Men. Type A blood was on the button—blood consistent with both Cooper and Doug Ryen. The button's color established that it came from a green prison jacket. When Cooper escaped from prison he was seen wearing a brown jacket by Lt. Cornelius Shephard, an employee of the prison who was driving near the prison in his truck. In his written report of the escape, Shephard stated that Cooper was wearing a jacket that was "brown in color." At Cooper's trial, Shephard testified that Cooper was jogging toward him and his "hair was in braids" and his jacket was "brownish." The unlikelihood of deputies finding a green, prison-issue button in the bedroom of the vacant house also points strongly to evidence planting.

In his opening statement to the jury, Public Defender David Negus referenced a detective who had lied under oath at two pre-trial hearings about not being in the empty bedroom where the hatchet sheath and blood-stained button were found. When D.A. Kottmeier called Detective Moran to testify, Negus thought he would get his opportunity to expose these fabrications.

On direct-examination, Moran said at the request of Larry Lease, who wanted to find out if anyone were hiding out in the vacant house, he and Detective Bob Hall entered the vacant house with their weapons drawn, but found no one inside it. Lease, who along with brothers Roger and Kermit Lang had purchased the house four years earlier from Dr. Mary Howell, entered the house with the detectives and waited in the living room while they searched it. Lease had testified earlier that Detectives Moran and Hall had checked all the rooms and "didn't see anything out of the ordinary."

As Negus began his cross-examination, he was like the cat toying with his not-quite-dead-yet, but disabled prey. In discovery provided by the prosecution to the defense after Moran's last pre-trial appearance in June of 1984, Negus had learned that three of Moran's fingerprints were lifted by deputies from inside the door of the closet in the empty bedroom where the hatchet sheath and blood-stained button were found the day after Moran and Hall's search of the hideout house.

On the witness stand, Moran was in a terribly awkward position. If he admitted he lied at two pre-trial hearings, he faced possible felony charges for perjury and dismissal from the sheriff's department. If he persisted in testifying that he had never been in the empty bedroom he would compound the perjury issues facing him. As Negus pressed him about whether he now recalled being in the empty bedroom, Moran took the only out open to him, saying that to the best of his recollection he did not remember ever going in that bedroom.

Following a number of other questions and evasive answers, Judge Garner interrupted the cross-examination for an in-chambers discussion. The judge said he questioned the relevancy of Negus's questioning, saying he was just setting up Moran as a "straw man to knock him down." He told Negus he wanted to let it go that Moran had said he did not see anything in the empty bedroom.

Negus responded that it was crucial to establish that Moran did go into the empty bedroom and did not see any evidence of a sheath or a button on the floor outside the closet and "that he was lying under oath about it."

Judge Garner clearly misunderstood the point Negus was trying to establish, saying, "I don't think either of you [Negus and Kottmeier] is going to contend that he [Moran] was correct. I think both of your positions would go to obviously there was something else there at the time."

In rebuttal, Negus said, "He [Kottmeier] knows my position is that there wasn't, that's the whole thing. I don't believe that a trained police officer would walk into a bedroom where there is all this evidence out in the open, have his fingerprints on there, and sees it and misses it. I can't believe Detective Moran would do that given all the training and background."

The judge asked Negus if he were trying to impeach Moran just to prove that he was there then.

NEGUS: WELL, YEAH. I THINK THAT'S BASICALLY WHAT THE EVIDENCE SHOWS. NO, THAT HE WASN'T THERE.

JUDGE GARNER: WASN'T THERE. THAT'S WHAT HE TESTIFIED. 'HEY, I WENT IN THERE, I DIDN'T SEE ANYTHING.'

NEGUS: NO, NO, NO. YOU DON'T UNDERSTAND. DETECTIVE MORAN HAS DENIED EVER GOING INTO THE BILBIA [EMPTY] BEDROOM…HE HAS DENIED IT THREE TIMES.

JUDGE GARNER: LISTEN, COUNSEL, HE'S AN IMPEACHER'S DELIGHT, THAT IS CLEAR. IT IS ABUNDANTLY CLEAR. WHY TAKE UP—ALL YOU ARE TRYING TO PROVE IS A NEGATIVE. ALL YOU ARE TRYING TO DO IS SHOW THAT THIS MAN IS INCOMPETENT.

NEGUS: NO, NO. WHAT I'M TRYING TO SHOW IS THAT HE LYING.

Negus argued that Moran's denying ever entering the empty bedroom "is circumstantial evidence that he lying; that in fact what happened is that he went in there, there wasn't anything in there on June 6th, later they had to explain how stuff which was found in there on June 7th was connected with Mr. Cooper, in fact, hadn't been there on June 6th."

"Tell me—explain this to me," the judge asked. "According to any other type of rational explanation, how did it [the sheath] get in there on the 7th"?

Negus said one rational explanation would be that the sheath was planted. "Circumstantially, I think that it is a certain inference which can be drawn from the evidence and I think one's entitled to bring that evidence out, and in front of the jury."

Back in open court, Negus's remaining questions failed to establish anything other than Moran's memory was selective. With a major assist from Judge Garner, Moran stepped down without Negus being able to develop the connection between Moran's previous false testimony and the likelihood that the sheath and button were planted evidence.

D.A. Kottmeier's next witness, Detective Robert Hall, reopened the door for Negus to expose Moran when he testified that he had not personally searched the bedroom where the sheath and green button were found because he had seen Moran "coming out of this area by the hallway." Hall further stated that after he was informed the next day that "there had been a substantial amount of evidence located in the residence" that he returned to the house that day, explaining, "I myself was rather curious to see what it might have been that we had overlooked." Negus's attempts on cross-examination to use what Hall had just said to cast aspersions on Moran went nowhere.

The best Negus could manage occurred a number of witnesses later when Deputy Ann Punter testified about lifting Cooper's fingerprints and his left footprint from a shower in the hideout house. On cross-examination, Negus asked her if three of the prints lifted from the hideout house were from inside the closet of the empty bedroom and were the prints of Detective Moran. "Yes, sir, they are," she answered. He then asked her when she discovered that they were Moran's prints. She said in June of 1984—a year after they were lifted.

If the hatchet that killed the Ryens and Chris Hughes had come from the hideout house, Kevin Cooper was almost positively guilty of their murders. To establish that it did, the prosecution put on a number of witnesses to suggest that it had. In an in-chambers conference while Roger Lang was testifying on cross-examination, Negus told the judge that he knew for a fact that Mary Ann Hughes, the mother of victim Chris Hughes, thought Cooper was guilty and very much wanted him convicted. She had spoken with a number of witnesses, including Roger Lang, questioning them about what they had told defense investigator Ron Forbush and relating that information back to Sergeant Arthur. Negus said he felt such activity on her part biased these witnesses and he should be allowed to bring out that bias by cross-examining them about their dealings with Mrs. Hughes.

Even though Lang, moments before the in-chambers session, had admitted speaking with Mrs. Hughes, Judge Garner refused to allow such questioning.

In addition to the testimony of Mr. and Mrs. Roger Lang and Larry Lease, all the other witnesses who would testify about the hatchet worked for them.

Kathy Bilbia, the ranch manager who lived in the house the previous eighteen months, testified that she saw the hatchet, in its sheath, while she was cleaning the house prior to vacating it. When asked where she saw it, her answer was less than straightforward, "It was kept by the fireplace on the hearth." The best she could do when asked to identify the hatchet and sheath in evidence was to say they looked like the ones in the hideout house.

Richard Sibbitt, Roger Lang's ranch foreman, testified that when he assisted Bilbia's move out of the Lease house he noticed the hatchet by the fireplace. Unlike Bilbia, Sibbitt positively identified the hatchet and sheath on exhibit as coming from the Lease house.

Perry Burcham, who worked under Sibbitt, testified that about a couple of weeks before the murders were discovered, Kathy Bilbia had called him to remove a snake that had fallen into the Lease house by the fireplace. While there he saw a hatchet in a sheath by the fireplace. Asked by Kottmeier if the sheath Sibbitt and he saw later in the empty bedroom was the same type as the one he had seen by the fireplace, he said, "Yeah. Just basically it did."

Larry Lease testified that the hatchet was normally kept outside the back door by the wood pile.

Virginia Lang, who periodically lived in the Lease house with her husband Roger, testified that about two months before the murders she stored the hatchet in a kitchen drawer, thinking that with the warmer months approaching she would not have need of it for some time.

Roger Lang positively identified a photograph of the hatchet in evidence as belonging to him and that he kept it near the fireplace, but when Kottmeier showed him the actual hatchet in evidence he qualified his answer by saying, "Yes, I believe it is."

If the judge had allowed Negus to probe the potential for bias exerted on these witnesses—directly or indirectly through Mrs. Hughes—the jury may have been better equipped to filter through many of the highly hedged answers these witnesses provided. Without such a perspective, the hatchet testimony along with the shoe impressions became the most damning evidence against Cooper the jury would hear.

One fact that would appear to discount the possibility of the hatchet from the Lease house being one of the murder weapons would not surface until Dr. Root, the medical examiner, testified later in the trial. In performing Peggy Ryen's autopsy, he noticed that there was a trace of black pigment—a couple of tiny black dots—on her face left by a hatchet wound. The hatchet from the Lease house had no black paint or pigment on its steel blade.

CHAPTER TWENTY-NINE

Luminol Tests

The prosecution would contend at trial, based on Luminol testing of the shower in the vacant house, that in washing up after the murders, Cooper had left traces of the victims' blood in the shower he used there. Possible blood traces were detected on the shower walls in a broad swatch that went from two feet to approximately five feet above the shower's floor, but there were no signs of the blood draining on the floor itself. The test results were quite strange in that regard. A shower would cause the blood on a person splattered with blood to run down his body to the shower's floor, not aggregate on the shower's walls in a three-foot band ending some two-feet above the floor.

The day before Cooper occupied the vacant house, Kathy Bilbia, the previous tenant, finished moving out, but not before cleaning the shower with bleach, a substance that reacts to Luminol testing in the same manner blood does—it shows up.

A two-stage test is required to determine if a Luminol positive is caused by bleach instead of by blood. It would appear, considering how counterintuitive it is for traces of blood to be in a tight swatch on the walls of a shower and not on the shower's floor, that either the crime lab deputies only conducted the first stage of the test and were satisfied with that or they simply withheld the findings from the second-stage results.

CHAPTER THIRTY

Josh Testifies

Near the end of the prosecution's presentation, a video-taped interview of Josh Ryen was played for the jury on December 13, 1984. Although Public Defender David Negus wanted Josh's testimony taken under oath before the jury, the prosecution argued that the ordeal of testifying in public about the murders of his family and best friend would be too traumatic for the now ten-year-old boy. Judge Garner agreed.

As the sole survivor of the brutal attack, what he saw would carry enormous weight with the jury. The jury had not yet heard testimony from hospital emergency room personnel regarding what Josh had communicated to them and to a sheriff's deputy shortly after his arrival at the hospital on June 5, 1983.

The interview with Josh had been conducted four days earlier at his grandmother's home. Present were his grandmother, Dr. Mary Howell, D.A. Kottmeier, and Negus. Dr. Howell administered the oath to Josh. For the interview with Josh, Kottmeier and Negus had formulated the opening questions in advance.

The first set of questions Kottmeier posed was intended to elicit some basic information. Josh said his father smoked a pipe in the car, his father slept on the right side of the bed, nearest the closest and furthest away from the sliding doors leading out to the patio, and that the family had four dogs.

When the family returned from the cookout they attended on the night of June 4, 1983, Josh said his mother was the first to enter the house through a locked door. Josh and Chris Hughes slept in sleeping bags on the floor of Josh's room. Before going to sleep, Josh and Chris talked and read magazines. Then both his parents came in to say goodnight.

Josh said his father stayed up a little later, watching television in the family room.

During the night he heard his mother scream. He got up, woke up Chris, and the two of them walked down the hallway toward his parents' bedroom. It was dark; he said he did not hear any other sounds. He saw his sister in the doorway. He said he did not go into the laundry room, something he had previously told his grandmother, Detective Hector O'Campo, Sergeant Arthur, his psychiatrist, Dr. Lorna Forbes, and others that he had done.

When Kottmeier asked if he remembered Chris calling out to him or Chris running through the house, he said he could not remember anything. Over and over, he told Kottmeier that he did not remember anything.

When Negus began his questioning, he did not ask Josh anything about what he had told various people at the hospital about his attackers being three white men, asking Josh only if he liked Detective O'Campo—Josh said he did—and if he had talked with O'Campo. Yes, he had.

Kottmeier waited until the end of the interview to ask Josh the question he most wanted the jury to hear: Did he see anyone in the house that night. Josh said he "saw like a shadow or something" by the bathroom. He said he saw a shadow when he saw his sister and he only saw one shadow.

Kottmeier's eliciting of the "shadow" reference countered Josh's previous revelations to Dr. Forbes and his grandmother, both of whom he told in mid-1984 that he saw "a puff of hair" standing over his mother during the attack. Over the past eleven months Josh had morphed from recalling that three white men were the assailants to adopting the position of the sheriff's department that Kevin Cooper was the lone perpetrator. Most of the photos that Josh had seen of Cooper showed him wearing an Afro hairstyle.

On his own, in an effort to make some sense of the horrible tragedy that had befallen him, Josh began to move away from the three white men he originally reported to believing that the attackers were three Mexican men who had driven up to the Ryens' house just as the Ryens and Chris Hughes were getting ready to go to the barbeque. The men had asked his father about the possibility of work, but his father had hustled them off. Josh knew his father did not care for Mexicans and soon came to believe that it was the three men looking for work who returned out of vengeance.

Josh advanced this notion to Detective O'Campo a day or two after he was admitted to the hospital. At the time no one yet knew that an escaped prisoner had holed up in the house below the Ryens' house. In an October 27, 1983 interview Negus and Forbush conducted with Josh's grandmother, Dr. Howell, she said she was sitting at Josh's bedside when O'Campo began interviewing Josh for the first time. She said that when O'Campo asked Josh how many attackers there were that Josh held up three fingers. Dr. Howell also recalled Josh informing O'Campo that one of the assailants had sleeves and two were bare armed, wearing "like T-shirts or something." She also said, "If I remember correctly, I think he said whether one had a beard or mustache."

Of all the information that would come Negus's way about what Josh did or did not see, the descriptions of his attackers the little boy provided his grandmother should have stood out the most. It was clear from the various people at the Canyon Corral Bar the police interviewed that the unruly men there the night of the Chino Hills murders were wearing T-shirts; it was even more stunning that Diana Roper had said Lee Furrow had returned home early the next morning in sleeved coveralls smeared with blood and matted with horse hair; and that Roper had told investigator Forbush that Furrow had shaved off his Fu-Manchu mustache shortly after the murders.

A week later, and several days after Kevin Cooper had been named by Sheriff Tidwell as the lone assailant, O'Campo did an extensive, ninety-minute interview with Josh in the presence of Dr. Jerry Hoyle, a staff psychologist at the hospital. By now, O'Campo was convinced that Kevin Cooper was the lone perpetrator. Although Sergeant Arthur had instructed O'Campo to tape-record the interview, O'Campo instead just took notes, as did Dr. Hoyle. Most likely, the detective did not want a verbatim record of the interview to prevent the defense from obtaining a copy of it through discovery. As would be revealed by the notes Dr. Hoyle took, Josh referred to multiple assailants numerous times during the interview. In the typed report O'Campo did of the interview some five months later, not one mention was made of Josh using the plural in referring to his attackers. What O'Campo's actual notes contained would not be divulged. At trial, he claimed he tore up the notes after finishing his typed report.

During the interview with O'Campo in a pediatric playroom, Josh recounted how he was awakened by his mother's screams; he woke Chris up and they walked toward the master bedroom. They saw Jessica sprawled in the hallway right in front of the door to the master bedroom. Josh told O'Campo he knew Jessica was dead. "I bent down and put my hand on her heart and I couldn't feel anything; she was hurt in the head real bad."

Josh said he looked into the master bedroom and saw his father over by his father's closet, but he did not see his mother. He would later tell Dr. Lorna Forbes that the first time he entered the bedroom that his mother yelled for him to go hide. According to the notes Dr. Hoyle made during the interview with O'Campo, Josh said he then went to the laundry room to find some sort of weapon but there was nothing of use, so he hid behind the laundry room door until he heard his friend calling out to help him. Dr. Hoyle quotes Josh saying, "Couldn't find anything in the laundry room, didn't know what—if I killed 'em or something that I might get sued or get killed myself."

O'Campo's typed report references Josh telling him that he ran into the laundry room and hid and heard what sounded like Chris running around in circles. Then he heard Chris calling his name in a shrill scream. When Josh went back into the master bedroom he saw his mother lying on her back next to her desk. His father was in the same position by his closet and he also saw Chris, who was lying by the ironing board. He told O'Campo that Chris was making a gurgling sound as he stood next to him. He said he remembered getting hit on the head and did not remember anything else until he woke up the next morning and heard birds singing. He told O'Campo he hurt all over, especially the back of his head. He said he could see and hear, but not move. The next thing he remembered was seeing Chris's father, Bill Hughes, outside the glass doors of the master bedroom and soon after that he heard police CBs. In the handwritten notes Dr. Hoyle made, he quotes Josh saying, "They chased us around the house," and "They snuck up behind me and hit me."

Later in the interview, Josh told O'Campo about three Mexican men coming by his house looking for work. O'Campo pressed Josh for details about each of the Mexicans and the vehicle they drove. Josh's memory was quite vivid of their blue truck.

In the intervening seventeen months since June 4, 1983, Josh had undergone a whirlwind of emotions and experiences. Right after his release from the hospital on June 18, Richard and Sally Ryen, in compliance with the custody stipulation in Doug and Peggy Ryen's will, took Josh to New Jersey to live with them. In the interim, Josh's grandmother, Dr. Howell, initiated a bitter, family-rupturing custody battle, challenging the Ryens' will in San Bernardino County Superior Court. Josh was caught in the middle. Shortly after Josh returned to Southern California in September of 1983, a judge awarded custody of Josh to his grandmother during the school year and to Richard and Sally Ryen during the summer and other school vacations.

Dr. Howell did not approve of the Montessori school Josh had been enrolled in by his parents. For her, it was far too unstructured. She transferred him to a public school near her home in Temecula where he did not know one classmate. She also had him begin psychological therapy with Dr. Forbes. She diagnosed Josh as suffering from post-traumatic disorder brought on by his sense of guilt for being the lone survivor of the attack that had killed his family and best friend.

Partly out of his own sense of guilt as the lone survivor, he had grown to detest talking about the night of the attack, even with Dr. Forbes. During therapy sessions Dr. Forbes began conducting with Josh in October of 1983, Josh demonstrated great reluctance to revisit what he had seen take place that night. What he did tell her originally was that "three Mexicans chased us around the around" and that he "tried to fight them off...and they came and hit me."

In December of 1983, Negus was permitted to submit a list of questions for Josh to be asked in an audio-recorded session with only Dr. Forbes and Josh present. During the defense portion of the trial, Negus asked Dr. Forbes if Josh had shown resistance to answering his questions. Dr. Forbes said he did. "He asked me how long it would take. He watched the pages of the questions and kept asking me how many more he had to do and he at times became extremely nervous," including covering himself with his jacket and hiding his face from her.

Until this interview with Dr. Forbes, Josh had never claimed to actually having seen any of his assailants. In response to one of the questions posed by Negus, Josh told Dr. Forbes that he saw an attacker in the master bedroom with a "big puff of hair."

With Dr. Forbes on the witness stand, Negus attempted to account for Josh's about-face in switching from three assailants to only one. He led Dr. Forbes into exploring the possibility that Josh was now fantasizing, a notion the psychiatrist readily supported.

DR. FORBES: BECAUSE OF HIS DEEP GUILT THAT HE WAS THE SOLE SURVIVOR, IT WOULD BE POSSIBLE FOR HIM IN THE INTERVENTION OF TIME SINCE THE INCIDENT AND MY INTERVIEW [IN DECEMBER OF 1984] TO HAVE CREATED A FANTASY THAT HE SAW AN ATTACKER, WHICH WOULD DECREASE HIS GUILT ABOUT BEING ALIVE.

NEGUS: IF JOSHUA WAS FANTASIZING ABOUT SEEING AN ATTACKER IN THE BEDROOM, WOULD HE BE LIKELY TO ADOPT AS THE PERSON HE FANTASIZED ABOUT THE PERSON WHO HAD BEEN ACCUSED BY THE POLICE OF COMMITTING THE CRIME?

DR. FORBES: IF HE WERE EXPOSED TO ANY OTHER STIMULI WHICH WOULD MAKE HIM INTEGRATE THAT INTO HIS MIND.

NEGUS: WOULD TELEVISION BE SUCH A STIMULANT?

DR. FORBES: YES.

NEGUS: IN YOUR—IN HIS DESCRIPTION TO YOU OF HIS ATTACKER, HE—INDICATED THAT THE PERSON HAD BUSHY HAIR, IS THAT CORRECT?

DR. FORBES: THAT'S CORRECT.

NEGUS: IF ON THE TELEVISION THE PERSON THAT THE PROSECU-
TION HAD ACCUSED OF DOING THE CRIME, MR. COOPER, HAD ALWAYS
BEEN SHOWN WITH BUSHY HAIR, COULD THAT INFLUENCE JOSH IN HIS
DESCRIPTION?

DR. FORBES: YES.

A few questions later, Negus asked her if she could assign a probability to whether Josh was fantasizing about seeing an attacker with bushy hair. Dr. Forbes answered, "I believe so." After some further questioning, Dr. Forbes answered, "The probability I would assign is that he does not—or did not perceive the exact identify of the attacker or specifically whether he saw bushy hair."

Judge Garner then asked her, "Are you saying that the probabilities are he did not perceive a man with bushy hair"?

"Yes, Your Honor," Dr. Forbes responded.

CHAPTER THIRTY-ONE

The Confession

After a twelve-day holiday break, the much-anticipated testimony of Kevin Cooper was set to begin on the morning of January 2, 1985. Just before Cooper was scheduled to take the witness stand, Assistant D.A. Kochis turned over fifteen pages of new discovery to Public Defender Negus. The discovery, which was dated December 17, 1984 through December 21, 1984, was a report written by San Bernardino County Sheriff's Department Detective Gary Woods, Sergeant Arthur's top detective on the case. It documented a purported confession that Kenneth Koon, an inmate at California Medical Facility at Vacaville, made to cellmate Anthony Wisely. Wisely told Woods that he was in lockdown, smoking marijuana with Koon, when Koon implicated himself in the Ryen/Hughes murders.

In his report, Woods wrote that Wisely informed him that Koon was with two other men who were in the Aryan Brotherhood and they had driven to a residence in Chino to collect a debt for the gang, but hit the wrong house. Wisely said Koon told him "that after all this [the Ryen/ Hughes murders] blows over that the Brand [the Aryan Brotherhood] would take care of business in the right way."

The Aryan Brotherhood is a notorious white-supremacist prison gang that numbers over 15,000 members in and out of prison throughout the United States. Also known simply as "AB" or "the Brand," membership is for life. Paroled or released members are often directed to carry out the gang's retributions in the form of severe beatings or murders and to operate its significant drug trafficking, extortion, racketeering, dog fighting, and arms trafficking operations. For good reason, it is the most feared prison group in the nation, accounting for, according to the FBI, eighteen percent of the murders in federal prisons while numbering less than one percent of the inmate population.

Wisely told Woods that Koon said he had waited in the car outside the residence while his two companions entered the home carrying two hatchets and wearing gloves. Koon told him the men were in the home for about ten or fifteen minutes and that when they came out they said "the debt was officially collected."

Koon and Lee Furrow were acquaintances. After Diana Roper turned in Furrow's coveralls to the police, Furrow moved out and Koon moved in to live with Roper.

Some of what Wisely told Woods about what Koon had told him, Koon clarified when Detective Woods interviewed him the same day he had spoken with Wisely. Wisely had said that it was Koon who went to Roper's house to change out of his coveralls pre-dawn on June 5 when Koon knew it was Furrow who had done that because Roper had told him about it. Koon denied being with Furrow the night of the murders, saying he was in Gorman, California. In his report, Woods noted that Koon was six-feet-four-inches tall and weighed two-hundred pounds—a size that would seem to exclude him as one of the three men in the Canyon Corral Bar.

What Wisely had told Woods is known as "*Brady* material," information collected by the police and prosecution that tends to exculpate the person charged with the crime. (In a 1963 case entitled *Brady v. Maryland*, the U.S. Supreme Court ruled that the prosecution is compelled to turn over to the defense any information it has that tends to support the innocence of the defendant and failure to do so is grounds for a new trial.) This information not only excluded Cooper, but it directly implicated three other persons. Under the *Brady* rules, the prosecution should have turned over Woods's interviews with Wisely and Koon to Cooper's attorney the next day, but instead it waited two weeks, until the trial was already in the defense stage and Cooper was set to testify.

Judge Garner was not pleased by the delay in turning over Detective Wood's report. "Oh, golly, why couldn't you have given this to him before, gentlemen"?

Kochis said he had only received it that morning and had given it to Negus right after he made a copy of it. Negus told the judge he was sure it was not Kochis who held it back.

"Then the sheriff's office should have passed it to Mr. Kochis before the holidays," the judge correctly stated. As a partial remedy, the judge gave Negus an hour to go over the discovery.

In chambers after reviewing the discovery, Negus made the biggest strategic blunder of the case, telling the judge he was not going to request "any further delay at this point in time." Instead, he said, he would send his investigator, Ron Forbush, to interview Wisely later on because he needed Forbush on hand during Cooper's testimony. Depending on what Forbush found out, Negus said "there might be a time later on when I may need a day or two's delay to get it all together, but at the present time I don't, and I hope to be able to get it done without any delay."

Wisely's revelations were so exculpatory to Cooper that Negus should have asked for a delay in the trial so that both Wisely and Koon could have been interviewed. Interviewing either of them would have led the defense straight back to Diana Roper and her information about not just the bloody coveralls Furrow came home in but also the tan, Fruit-of-the Loom T-shirt Furrow had been wearing on the day of the murders and the hatchet missing from Furrow's set of tools. Had Negus taken this road, the trial would have taken a radical turn in Cooper's favor.

Ten days later when Forbush did get around to interviewing Wisely, he found him to be "wary." At first Wisely refused to speak with Forbush. Eventually he told him that the interview he had given Detective Woods was the beginning of his troubles and that he had been "in the hole" ever since, although he had committed no violation of prison rules. It was a reprisal. He then told Forbush that he knew Kevin Cooper had not committed the Ryen/Hughes murders and Forbush would know who the murderers were if he had been there and listened to Koon talk to him.

Negus, now engrossed in taking testimony from defense witnesses, did nothing with the information Forbush provided him, and asked for no delay in the trial to delve into these incredibly important revelations.

The sheriff's department's tactic of withholding the Wisely and Koon interviews for nearly two weeks had a major effect on Cooper's right to a fair trial. The jury never got to hear anything about Kenneth Koon's alleged confession.

Asked why he did not ask for the continuance the judge seemed more than willing to provide so he could get to the bottom of Wisely's revelations, Negus said in a 2011 interview, "I made that decision because Kevin was ready to testify and I wanted to get it over with. There was nothing in that discovery that would bear on his testimony." Negus also said that he did not consider Wisely "credible," although he could not remember why he thought that.

Negus said that bringing in Wisely as a witness would have been "a shotgun approach or an alternative theory [approach]. My theory was that three people from the [Canyon Corral] bar killed the Ryens…that's what I thought I had the most evidence of and I didn't want to put on other theories."

Negus had simply failed to make the connection between the three white men Wisely had told Detective Woods about and the three men in the bar. Far from being "an alternative theory" approach, the Wisely revelations were Negus's pathway to making the men in the bar real to the jury—men so drunk out of their minds they hit the wrong house and killed the wrong people.

CHAPTER THIRTY-TWO

Cooper Testifies

Many defendants at murder trials elect not to take the stand in their own defense—O.J. Simpson and Scott Peterson being notable examples—because they have reason to fear the merciless cross-examination of the prosecutor. Although jurors are instructed by the judge to make no inference from a defendant's not testifying, it is generally believed that jurors have a difficult time heeding that admonition. Cooper, knowing himself innocent, very badly wanted to testify. Despite all of his past arrests and sentencings, Cooper had never testified as a witness at any court proceedings.

Public Defender David Negus intended to start the direct-examination off by asking his client if he killed the Ryen family and Chris Hughes. It would have been an attention-grabbing way to begin, and good theater to boot. The jury had been waiting since the opening of the trial back on October 23 to hear from the defendant. Even D.A. Kottmeier would prove to be all ears, not making one objection during Cooper's day-long direct-examination.

Incredibly, Negus began by asking Cooper, "Do you have gum in your mouth"?

Cooper said "No."

"Oh, excuse me. Kevin, did you kill the Ryen family and Christopher Hughes"?

"No, sir, Mr. Negus, I didn't," he answered.

With this inauspicious, bungling beginning hanging in the air, Negus began by taking Cooper back to his days at the California Institute for Men and how he came by the pair of tennis shoes the prosecution had made a centerpiece of its evidentiary case against him.

Cooper, wearing a jacket and tie and dark, horn-rimmed glasses, did not appear at all to be the crazed, homicidal maniac that Kottmeier had portrayed him as in his opening statement. His answers to Negus's questions were direct and informative, delivered in a low-key, quiet voice. What little nervousness he displayed at the beginning of his testimony soon fell away as he settled in. The direct-examination quickly became more of a conversation than an interrogation.

Cooper told Negus that he remembered getting a pair of used, faded black or blue tennis shoes, size nine, in a box from a correctional officer in the lock-down section of the prison. (The Pro-Keds Dude tennis shoes the prosecution alleged he had acquired from inmate James Taylor and worn at the crime scene were black. Those shoes had come from gym section of the prison. Cooper had tossed the tennis shoes away at sea and could have said they were any color other than black.)

Asked if he knew James Taylor, Cooper said he had only seen him at the prison gym, but had never spoken with him and most certainly had never received any tennis shoes from him.

In the hideout house, he smoked Kools until he ran out of them and then began rolling his own cigarettes from the bag of prison-issued tobacco he brought with him. He said he did not smoke any Viceroy cigarettes at the hideout despite deputies finding a butt of one in the headboard in the empty bedroom. (Roger Lang, one of the owners of the Lease house, smoked Viceroys.)

He did not see a T-shirt and a towel in the closet where he slept in the hideout house. (The prosecution had a photo of the closet showing a T-shirt and a towel at the top of the closet.) "Positively they weren't there," he answered. He also did not see a hunk of rope, a hatchet sheath or a green button in the empty bedroom. Later on he said he never saw an ax in the hideout house.

Negus asked him what he did after a woman entered the hideout house on Saturday morning to pick up a sweater she had left there and then left without detecting him in the bathroom. "Kind of sighed and closed the door. I was kind of nervous."

Negus then took Cooper through how he spent his time in the hideout house, finally coming to the point where Cooper was preparing to leave.

NEGUS: AND DID YOU HAVE ANY SHOES ON?

COOPER: YES.

NEGUS: AND WHICH ONES WERE THOSE?

COOPER: THE PRO-KEDS.

NEGUS: THE ONES RIGHT HERE [PICTURED IN] EXHIBIT 120?

COOPER: YES.

NEGUS: AND WHAT DID YOU DO FOR THE REST OF THE DAY?

This series of questions greatly undermined the defense's position that Cooper had been given a pair of worn P.F. Flyers, not new Pro-Keds Dude tennis shoes at CIM. Negus's belated attempt to change the subject from Cooper saying he did have a pair of Pro-Keds tennis shoes to asking him what he did the rest of the day only proved the old courtroom maxim about never asking a question you do not know the answer to or do not want the answer to.

Negus wound up the direct-examination by asking Cooper a series of questions that elicited a "no" response each time: Had he ever been to Long Beach; had he ever dressed up as a woman; and, finally, did he kill Doug, Peggy, Jessica Ryen and Chris Hughes.

CHAPTER THIRTY-THREE

Cooper's Cross-Examination

he one bit of advice David Negus gave his client about how to handle
himself during the upcoming cross-examination was "to give only one
word answers to the district attorney. Do not give open-ended answers,"
Cooper said in an interview.

For D.A. Dennis Kottmeier, the cross-examination of Kevin Cooper
would be the highlight of his twenty-six year career in the San Bernardino
County District Attorney's Office.

Kottmeier would later recall that one of his early goals was to rattle
Cooper to the point where he would take off his glasses, something Cooper
would do from time to time during the cross-examination. Kottmeier, believing Cooper was evil incarnate, wanted the jurors to clearly see Cooper's
eyes. He planned to get Cooper to take his glasses off by intentionally
asking objectionable questions, questions meant to provoke Cooper that
Kottmeier knew Negus would object to and the judge would disallow.

Kottmeier did not like how comfortable, calm, and collected Cooper
had appeared during the direct-examination. The bulldog D.A. also did
not care for the fact that Cooper had undergone what he considered to
be "a college education" in his appearance, transforming from a menacing
man with a wild Afro and a mean stare in his Pennsylvania mug shots to a
respectable young man "with closed cropped hair, tinted glasses and a suit."

In his high school days, Kottmeier appeared in *Teenagers Battle the
Thing*, an hour-long 1958 horror film about a group of high school students
on an archaeological field trip who dig up a mummy that turns into a
monster. A review on the website Zombie Movie Data Base said the movie

was "so bad it's funny," terming the acting "hideous and flat." Twenty years later the movie was repackaged and released to TV as the *Curse of Bigfoot*. Reviews continued to be harsh. Amazon.com called it "ultra cheesy."

As Kottmeier began his cross-examination, he summoned his thespian inclinations, sauntering over to the exhibit's table and dramatically picking up the hatchet allegedly used in the assault at the Ryen house. Waving the ax around, he posited his first question: "Mr. Cooper, there is no doubt in your mind that the hatchet, Exhibit 42, was used to kill the Ryen family, is there"?

Cooper answered, "I don't know." His attorney objected to the question, saying it was irrelevant what his client's "state of mind as to what the hatchet is." Judge Garner allowed Cooper's answer to remain.

Kottmeier, somewhat encouraged by the ruling, pressed on:

KOTTMEIER: DO YOU -- HOW DO YOU EXPLAIN TO THE JURY, MR. COOPER, THAT THIS HATCHET, EXHIBIT 42, THAT HAS THE BLOOD ON IT, CAME FROM THE HOME THAT YOU USED AS A HIDEOUT?

NEGUS: OBJECTION. THAT'S ARGUMENTATIVE AND IRRELEVANT. IT IS NOT THE SUBJECT OF HIS TESTIMONY TO TRY AND EXPLAIN THINGS; MERELY HE HAS NO WAY OF KNOWING HOW IT CAME ABOUT.

JUDGE GARNER: MR. KOTTMEIER?

KOTTMEIER: YOUR HONOR, IT IS OFFERED BECAUSE THIS PAR-TICULAR DEFENDANT HAD ACCESS TO THE HOUSE AS ILLUSTRATED BY THE TESTIMONY, GIVING MR. COOPER A CHANCE TO EXPLAIN VARIOUS ASPECTS.

JUDGE GARNER: NO, I THINK THE OBJECTION IS GOOD, SIR. SUSTAINED.

Time and again, the prosecutor would advance obviously inappropriate questions, asking Cooper, for example, how could he explain Doug Ryen's hair in the drain of the shower in the hideout house, or the prison tennis shoe footprints, or his blood being in the Ryen house. Each time Negus would object and the judge would sustain the objection. The judge told the D.A. that it was not the witness's role to explain anything.

Kottmeier remained undeterred. A number of questions later he asked Cooper to explain the Role-Rite tobacco found in the Ryens' stolen station wagon. After the judge sustained Negus's objection, Negus asked the judge, "Could Mr. Kottmeier be admonished to not keep doing it"?

Although Judge Garner should have admonished the prosecutor long before, he made no response.

Asked what effort he made at the hideout house to avoid leaving any fingerprints, Cooper said, "None." This was a particularly odd question because Cooper's fingerprints were all over the hideout house.

KOTTMEIER: DIDN'T WEAR ANY GLOVES?

COOPER: NO.

KOTTMEIER: DIDN'T WIPE ANYTHING OFF?

COOPER: NO.

KOTTMEIER: HOW DO YOU EXPLAIN NO FINGERPRINTS BEING ON THE GLASS YOU HAD COFFEE IN, EXHIBIT 124?

COOPER: I DON'T EXPLAIN.

The answer was astute: It put Kottmeier in his place without Negus even having to make an objection. Cooper, to the veteran prosecutor's surprise, was holding his own extremely well. His responses were direct and generally respectful and polite; he often included the word "sir" in his answers. Something else that surprised and impressed Kottmeier was Cooper's realigning his chair to face the roaming D.A. as he answered his questions.

Earlier on in the cross-examination, Kottmeier tried to get before the jury that Cooper had charges pending against him in Pennsylvania that included house burglary, auto theft, kidnapping and rape. When Kottmeier obliquely approached the subject by asking Cooper if there were some places he wanted to avoid after he escaped from the California Institute for Men, Negus objected and the judge subsequently agreed, at Negus's request, to hold an in-chambers conference. The judge had already ruled that all charges against Cooper from Pennsylvania were inadmissible and now reiterated that ruling.

The attempt by the prosecutor to have inadmissible evidence entered is an ethical violation of his status as an officer of the court, a fact the judge should have, but did not, point out. With the overwhelming resources of the district attorney's office and the sheriff's department at his disposal, along with the alleged evidence of Cooper's blood and footprints at the crime scene, Kottmeier's stooping to this tactic was an over-the-top, bad-faith effort to prejudice the jury against Cooper.

Demonizing and demeaning Cooper had been a mainstay of the sheriff's department ever since Sheriff Tidwell had named him as the sole perpetrator of the Chino Hills murders back on June 9, 1983. The news media had quoted sheriff's officials saying Cooper was an escapee from a mental asylum, a homosexual and a cross-dresser. Kottmeier was not above trying to extend this vile image of Cooper by asking him about the semen found on the green blanket he had wrapped around himself while sleeping nude on the floor of the closet in the hideout house. During Negus's direct-examination, Cooper had testified that he deposited the semen during a wet dream. "The only reason you've come up with this particular story [about sleeping nude] is to explain the masturbation on the green blanket. Isn't that correct"?

"I don't masturbate," Cooper replied.

One of the most difficult things for any objective person to grasp about the horrible murders inflicted on the Ryens and Chris Hughes was the undeniable fact that multiple weapons had been used during the assault on all of the murder victims and Josh Ryen as well.

In his opening statement, Negus made great issue of the multiple weapons pointing to multiple assailants. For the individual jurors, the questions raised by the multiple weapons issue could become like the elephant in the room if not explained away by the prosecution.

To help Kottmeier deal with this question, two weeks before the trial's opening, Sergeant Arthur wrote up a five-page report entitled, "Cooper's Ambidextrous Nature." Arthur claimed he had observed Cooper during the many pre-trial hearings using both his right and left hands interchangeably. For example, Arthur noted Cooper poured water with either hand. Some of the dates Arthur cited in the report were days Cooper was not even present in the courtroom—total fictions in other words. The best Kottmeier could do would leave the issue in serious doubt:

KOTTMEIER: YOU ARE LEFT-HANDED?

COOPER: YES.

KOTTMEIER: DO YOU USE A FORK IN YOUR LEFT HAND?

COOPER: YES.

KOTTMEIER: WHEN YOU USE A KNIFE, DO YOU USE IT IN YOUR RIGHT HAND?

COOPER: YEP.

KOTTMEIER: WHEN YOU POUR WATER HERE IN COURT, FOR EXAMPLE, DO YOU USE YOUR LEFT HAND TO POUR WATER?

COOPER: SOMETIMES. SOMETIMES I USED MY RIGHT HAND TO POUR WATER.

KOTTMEIER: WHEN YOU WRITE ON THE DIAGRAM SOMETIMES YOU WOULD USE YOUR LEFT HAND?

COOPER: YES. I ALWAYS USE MY LEFT HAND TO WRITE.

KOTTMEIER: OR DRAW?

COOPER: OR DRAW, YES.

KOTTMEIER: HOWEVER, YOU DO HAVE THE ABILITY TO USE YOUR RIGHT HAND MORE THAN SAY A NORMAL LEFT-HANDED PERSON?

COOPER: NO.

Even as experienced a prosecutor as Kottmeier is not immune from asking questions that backfire in the sense that if the jurors had not heard the answers they would have had no way of being able to consider the new information imparted. Such a development occurred when Kottmeier bungled into asking Cooper about the jacket he wore when he escaped. Cooper explained that he had stolen the jacket the day of his escape out of the TV room in Cedar Hall. Unlike all three of the prison jackets on exhibit in the courtroom, Cooper said this one did not have "CIM" stenciled on it, nor did it have fur around the collar, and it had a different type of lining.

Furthermore, it was brown, not green. The telling detail Cooper provided was that the jacket did not have any buttons on the front, just a zipper. Cooper said he thought the jacket was the private property of an inmate.

Another gaffe was asking Cooper if he left the hideout house with Role-Right tobacco. Cooper answered that by the time he made his getaway he had smoked all of it and had used up all the paper to roll it in as well.

A great deal of the information Kottmeier covered in his cross-examination was information Cooper had provided during his direct-examination by Negus. Kottmeier was mining for inconsistent statements to demonstrate that Cooper was a liar, going into great detail about Cooper's movements in the hideout house, even asking him such trivial things as the ingredients of the sandwiches he made for himself or whether the door to the kitchen in the hideout house had curtains on its windows. On direct-examination, Cooper had said he thought it did which allowed Kottmeier to show him a photo of the door and have him admit it did not have curtains. At many junctures, Cooper said he could not precisely remember the exact details, responding once, "...I do not remember detail by detail by detail. The only thing I know is what I didn't do."

Kottmeier fell for the bait, asking him what he did not do.

"I did not kill the Ryens, and I did not attempt to kill Christopher Hughes and I did not attempt to kill Josh Ryen," Cooper said.

Toward the end of the first day of cross-examination and well into the second day, Kottmeier began trying to establish that Cooper's escape from CIM had been part of a grand plan Cooper had devised well in advance. His relentless questioning of Cooper would establish just the opposite. Kottmeier began by asking Cooper when he first made up his mind to try to escape from CIM. Cooper said the thought came to him as he lay on his bunk in his first night in the minimum-security section.

Kottmeier thought he had caught the defendant in a lie, asking him to explain why he mailed some documents to a woman friend, Yolanda Jackson, a few days before he was switched to minimum.

KOTTMEIER: YOU DIDN'T WANT THE PRISON AUTHORITIES TO KNOW THAT YOU WERE KEVIN COOPER?

COOPER: I BELIEVE THEY ALREADY KNEW.

KOTTMEIER: WELL, THAT'S WHY YOU SENT THE PAPERS OUT TO YOLANDA JACKSON?

COOPER: WELL, IT'S MY UNDERSTANDING THAT WHEN YOU SEND STUFF OUT THROUGH THE JAIL THEY READ IT AND THEY GO THROUGH IT ANYWAY, SO THEY KNEW BECAUSE WHEN LEGAL STUFF COMES IN SOMETIMES THEY GET A COPY OF THEIR OWN.

At 7:53 p.m. on the night he left the hideout house, Cooper placed a call to Diane Williams in Pittsburgh, Pennsylvania to see if she had been able to put together any money to send him. She told him she had not. The call terminated at 8:30 p.m. and Cooper left the hideout house shortly thereafter.

KOTTMEIER: WHAT IS YOUR PLAN AT THIS POINT IN TIME WHEN YOU STARTED TO MAKE YOUR PHONE CALL TO DIANE WILLIAMS?

COOPER: JUST BASICALLY WAIT UNTIL IT GETS DARK ENOUGH TO LEAVE.

KOTTMEIER: WHERE ARE YOU GOING?

COOPER: TO MEXICO.

KOTTMEIER: WHAT OTHER PART OF THE PLAN DID YOU HAVE AT THIS TIME?

COOPER: BASICALLY NONE.

KOTTMEIER: ALL YOU'RE GOING TO DO IS GO DOWN TO MEXICO AND HAVE DIANE WILLIAMS HOLD MONEY FOR YOU?

COOPER: I WOULDN'T SAY IT IN TERMS LIKE THAT, BUT BASICALLY YES.

KOTTMEIER: WHAT OTHER PARTS TO THE PLAN WERE THERE?

COOPER: THERE WASN'T—YOU MAKING IT SEEM LIKE IT WAS A REAL SET-OUT, THOUGHT-OUT PLAN. IT WASN'T NO PLAN LIKE IT WAS A CONSPIRACY. IT WASN'T A CONSPIRACY. YOU MAKING A MOUNTAIN OUT OF A MOLEHILL. ALL I DID, YOU KNOW, WAS TELL THE GIRL IF SHE HAD THE MONEY, JUST HOLD IT FOR ME AND I WILL BE BACK IN TOUCH WITH HER—TELL HER WHERE TO SEND IT TO ME AT A LATER TIME.

Part of Kottmeier's courtroom theatrics was to set up the haymaker types of questions he relished hurling at Cooper with a seemingly innocuous lead-in question. Just after he asked Cooper why he changed his mind about going to Los Angeles—Cooper explained that Yolanda Jackson told him on the phone that the police would be looking for him there—this exchange took place:

KOTTMEIER: YOU CHANGED YOUR MIND ABOUT LOS ANGELES AFTER YOU KILLED THE RYENS AND CHRISTOPHER HUGHES, DIDN'T YOU?
COOPER: NO, SIR.
KOTTMEIER: AFTER YOU LEFT CHINO HILLS YOU HAD TO GET FURTHER AWAY FROM THAT THAN JUST LOS ANGELES?
COOPER: EXCUSE ME, I DON'T UNDERSTAND.
KOTTMEIER: AFTER YOU LEFT CHINO HILLS YOU HAD TO GET FURTHER AWAY FROM THE MURDERS THAN JUST GOING TO LOS ANGELES?
COOPER: I DIDN'T KILL ANYBODY.

In repeatedly fending off such hostile questions, Cooper was in his own way leveling the playing field, showing himself to be adept and poised under fire—just the opposite impression the venom-spewing prosecutor was working to create. The longer Kottmeier kept Cooper on the witness stand, the more the under-educated, reviled defendant established his credibility.

Some of the answers Cooper provided were so full of telling detail that they carried a ring of great authenticity to them. Certainly without intending to, Kottmeier's insistence on detail only served to buoy Cooper's credibility. A perfect example occurred when Kottmeier asked him about how he was carrying the two bags Cooper said he took with him when he left the hideout house.

"Well, at one particular point in time that green bag had a yellow strap just like it had yellow handles, so I put it over my shoulder. At some point in time, maybe weight from the bag, whatever, it ripped. But at that particular time, the shoulder—the shoulder bag—shoulder handle part of it worked," he said.

Kottmeier was the master of the read-between-the-lines type of question. When his question expressed incredulity he hoped the jurors would pick up on that and discount whatever Cooper had to say. Kottmeier made it clear that it found it hard to believe that Cooper, an escaped convict, would be brazen enough to approach a busy intersection and ask a man in a convertible stopped at traffic light which way Mexico was.

KOTTMEIER: YOU'RE NO LONGER HIDING AT THIS POINT?

COOPER: NO.

KOTTMEIER: WELL, WHAT CAUSED THE CHANGE? HOW ALL OF A SUD-DEN ARE YOU ABLE TO COME OUT AND STAND ON THAT BUSY ROAD AND WALK UP AND START TALKING TO PEOPLE?

COOPER: WELL, THE WAY I LOOKED AT IT, FIRST OF ALL, I WAS NO LONGER IN PRISON CLOTHES, EVEN SO, I HAD SOME IN THE BAG. NO ONE OTHER THAN MYSELF KNEW THEY WERE IN THERE. AND SECOND OF ALL, MY APPEARANCE HAD CHANGED. I HAD SHAVED MY PARTIAL BEARD OFF, MY MUSTACHE, RE-BRAIDED MY HAIR. I'M QUITE SURE SOMEWHERE IN HISTORY I WASN'T THE ONLY BLACK MAN WITH TWO BAGS TO BE STANDING THERE HITCHHIKING. SO I WAS LOOKING AT ALL THAT.

Try as he might, Kottmeier's grueling, no-holds-barred cross-examination had turned up nothing but petty, meaningless inconsistencies from what Cooper had testified to under direct-examination. The story he had told Negus about his escape from CIM, his two days in the hideout house, and his leaving that house shortly after dark—hours before the Ryens and Chris Hughes were murdered—was the same story he was telling the prosecutor about his escape.

When Cooper stepped down from the witness stand after three rigorous days of cross-examination, his credibility was intact. The hard-driving prosecutor had succeeded periodically in getting the defendant to remove his glasses, but had failed to unmoor him. "Despite three grueling days of cross-examination by Kottmeier, Cooper remained cool and confident and steadfastly maintained his innocence," the trial reporter for the *Los Angeles Times* wrote. Cooper came off essentially as he truly was: a catch-as-catch-can opportunist with no grand plan, a laid-back, ne'er-do-well of a young man who survived on his wits with absolutely no motive to murder the Ryens and Chris Hughes to aid his escape.

RYEN FAMILY TAKEN IN 1983

CHRISTOPHER HUGHES FROM
1983

RYENS' HOUSE FROM BELOW

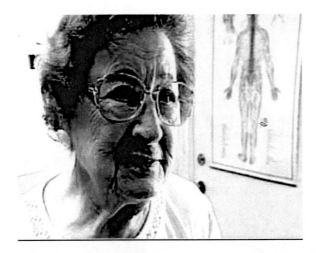

DR. MARY
HOWELL, PEGGY
RYEN'S MOTHER
(2003)

RYENS' MASTER
BEDROOM AFTER
BODIES WERE
REMOVED ON
JUNE 5, 1983

SHERIFF FLOYD
TIDWELL IN
RYENS' MASTER
BEDROOM AFTER
THE BEDROOM
HAD BEEN
DISMANTLED

FOLDED MONEY AND LOOSE CHANGE SITTING ON THE KITCHEN COUNTER AT THE RYENS' HOUSE

HANDGUNS IN RYENS' MASTER BEDROOM

INTERIOR VIEW OF THE CANYON CORRAL BAR

MUG SHOT OF KEVIN COOPER FROM PITTSBURGH, PA., POLICE DEPARTMENT IN 1982

ANOTHER MONKEY HANGED IN EFFIGY OUTSIDE SAN DIEGO COURTHOUSE IN 1985 THAT STATES, "HANG THE AFRICAN TROGLODYTE."

MONKEY HANGED IN EFFIGY OUTSIDE ONTARIO COURTHOUSE IN 1984

HATCHET FOUND IN THE WEEDS JUST OFF THE ROAD LEADING AWAY FROM THE RYEN HOUSE ON JUNE 5, 1983, THE DAY THE MURDERS WERE DISCOVERED

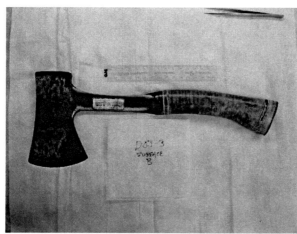

HATCHET THAT WAS ENTERED IN EXHIBIT AT COOPER'S TRIAL AS THE MURDER WEAPON -- THE SAME HATCHET FOUND IN THE WEEDS OFF THE ROAD LEADING AWAY FROM THE RYENS' HOUSE

TAN T-SHIRT

THE LOCATION
OF A-41 IN
HALLWAY LEAD-
ING TO RYENS'
LIVING ROOM

REMAINS OF
A-41 AS OF
7-11-84

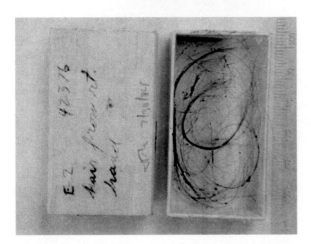

THE BLONDE OR
LIGHT BROWN
CLUMP OF HAIRS
CLUTCHED IN
JESSICA'S RYEN'S
RIGHT HAND

NEW PRO-KEDS
DUDE TENNIS
SHOE

DANIEL J.
GREGONIS FROM
2001

ARTIST'S DRAWING
OF ORRICK ATTORNEY
NORM HILE DURING
ORAL ARGUMENTS
BEFORE AN ABSENT
THREE-JUDGE
PANEL OF THE NINTH
CIRCUIT COURT OF
APPEALS ON JANUARY
9, 2007. ATTORNEY
DAVID ALEXANDER
IS IN BOWTIE AT
DEFENSE TABLE

JOSH RYEN
IN 2003

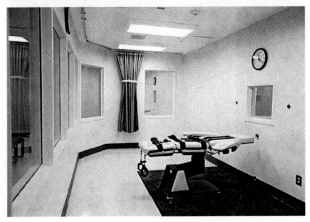

NEW DEATH
CHAMBER AT
SAN QUENTIN

KEVIN
COOPER FROM
2011

CHAPTER THIRTY-FOUR

Josh in the Emergency Room

Following Cooper's testimony, Negus called Don Gamundoy, the clinical social worker who communicated with Josh in the emergency room at Loma Linda University Hospital, and then the San Bernardino County Sheriff's Department deputy, Dale Sharp, who interviewed Josh right after Gamundoy had finished.

Negus needed both of these witnesses to counteract the videotaped testimony of Josh saying he could not remember what happened at his home during the assault and that all he had seen was "a shadow on the wall." The truth was that if Josh had stuck to what he communicated to Gamundoy and Deputy Sharp, the D.A.'s Office would have been forced to drop its murder and attempted murder charges against Cooper.

Gamundoy was one of the most credible witnesses the jury would encounter. Friendly and personable, he was well suited for his job of clinical social worker and very experienced at it. Before working with Josh, Gamundoy had tended to more than twenty other survivors of violent crimes.

When Josh arrived at the emergency room at Loma Linda University Medical Center, he could neither speak nor write legibly. The hospital staff did not even know his name. As Gamundoy began questioning Josh at 2:23 p.m., other hospital staff were monitoring his pulse and blood pressure and taking some X-rays. Despite the severe injuries he had sustained, the staff found Josh to be amazingly stable and alert. Throughout his time in the emergency room his blood pressure and pulse held steady and he never lost consciousness.

A tube to assist breathing had already been inserted in Josh's windpipe, so Gamundoy first asked the little boy to just blink his eyes once if the answer was "yes." When that method soon proved unreliable, Gamundoy asked Josh to write out his name and birth date, but no one could read his writing. At that point Gamundoy improvised by writing all the letters of the alphabet, the numbers zero through nine, and the words "yes" and "no" on a sheet of paper he attached it to a clipboard he held above Josh's head. He told Josh, who was lying flat on his back on a gurney, to just point to the letters, the numbers or words to give his answers.

By pointing at the letters and numbers with his right hand, Josh correctly provided his name, his date of birth, and his telephone number. When Gamundoy asked him if "Josh" was short for "Joshua," Josh pointed to "yes." Once the staff knew that Josh was able to communicate lucidly, some of them, including the charge nurse, Marion McQuinn, began suggesting questions for Gamundoy to ask Josh.

Gamundoy proceeded to ask him how many people attacked him. Josh pointed to "3", and then to "4." Next Josh indicated the attackers were male. Gamundoy then asked him if they were black. Josh pointed to "no." Because Gamundoy is Hawaiian and is frequently mistaken to be Mexican or Spanish, he asked Josh if the attackers looked like him, had his skin color. Josh pointed to "no." Josh pointed to "yes" when asked if they were white.

As Josh responded to these questions his face was taut with emotion, he cried, and several tears ran down his face.

To make sure that he was getting accurate answers, Gamundoy asked most questions twice in a row, having Josh reconfirm his first response.

During Gamundoy's questioning of Josh, an emergency room staff member took notes recording Josh's responses and so did Deputy Dale Sharp who had entered the emergency room around 2 p.m. and stood off to the side as medical staff worked on Josh.

Within the hour, Gamundoy prepared a written report of his session with Josh. One would think that what Josh had communicated to Gamundoy in the presence of various emergency room staff about his assailants would have been of great interest to law enforcement investigators. As

Negus brought out in direct-examination, this would not be the case. Seven months would elapse before Detectives Hector O'Campo and Gary Woods came to the hospital to interview Gamundoy. Their visit was not to find out what Josh had told him, but to inquire about what questions defense investigator Ron Forbush had asked Gamundoy in October of 1983.

During the cross-examination of Gamundoy, D.A. Kottmeier attempted to make a case for mass confusion in the ER and Josh passing in and out of consciousness.

In an interview in 2010 at Loma Linda University Hospital, Gamundoy recalled "being pissed" at Kottmeier for attempting to undermine the clarity of the answers Josh gave. "There were people in the room who saw Josh give the answers he did. I didn't make anything up."

Deputy Sharp got his chance to question Josh at about 2:30 p.m. and continued for the next fifteen minutes. Instead of using Gamundoy's method of communication, Sharp deployed a hand-squeeze technique. A squeeze meant "yes" and no squeeze meant "no." In his written report of the two initial interviews he conducted, Deputy Sharp stated, "The victim first advised me that there were three white male adult suspects in the residence and he had been asleep." He resumed questioning Josh in the CAT scan room at 3:45 p.m. just before Josh went into surgery. During the two interviews, Sharp called Sergeant Arthur, the lead detective on the case who was at the crime scene, three times. A police log from that time period—most likely the result of information supplied to Arthur by Sharp—described the suspects as "three young males" driving the Ryens' station wagon.

Deputy Dale Sharp was a most reluctant defense witness. The night before he testified, he had gone over his upcoming testimony with Kottmeier on the phone and had gone over it again with the district attorney that morning. Under questioning from Negus, Sharp said he arrived at the hospital and notified dispatch he was there at 1:50 p.m. Sergeant Arthur called him a minute or two later and told him to get any information he could from Josh. Ten minutes later he saw Josh being treated in the emergency room and stood off to the side waiting for his opportunity to approach

Josh. As Josh was providing information to Gamundoy, Sharp was taking notes of the boy's age, birth date, and home phone number—information he would provide in a report he wrote up later that day at 6 p.m.

It is difficult to believe that a sheriff's deputy could be so confused or forgetful about what he saw going on in the emergency room. Instead of seeing Don Gamundoy—whom Sharp denied ever seeing in the ER—he testified that he saw a female nurse with the clipboard getting information from Josh. As misleading to the jury as this was, it was an improvement over Sharp's testimony at a preliminary hearing when he had denied under oath seeing anyone in the ER using a clipboard to elicit information from Josh.

Sharp also misstated the time he was with Josh in the ER, claiming he had interviewed him from 2:15 until 2:30 that afternoon when, in fact, he did not approach the boy until after Gamundoy had finished interviewing Josh at around 2:35 p.m. When Negus pointed out to him that hospital records showed Josh being sent to get a CAT scan at 2:45 p.m., Sharp backed off and now said he spoke with Josh from 2:30 to 2:45 p.m.

Sharp had less wiggle room when Negus questioned him about the information Josh imparted to him because the defense attorney had a copy of Sharp's report about his interviews with Josh. To compel Sharp to state the report's contents accurately, Negus had the deputy read directly from it. The report began, "The victim first advised me that there were three, white male adult subjects in the residence and he had been asleep." Further on his report, Negus had him read this revelation, "The victim did not know who the suspects were."

At 3:45 p.m., after Josh's CAT scan, Sharp interviewed Josh for the next forty-five minutes in the CAT scan room. It was during this session that Josh somehow communicated to the deputy that three Mexican men had approached his father as the family was about to leave for the party they would attend in Chino that evening.

Under direct-examination, Negus asked Sharp about Josh's switch from three white males to three Mexican men.

SHARP: I ASKED THE VICTIM IF HE WAS SURE IT WAS THREE MEXICANS RATHER THAN THE THREE WHITE MALE ADULTS. THE VICTIM ADVISED OF THREE MEXICANS. THE VICTIM MOVED UP HIS SHOULDERS THEN APPEARED TO BE CONFUSED.

NEGUS: TOWARD THE END [OF THE FORTY-FIVE MINUTE INTERVIEW] JOSH WAS DRIFTING AWAY, TIRED, PERHAPS CONFUSED BY THE QUESTIONS YOU'D ASKED HIM?

SHARP: I WOULDN'T KNOW. YOU KNOW, HE APPEARED TO BE CONFUSED TO ME AS FAR AS THAT PARTICULAR QUESTION, YES, SIR.

The confusion that Josh communicated to Sharp due to the inherent limitations of the hand-squeeze method Sharp deployed would form the basis for both the investigators and the district attorney's office to discount utterly the information Josh provided in the emergency room about the attackers being three white men.

CHAPTER THIRTY-FIVE

Jessica Outside Ryens' House

Without realizing it, or at least not making it clear to the jury, Public Defender Negus had a great opportunity to advance the multiple-assailant theory when he called Dr. John Thornton as a defense witness. At Negus's request, the prosecution had sent Dr. Thornton, a forensic science professor at the University of California with a doctorate in criminalistics, Jessica's nightgown, underpants and the white vinyl body bag used to remove her corpse from the Ryens' house.

Inside the body bag was a beetle; two burrs and a fragment of a foxtail adhered to her nightgown. Foxtail is a perennial weed with dense, cylindrical, often brush like, flower clusters that resemble foxes' tails. The burrs were close together, lodged about ten inches from the bottom of the nightgown's hem, along the right-hand seam.

When Negus asked him what inferences he drew from the evidence sent him, Dr. Thornton said, "Jessica had been outside of the residence prior to her death." He said the burrs would have been such "a great annoyance to Jessica" that he could not imagine her going to bed with them inside her nightgown. Further, he said the beetle is nocturnal and lives outdoors.

If an assailant had brought the burrs into the house, the burrs would be on the outside of Jessica's nightgown, Dr. Thornton said, and they would not likely be found in such close proximity to each other. Further, Dr. Thornton said it would be unusual for such burrs to transfer from one fabric surface to another; once the burrs have adhered to a surface, they typically must be physically plucked in order to be removed.

He said the burrs are a species of a family called medicheo, a large family of grasses that includes alfalfa and are used in horse and cattle feed. The plant that produces the burrs is common in Chino Hills.

To provide the jury with more detailed and expert testimony about the beetle in the body bag, Negus called John T. Doyen to the stand, a professor of entomology at the University of California with a specialty in coleoptera, commonly known as beetles. Within the order of coleoptera, Dr. Doyen specializes in a family called tenebrionidae—darkling ground beetles.

Dr. Doyen testified that the beetle in Jessica's body bag was from Central and Southern California, in the woodlands and grassland areas, not in the desert, but near the coast. He said Chino Hills would be within its habitat.

He explained that during the warmer months these beetles spend their days hiding down among the roots of plants, under boards and rocks and become active at night, crawling around the ground.

When Negus asked him if this type of beetle is normally found inside a house, Dr. Doyen said, "No. These are not domiciliary insects at all. They might be in a stable, but they would not be inside a house." On cross-examination, Dr. Doyen said if one of them happened to get attached to an animal, it would try to get off because they are secretive and reclusive."

By inference, what Dr. Doyen said meant that the beetle attached itself outside the Ryen house to Jessica but did not have enough time to detach itself before Jessica reentered the house. Somehow, in all the mayhem going on inside the Ryen house, Jessica had managed to escape outside.

This testimony presented Negus with a once-in-a-trial opportunity to destroy the single-attacker theory the prosecution had predicated its case upon. All he needed to do was put the medical examiner, Dr. Root, back on the stand and have him reiterate what he had testified to during direct-examination earlier in the trial about the distribution of blood on Jessica and Peggy Ryen. Dr. Root had testified that in conducting their autopsies, he observed a large blood smear across Jessica's face. He said his impression at the time was that the smearing of blood on Peggy's chest, arm and armpit areas "corresponded to blood on Jessica's face." He said Jessica also had blood smears on both her legs and thighs and on her right thigh there were a couple of drops of blood—drain patterns—suggesting "that someone bleeding was standing over her." He also testified that Peggy sustained some of her worst wounds while standing.

If Negus had orchestrated the testimony about Jessica being outside with the blood distribution patterns on her and her mother, he could have raised considerable doubt that a lone assailant was responsible. Proceeding in this manner would have set him up to argue in his summation to the jury that it was too far-fetched for one assailant to have tracked down Jessica and brought her back to the doorway of the master bedroom while her mother was still alive and standing within feet of a loaded .22 Ruger pistol.

Negus could have further argued that with all of this hyper, frantic activity taking place in just a matter of three or four minutes, the notion that a single perpetrator could have controlled two strong, able-bodied adults who were mobile for at least part of the attack, one child who ran outside the house, and two boys scurrying in and out of the master bedroom while at least Peggy Ryen was alive begged credulity.

Establishing these possibilities for the jury would have brought back in focus the three men Josh originally said perpetrated the attack, the three or four men the married couple saw driving away from the direction of the Ryens' house around midnight on the night of the murders, and three strange men at the Canyon Corral Bar.

Negus could have also used Dr. Root to support the multiple-assailant theory by having him revisit his prior testimony about Doug Ryen's having made it back and forth from one side of the bed to the other during the attack, meaning that while he was being besieged Peggy would have been free to get the Ruger out of the nightstand drawer if there was only one assailant in the bedroom.

The blood evidence that Dr. Root noted in his earlier trial testimony would make a good case for postulating that Doug Ryen was attacked first. There was a heavy trace of blood in the middle of his pillow. Somehow he was able to get to the other side of the bed where a stab wound to his carotid artery caused his blood to spray high up on the wall behind the bed. Still mobile, he made it back to his own side of the bed where he was found kneeling, just two feet from the closet that contained his loaded rifle.

Dr. Thornton was not alone in thinking that Jessica was outside the house at some point during the attack. Lillian Shaffer said in a 2010 interview that Sergeant Billy Arthur, the lead detective on the case, called her on the phone a few days after she returned from attending the Ryens' funerals and told her that Jessica had been outside during part of the attack. On June 6, the day after the murders were discovered, Shaffer had sat at Josh's bedside. Arthur was there and the two established a bond consoling Josh. While she held one of Josh's hands, Arthur held the other. The sergeant told her he had a son the same age as Josh.

CHAPTER THIRTY-SIX

Investigative Bias

In an ideal world, investigative work by law enforcement officials would be transparent. They would tape the interviews they did with key witnesses, preserve their original notes, and write their reports as soon as possible following each contact. The information they collected would, in due time, become part of the discovery material the prosecutor is compelled to turn over to the defense. Having such information would allow the defense something of an equal footing in preparing a defendant's case for trial.

In the real world, law enforcement officials by-and-large view the justice system as an adversarial undertaking, where racking up convictions supersedes all other considerations, including searching for the truth and respecting a defendant's constitutional rights to a fair trial. Once a suspect is indicted, the battle to suppress favorable information takes center stage: interviews that should have been taped are not, handwritten notes that should have been preserved are thrown away, and once called to the witness stand an incredible amnesia befogs the deputy, the detective or the sergeant on direct or cross-examination by the defense attorney.

No one more so than Detective Hector O'Campo personified the bias against Kevin Cooper that pervaded the San Bernardino County Sheriff's Department investigation into the Chino Hills murders. More than any other officer involved in the investigation, O'Campo truly vexed Negus. As the detective assigned to both befriend and debrief Josh during his hospital stay, O'Campo played the key role in moving Josh away from his initial communications that his attackers were three white males. From the day Cooper's fingerprints were discovered at the hideout house below the

Ryens' home, O'Campo became unshakably convinced that Cooper was the lone perpetrator. Over the course of some twenty personal visits with Josh in the hospital, visits which began on June 6, the day after Josh was admitted to the hospital, O'Campo was able to turn Josh's recollection of three white males into three young Mexicans, and eventually into a lone, unseen assailant, "a shadow on the wall."

Right after Deputy Sharp finished testifying, Negus called O'Campo to the witness stand for the purpose of demonstrating the extreme bias the detective harbored for his client. O'Campo, normally disingenuous, was not coy about having his prejudice against Cooper known to the jury. He told Negus that sometime between June 6 and June 9 he became convinced of Cooper's guilt.

NEGUS: DID YOU, IN FACT, FORM A CONVICTION STRONGER THAN JUST A MERE BELIEF ON JUNE THE 9TH THAT KEVIN COOPER WAS RESPONSIBLE FOR THE CRIME?

O'CAMPO: I WOULD HAVE TO SAY YES. I HAD MORE THAN A MERE BELIEF.

NEGUS: YOU TOLD YOLANDA JACKSON [A FRIEND OF COOPER'S] ON JUNE THE 9TH, DID YOU NOT, THAT: "I KNOW THAT HE SLAUGHTERED THOSE PEOPLE." IS THAT THE WORDS YOU USED?

O'CAMPO: WORDS TO THAT EFFECT, YES, SIR.

Detective O'Campo, with thirteen years in the employ of the San Bernardino County Sheriff's Department, was a virtuoso of cool, calculated elusiveness. (His career would go on another twenty years. When he retired in 2005 he held the rank of sergeant.)

For Negus, examining O'Campo was like trying to put toothpaste back in the tube. O'Campo denied having a conversation about Mexicans with Josh on June 6 when ICU nurse Linda Headley was in the room; he denied Josh communicating about hearing his mother's screams, or his being asleep, or it being dark outside when he awoke, or Josh holding up three fingers to him, or Josh saying he tried to fight to beat someone up with his fists.

NEGUS: DO YOU REMEMBER HOW MANY TIMES THAT YOU TALKED TO
JOSH ON JUNE THE 7TH, THE SECOND DAY THAT YOU KNEW HIM?

O'CAMPO: NO, I DON'T.

NEGUS: YOU DID GO OUT TO SEE HIM ON THAT DAY, DID YOU NOT?

O'CAMPO: I DON'T REMEMBER.

NEGUS: WOULD YOUR ANSWERS TO ALL THE QUESTIONS I ASKED ABOUT
CONVERSATIONS, ABOUT MEXICANS, RED SHIRTS, MOTHER SCREAMING,
BEING ASLEEP IN HIS ROOM, BEING DARK OUT, APPLY TO THE 7TH AS
WELL AS TO THE 6TH? DO YOU UNDERSTAND MY QUESTION?

O'CAMPO: I THINK SO. NOT KNOWING I WAS THERE ON THE 6TH,
NOT REMEMBERING WHETHER I WAS THERE ON THE 7TH, SPECIFICALLY,
TAKING INTO CONSIDERATION, I'D SAY THAT THERE WAS SOMEWHERE
BETWEEN ONE AND AS MUCH AS THREE DAYS THAT I MISSED. I DON'T
THINK I CAN ANSWER THAT.

Negus followed up by asking O'Campo if he had ever talked to Josh about the above referenced questions prior to the June 14 interview. "No, sir," was the answer.

"Mr. O'Campo, are you trying to cover up some information that you received from Josh which you now feel is harmful to the prosecution's case," Negus asked.

"Not at all," O'Campo said.

It did not appear to daunt him that Dr. Mary Howell and RN Linda Headley had observed him asking Josh numerous questions about the night of the attack and taking notes as Josh responded while Josh was in ICU from June 6 through June 9. Those witnesses, who would in short order follow O'Campo to the witness stand as defense witnesses, would contradict almost everything O'Campo testified to about his interaction with Josh in his ICU room.

Nurse Linda Headley's testimony undermining O'Campo would carry special weight because, as she told Negus on the witness stand, the attachments she had established with both Josh and Dr. Howell made her not want to testify at all, fearful that anything she said might be of help to Cooper. Negus had to subpoena her to get her to testify at trial.

O'Campo also testified that he took no notes during the initial interview, Linda Headley testified that he did; Dr. Howell said she thought it might have been June 7 or June 8, but she observed O'Campo taking notes with a pencil and a pad and that Josh also wrote on the detectives' pad. O'Campo said he did not ask Josh any questions about the attack, both Dr. Howell and Headley said he did. Nurse Headley testified that her notes from June 6 indicated that O'Campo began speaking with Josh at noon. Reading from her notes, Headley said, "Patient answering questions of detective by mouthing words and writing." O'Campo testified he asked no questions about Mexicans, Headley said she remembered Josh communicating that there were three attackers and that one was a Mexican. "He pointed to the detective, you know, that he was the same as the detective [Hispanic]. I remember Josh pointing at him," Headley said. Dr. Howell said O'Campo asked Josh about Mexicans and recalled her grandson holding up three fingers to indicate how many there were.

It would not be until November 17, 1983 that O'Campo even wrote up a report that referenced his ICU interviews with Josh. Negus asked him if he normally waited five months to prepare reports of his interviews with surviving victims of murders. "No, sir, not normally," the detective answered.

That report, written at the request of Sergeant Arthur, made no mention of his even talking with Josh on any occasion other than the extended interview he conducted in the pediatric playroom on June 14 in the presence of Dr. Jerry Hoyle, a staff psychologist at the hospital. O'Campo had visited Josh some nineteen other times in the hospital, frequently more than once a day, and although he was particularly fuzzy about what days he might not have seen Josh at all, it appeared from what Negus could get out of him that June 9 – the day Josh was transferred from ICU to the pediatric ward – was the only day he missed.

Sergeant Arthur had instructed O'Campo to tape the June 14 interview with Josh in the pediatric playroom. By this time, Josh had recovered sufficiently from his neck slashing that the endotracheal tube had been removed and he could now speak and sit up. Josh's grandmother wanted to be with Josh during this extended interaction with the detective, but O'Campo told Dr. Howell she would have to wait outside. With only staff psychologist Dr. Hoyle present to protect Josh's interest, O'Campo conducted an exhausting, ninety-minute interview that was not recorded. O'Campo simply took notes, as did Dr. Hoyle.

Negus would encounter the same problem in examining O'Campo about this extended interview as he had in questioning the detective about his ICU interviews with Josh. From reading the two pages of notes that Dr. Hoyle provided both the prosecution and the defense, Negus knew that Josh had frequently referred in the plural to his assailants. In reading O'Campo's report of the interview, not one reference was made to more than one attacker. Dr. Hoyle's notes reflected that Josh had told O'Campo that "They chased us around the house." Dr. Hoyle quotes Josh saying that he "tried to fight them off, tripped 'em up, fell on, but it loosened them up." Dr. Hoyle testified he took the "loosened up" as a reference to teeth. The last quote Dr. Hoyle recorded has Josh saying that after he went into the master bedroom in response to Chris calling out his name and that "They snuck up behind me and hit me."

NEGUS: HOW MANY TIMES DID JOSH USE THE WORD "THEY" IN DESCRIBING THE ACTIONS OF HIS ATTACKERS WHEN HE WAS TALKING TO YOU?
O'CAMPO: HE DIDN'T.
NEGUS: NONE AT ALL?
O'CAMPO: THAT'S CORRECT.

Negus got O'Campo to agree that this formal session with Josh was "an exceedingly important interview in the Ryen investigation." Negus asked him if his preparation for the interview had included his reading Deputy Sharp's June 5 report about Josh saying three white men were his attackers. O'Campo said he was not sure Sharp did a report. Nor did O'Campo interview any of the emergency room staff who had observed Josh providing information about three white assailants.

Without saying it directly, what O'Campo was revealing was that it did not matter to him what Josh had told anyone in the emergency room about his attackers because O'Campo already knew Kevin Cooper was the long assailant. And as Negus would soon bring out, it also did not matter to him that Reserve Deputy Luis Simo had told O'Campo that when Cooper's picture appeared on the television in Josh's hospital room that Josh had told Simo, "He didn't do it." That mattered so little to O'Campo that he did not even write a report about Simo calling him or tell anyone else in homicide about the call until months later when Simo called him during the preliminary hearing and told him again about what Josh had said. This call forced O'Campo to take the time to interview Simo in person at his homicide office and write up a report to appease the reserve deputy.

Like any other hierarchical organization, a homicide division reflects its leadership. Sergeant Billy Arthur, once Sheriff Floyd Tidwell had named Kevin Cooper as the lone perpetrator of the Chino Hills murders, centered the entire investigation on supporting that hypothesis and proving that Cooper was guilty. Judging by the way every detective testified, all the detectives reporting to Arthur took their lead from him.

On the stand, Arthur's favorite way to evade a question by Negus was to say "I don't know" or he could not remember. Asked by Negus when he received a report from Deputy Rick Eckley about the coveralls turned in by Diana Roper, he said, "I don't know."

"Was it not in the month of June"? Negus asked.

"I don't know," Arthur said.

Negus asked him if he remembered when he first viewed Eckley's report. "No, I don't," was the reply.

Negus's direct-examination of Arthur brought out the same mindset Detective O'Campo's questioning showcased: There was no need to look at any evidence that implicated other possible perpetrators because Cooper was guilty.

After Negus established that Arthur never saw the coveralls or ordered any tests of the blood on the coveralls, he asked the lead detective if that was "because of neglect."

"Yes," Arthur said. When Negus attempted to determine Arthur's motive for his total lack of interest in the coveralls, Judge Garner cut off that line of questioning, ruling that the sergeant's motives were off limits.

CHAPTER THIRTY-SEVEN

Prosecution's First Summation

C *alifornia Penal Code 1095* stipulates that both the prosecution and
the defense in a capital case have the right for two attorneys to present
summations to the jury in the guilt phase of the trial. In an in-chambers
session with Judge Garner prior to the opening of the trial on February 7,
1985, Negus said he wanted to be allowed to respond to both prosecutors,
and, if that were not allowed, then he thought only one prosecutor should
argue to the jury.

"Mr. Negus, you and your client were well aware of the two versus one,
that is two prosecutors versus one defense counsel from the very beginning.
You've not requested any assistants. You may have even declined it," the
judge responded. As it had plagued him throughout his representation of
Kevin Cooper, from the arraignment through the trial, Negus's penchant
for going-it-alone now tilted the deck sharply against his client. Instead
of the defense getting two shots in closing argument, Negus's summation
would be sandwiched between those of Assistant D.A. Kochis and D.A.
Kottmeier.

Holding up an enlarged color photograph of the Ryen family smiling
and posing together and another one taken of a smiling Chris Hughes,
Kochis began by saying, "All of these hopes and dreams were lost by the
nightmare that Kevin Cooper brought to Chino Hills." Next he showed
the jury graphic crime scene photos of the deeply lacerated, blood-caked
victims. The face of Chris Hughes was covered in blood from the hatchet

wounds to his head and face. His parents, Bill and Mary Ann Hughes, "wept quietly in the courtroom audience," according to a report in the Los Angeles Times.

By injecting pure emotion so early in his summation, Kochis was showing signs of being around the dramatic Kottmeier too long. To an objective, disinterred observer, Kochis's evoking open weeping from the parents of one of the victims in the very opening of his summation was a subterfuge, a smokescreen to fog over just how little actual evidence there was linking Cooper to the crime.

The evidence that Kochis said he would go over with the jury—the hatchet, prison-shoe sole prints, the blood sample labeled "A-41," plant burrs, and hair—"will proved beyond any doubt that Kevin Cooper is guilty of the crimes charged."

He moved first to the hatchet and the hatchet sheath, saying, "With these two items of evidence, we will be able to follow Kevin Cooper from the hideout to the murder scene, to the Ryen car."

Summations, by rule, are limited to evidence introduced at trial. This does not mean that the evidence discussed may not be spun or cast only in a favorable light. When Kochis said that numerous witnesses testified that the hatchet was kept by the fireplace in the Lease house, he was under no obligation to say that Larry Lease testified that it was kept out back by the woodpile or that Vickie Lang, who lived in the house periodically, said she kept it in a kitchen drawer.

When he said "We know the sheath ends up" in the empty bedroom where Cooper slept in the closet, he was under no compunction to say it was not there when Detectives Moran and Hall searched the Lease house the day after the murders were discovered and that Detective Moran had been caught misrepresenting that he had ever been in the room where the sheath was "found."

When Kochis next claimed that a knife belonging to Roger Lang had been stolen from the Lease house, he had no evidence to support that.

Kochis, who is now chief deputy district attorney for San Bernardino County, would not answer any questions about the Chino Hills case when he was called in 2010, so it is unknown whether he was aware of CIM

Warden Midge Carroll's informing one of the two lead detectives on the case that Pro-Keds Dude tennis shoes were not shoes made specifically and exclusively for institutional use.

The Pro-Keds shoes were the single most important link the prosecution had to place Cooper at what Kochis said was "the center of the slaughter." Kochis told the jury that it was a shoe that "can't be purchased in any store anywhere in this country. A shoe manufactured only for institutions, a shoe Kevin Cooper escaped in." If anything showed just how thin the prosecution's case against Cooper was it was this totally spurious claim.

During his direct and cross-examination, Cooper had provided significant detail about the tennis shoes he had on when he escaped from CIM. What he remembered most about the shoes was how worn they were, how their lack of traction caused him to slip and fall repeatedly as he made his way up the hill to the Lease house. When he got to Tijuana he purchased a new pair of soft-soled shoes and began wearing those. At sea, he tossed away his prison clothes and tennis shoes. Kochis—again with no evidence to support his claim—said Cooper had no reason to get rid of his tennis shoes unless "they were covered in blood."

As Kochis went deeper into laying out the evidence against Cooper, the well was running dryer and dryer. "You won't need an expert, you won't need anyone to tell you that the button found in Cooper's bedroom is the same type of button that came off the state prison jackets."

No piece of evidence suggested the planting of evidence against Cooper more than this green button. It was undisputed, based on the trial testimony of the CIM officer who had seen Cooper escaping from prison, that the jacket he had on was brown. Having a green button, with blood consistent with both Cooper's and Doug Ryen's blood on it, found next to the hatchet sheath was simply—save for being planted—inexplicable.

Total speculation filled a good part of the assistant district attorney's summation. He made numerous unsupportable claims that he had no way of proving. He said Cooper stole Viceroy cigarettes from the Lease house, leaving one in the empty bedroom's headboard and one in the Ryens' station wagon; he said Cooper, after assaulting Josh, went to the refrigerator in the Ryens' kitchen and took two cans of beer out of it, tossing one of them in the field between the Ryen house and the Lease house; he said "there was no question" that Cooper brought a rope with Doug Ryen's blood on it into the closet of the empty bedroom and then attempted to link that rope to a piece of rope found outside the Ryens' house where the station wagon had been parked.

This linkage was more than a stretch. Kochis admitted that one of the ropes had a cord in the center and the other did not, but said the ropes were the "same color and material."

Later on he postulated from Dr. Root's testimony that Cooper inflicted fewer blows on Josh than any other victim "because Josh came last, because Cooper is tired."

Kochis was going for tonnage. His approach to the summation seemed to be if he threw enough mud at the wall, some of it was bound to stick. He mentioned a pubic hair found in the Ryens' station wagon. The single specimen was so minuscule the lab was not even sure it was a pubic hair, or even if came from a black person. He claimed that Jessica's hair was found in the bathroom sink of the Lease house and Doug Ryen's hair was in the Lease house shower. It was grossly misleading for Kochis to assert anything about these hairs because no mitochondrial DNA testing of them was ever conducted.

The blood evidence, Kochis said, "will forever stain Kevin Cooper with the guilt of these crimes." He said Jessica and Peggy Ryen's blood was on the driver's side of the station wagon—"in the same front seat where the hand-rolled cigarette butt was found." Kochis may have been hoping that the jurors had not been paying attention when trial testimony established that the rolled butt was in the passenger side seat, pressed into the crevice by the vertical and horizontal portions of the seat. As to the Viceroy butt Kochis had referenced moments before, it was found under the passenger seat. The location of both the rolled butt and the Viceroy butt suggested someone sitting in the passenger seat had deposited them.

The blood evidence in the car also supported the probability that someone had sat in the passenger seat. When Luminol testing of the car was conducted the day after it was found, a positive reaction for blood was detected from the passenger compartment, seat and floorboard. There was also blood on the lower portion of the driver's door, the driver's headrest, as Kochis had just said, but there was blood in the back seat area as well. Blood in three separate areas of the station wagon would support the eyewitness testimony of Mr. and Mrs. Leonard, who reported seeing three or four white men driving rapidly away from the direction of the Ryens' house around midnight the night of the assault at the Ryens' house.

The blood evidence in the station wagon—that Kochis said would "forever stain Kevin Cooper with the guilt of these crimes"—actually undermined entirely the prosecution's position that Cooper showered in the bathroom of the hideout house after committing the murders. (Negus neglected to point out this inherent contradiction in his summary.)

The linchpin of its forensics' case against Cooper was the blood sample labeled "A-41." During cross-examination, Public Defender Negus had so discredited criminalist Dan Gregonis's handling and testing of A-41 that the evidence about it was the most confusing the jury had heard. As a result, Kochis was now in the position of attempting to rehabilitate the incriminating value of the lone drop of blood. He began by saying A-41 could only have come from someone who is black, and then threw the hammer down: "That drop of blood could not, under any circumstances, have ever come from any one of the group of three young men who happened to be at the Canyon Corral Bar on the night of the murders having a glass a beer. Nor could it have come from the three Mexicans who were looking for work on June 4th."

Interrupting his scathing indictment of the defendant to remind the jurors that there were other possible suspects was a high risk ploy for the young prosecutor to take.

Both Kochis and Kottmeier believed that Cooper was some sort of master of deception and an inveterate liar. Pursuing this theme would bring his summation to a powerful close. To set the mood, Kochis referred to the trip the jurors made by bus to the crime scene toward the end of the trial. The jurors viewed the insides and outsides of both the Ryen and Lease houses. Cooper had testified he had never seen the Ryen house. Other witnesses who had lived or been in the Lease house said they could see the roof jutting out from the Ryen house. Cooper had been there in early

June when the foliage was in full bloom while the jurors had seen it in the dead of winter. The jurors, without the obstruction of the foliage, could see the top of the Ryens' house from the living room of the Lease house so to Kochis that proved Cooper was untruthful.

As a convicted felon, Cooper's credibility is in question, Kochis said, adding that the judge will instruct them about that later. Kochis said the jury knew that Cooper lies about who he is to the DMV, the courts, CIM, to the Handys on the boat, and to his girlfriend in Pittsburgh, telling her he was out of prison because of a new law passed in California.

"You know that Kevin Cooper lies about who he is and what he does, where he comes from. He lies about what he's done. He's good at lying. Don't let him fool you," Kochis said.

Kochis said Cooper lied about seeing the hatchet in the hideout house, about seeing the Ryen house.

"Kevin Cooper told you he didn't kill the Ryens. That's a lie," Kochis said, and then asked them to reach "the only conclusion which the evidence allows you to reach: Kevin Cooper is guilty as charged."

CHAPTER THIRTY-EIGHT

Defense Summation

After a short morning break, Public Defender David Negus addressed the jury. Due to the closeness of the noon hour, his summation would be interrupted midway through and resumed at after lunch, heaping on him another disadvantage.

Negus began by saying that trying to get to the truth of the Ryen/Hughes murders was something like trying to put together several jigsaw puzzles after the boxes have been dropped and the pieces all mixed up. "... some of the pieces were carted away, some of them were left behind, some of them were now forced into place, some of them actually been changed, altered, cut down, painted over, lied about, according to the evidence," he said.

Negus was off to a good start. The jigsaw analogy was an apt one and one that had legs, considering the incredible amount of bungling at the crime scene and in the crime lab. The basic problem he would run into would be trying to sustain the momentum of that theme by giving it specifics to illustrate it and keep the image fresh in the jurors' minds. But instead of staying right on message, he immediately took off in a tangent, telling the jury that because the evidence against his client was entirely circumstantial it was their duty—under the law of circumstantial evidence in California and in the United States—that in the event there are two viable interpretations of the evidence to adopt the interpretation of that evidence which points to a defendant's innocence.

This was a lot for the jurors to mull over so early in the summation. They had no foundation for knowing what Negus was referring to and would not until the judge gave them instructions after Kottmeier concluded his summation later that day.

In his opening statement, Negus had told the jurors he would not be able to prove his client's innocence or who committed these crimes. It was an unfortunate way to begin his defense. It left the jurors with the idea that it would fall to the prosecution to provide those answers. Now, he reiterated those same words, adding, "I think the reason that I'm not going to be able to do that has become clear: There are too many pieces that have been changed, too many pieces that have been forced together, too many pieces that are missing."

Two of the missing pieces he mentioned were Deputy Sharp not using a tape recorder when he interviewed Josh in the emergency room and in the CAT scan room; another was Detective O'Campo not using a tape recorder when he conducted the ninety-minute interview at the hospital on June 14.

While he excused Sharp's failing—he was young and only a deputy— he said that O'Campo's not tape recording that interview was "a deliberate decision" to conceal what Josh had actually told him about multiple assailants. "Why did Mr. O'Campo not bring in a tape recorder? Because the evidence shows that Mr. O'Campo lied about his conversations with Josh," Negus said.

"Why is he [O'Campo] lying? Again, we will never know, he's not going to tell us. The inference you can draw from it is that the information he got from Josh when Josh was in that impressionable state is not going to help the prosecution in this particular case," Negus said. "The inference is that it will establish another rational interpretation of the evidence, one which points toward innocence."

After calling O'Campo a liar, he moved on to lab criminalist Dan Gregonis, saying he "has demonstrated some areas of significant ignorance," and to crime lab technician David Stockwell, characterizing his work on the case as deficient due to his "inexperience and ignorance."

Using such forceful words about law enforcement personnel—even if they are true—can easily alienate jurors. It can make the attorney uttering them appear to be a bully. If Negus's summation were the last words the jury would hear before the judge gave them instructions, he might have been able to get away with such inflammatory broadsides. But Kottmeier was dutifully making notes as Negus spoke and would soon make him pay when he got the last word.

When Negus got back to his jigsaw puzzle theme, he hit his stride. Taking up the issue of "forced pieces" in the puzzle, he said, "One of the things that is most interesting about the evidence in this particular case is that as to the major issues of prosecution's evidence there is something fishy about each one. Let's go over them one by one."

--A-41: Detective Mike Hall's exhaustive report about evidence at the crime scene does not reference A-41. Gregonis claimed to test it blind, but then admitted he tested it along side Cooper's own blood. He admits to wasting a great part of the sample, preventing the defense experts to test it. He miscalls one of the elements of the sample and then changes his lab notes to correct the mistake. "He sees what he wants to see."

--Viceroy cigarette in Ryens' station wagon: Gregonis says the saliva in it is consistent with coming from Cooper, but Dr. Wraxall testifies it could have come from any person on earth.

--Shoe impression on bedspread: Detective Hall's report makes no mention of it.

--Shoe impression of the Jacuzzi cover: Hall does not mention any tennis shoe impressions on the cover. The deputy in charge of diagramming all the footprints on the Jacuzzi cover does not see this impression. Later it is pointed out to her. There are photos of the Jacuzzi cover when deputies first arrived showing it to be in place. Later that afternoon, photos show it dislodged. Detective Robert Hall testified he was tromping all over the Jacuzzi cover because it was not considered to be of evidentiary value.

--Lease house: Detectives Moran and Hall enter it on June 6, search every room, and find nothing of evidentiary value. The next day a hatchet sheath and a prison button are found on the floor in the empty bedroom where Cooper slept. Moran testified at pre-trial hearings he never entered that bedroom, but his fingerprints are found on the closet door. "Why didn't Moran see the ax sheath"?

--Ryens' station wagon: The security manager at a motel in Costa Mesa sees a station wagon with the Ryens' license plate on it on June 7. Cooper has been in Tijuana since June 5.

--Pro-Keds Dude: Are available to the Navy, to the forestry service, "and to all kinds of different people besides prisoners."

--Doug Ryen's hair in drain of sink in Lease house bathroom: Prosecution's own expert testified the hair in the sink had not been chopped off, that it had fallen out naturally. He said there was no way to determine that the hair had come from Mr. Ryen.

--Pubic hair in station wagon: Prosecution's own expert said he could not tell if the pubic hair from Ryens' station wagon even came from a black person

--Knife allegedly stolen from Lease house and used in attack on Ryens and Chris Hughes: Roger Lang told investigator Ron Forbush, on tape, that other than the ax, nothing was missing from the Lease house. He said he kept the knife in question at his primary home.

--Bloody rope in closet in empty bedroom: The woman who lived in the Lease house for eighteen months prior to Cooper holing up there said no such rope was kept in the Lease house—just in the breeding area of ranch.

More than any other aspect lacking in the prosecution's case against Cooper was his utter lack of motive to kill the Ryens, Chris Hughes, and attempt to murder to Josh to aid his escape. In the afternoon part of his summation, Negus featured this element.

THERE IS ONE PIECE OF THE PUZZLE THAT IS MISSING BECAUSE THERE IS NO EVIDENCE ON IT. THAT IS MOTIVE. MR. KOTTMEIER, IN HIS OPENING STATEMENT, MR. KOCHIS IN HIS CLOSING STATEMENT, HAVE BOTH INDICATED THAT WE HAD THE ACTION OF A DESPERATE MAN WHO HAD BEEN TURNED DOWN. HE COULDN'T GET A CAR, HE COULDN'T GET MONEY, AND THEREFORE THE RYENS WERE MURDERED. THE PROBLEM IS THAT DOESN'T COMPUTE.

THERE WAS MONEY IN PEGGY RYEN'S PURSE; THERE WAS MONEY ON
THE COUNTER, IN PLAIN VIEW. HAD THE CRIME BEEN ONE OF ROBBERY,
THE MONEY WAS AVAILABLE; HAD THE CRIME BEEN ONE TO TRY TO GET
SOMETHING VALUABLE FOR A PERSON LIKE MR. COOPER, WHO HAD NO
MONEY AT THAT POINT IN TIME, THERE WERE MANY VALUABLE THINGS
IN THE RYEN HOUSE WHICH WERE NOT DISTURBED, WHICH WERE NOT
TAKEN.

With his past record of burglaries and his escape from prison, Cooper
was not a sympathetic figure to the jury and Negus wanted to face that
animosity head-on. "Mr. Cooper is obviously not the kind of person that
any of you are going to particularly like," he admitted, "...but that does
make him guilty of this particular crime."

Returning to Cooper's lack of motive, Negus discussed how the defendant had managed to elude authorities after his prison escape by first laying
low for hours in a lumber yard and then hiding out in the Lease house for
two full days waiting to make his escape to Mexico. He said the district
attorney would have them believe that "a person who takes that kind of
care to avoid directing attention to himself would do the one thing in the
world that would ensure that at some point in time he would be caught...
[by committing] a crime which would cause international pursuit for his
capture."

Negus said it made no sense that Cooper, who would most likely still
be at large if it were not for the Chino Hills murders, would commit these
horrible crimes for no reason and guarantee he would be eventually apprehended and severely punished.

"There is no evidence—there may be speculation, there may be rhetoric,
but there is no evidence to explain why Mr. Cooper would have done that,"
Negus said.

On balance, the summation Negus delivered gave the jurors a great
many reasons to find reasonable doubt about the prosecution's case. If his
closing argument had been the final words the jurors heard before beginning their deliberations, the chances of Cooper's acquittal would have been
quite promising.

CHAPTER THIRTY-NINE

Judicial Bias

In an in-chambers discussion with all three trial attorneys and Cooper present prior to the summations, Judge Garner revealed a stunning bias against the defendant. The issue under discussion was whether the judge should instruct the jury to consider both first and second-degree murder verdicts. The fact that other possible perpetrators—the three white men at the Canyon Corral Bar, the three Mexican men who appeared at the Ryen house just before they left for a cookout—made the topic of second-degree murder viable in the sense that others may have participated in the killings. Negus was adamantly opposed to having a second-degree instruction given because he thought it would allow the jurors to compromise their verdict.

With the judge more than willing to allow the jury to consider both a first and second-degree murder charge, Negus's opposition to the second-degree charge was a major strategic gamble he was willing to wage, most probably on the belief that the prosecution had not proved its case against Cooper beyond a reasonable doubt. Negus also mistakenly thought that a second-degree murder conviction could also result in a death sentence; this misconception made the inclusion of a second-degree charge even more onerous to him. (Under California law, a conviction for second-degree murder can never support a death sentence. For Cooper, a second-degree conviction would have spared him the eventual death sentence the jury imposed and, under California's sentencing procedures, allowed him to apply for parole at various intervals down the line.)

In arguing against the instruction, Negus incredibly said there was no evidence of other perpetrators. "If Mr. Cooper is the one that did the crime, all the evidence points Mr. Cooper did it alone. If someone else did the crime then that's something else again. But as far as the evidence in this particular case, there is no evidence that would..."

Judge Garner cut Negus off to say, "I am not insisting upon giving these two instructions. I suggested it because it is the defense that all the time says, 'Hey, it wasn't me it was three other guys,' and I think that there is evidence that the jurors could say, 'Hey, it could have been more than one guy there.' If there was anybody else there, I don't know, but I am certain that the defendant was right there in the middle of it."

For a judge, in front of the defendant and his counsel, to say he was "certain that the defendant was right there in the middle of it" was totally out of bounds and unprofessional. He had dispensed with the most basic tenet of criminal law: A defendant is to be presumed innocent until deemed guilty by a jury.

CHAPTER FORTY

D.A. Kottmeier's Summation

Following a short recess after Negus concluded his closing argument, D.A. Kottmeier strode to the well of the courtroom. Negus's raising his client's complete lack of motive for the attack at the Ryen house was one of the first issues the district attorney took up in his closing argument. Contrary to what Negus said about the importance of motive, Kottmeier said the judge will instruct the jury that motive is not an element of the crime. "Why a crime occurs is something that is very difficult, at time impossible, to explain."

He argued there could be no explanation for a crime of such extreme violence. In actuality, the extreme amount of violence and the murdering of children would indicate a vendetta of some sort being meted out.

Because Negus had spurned using Diana Roper as a witness and had decided against putting before the jury information about the inmate who claimed that Kenneth Koon confessed his involvement in the murders to him, Kottmeier's next claim was true when he said there was "no reasonable evidence that you've heard" to show that any multiple group of individuals was responsible for these crimes.

Logic seemed to abandon the district attorney when he tried to explain why one attacker was more probable than multiple attackers. "…is it likely that all the attackers would decide that they would leave the valuables behind, such as the video camera, such as money"?

The fact that children were murdered, to Kottmeier the drugstore psychologist, also proved a lone assailant because "I submit to you, ladies and gentlemen, that the killing of children is something that you will not find multiple individuals casually out to commit a crime such as this that they could agree on even let one of their group accomplish." He expanded this thought to add, "There is a special coldness associated with killing children. It is the kind of frustrated anger that lashes out from a mind of a single person." Kottmeier had apparently forgotten Leopold and Loeb's murder of Bobby Franks.

The district attorney loathed Kevin Cooper and wanted the jury to buy into his loathing. "You were able to see the killing countenance of Mr. Cooper [during his trial testimony]. You could look into his eyes. You could see the change between the time that Mr. Negus is asking the questions and the time that I am asking the questions. You could see, I submit to you, each time Mr. Cooper felt that he was damaged, each time that it looked like the lie was not going to work."

If anything, Cooper's demeanor during Kottmeier's relentless, often insulting cross-examination showed the jury a controlled, straight-forward young man able to withstand broadside attacks and accusations without overreacting.

Kottmeier spent most of the rest of his argument attempting to re-habilitate the San Bernardino County Sheriff's detectives, deputies, and crime lab personnel Negus had skewered in his summation.

The best the district attorney could offer in defense of crime lab techni-cian David Stockwell was gibberish, "Mr. Stockwell it was suggested is inexperienced, ignorant; he has biases, motives...I submit to you, ladies and gentlemen, that when an expert testifies, you may communicate your information at different levels of detail."

He could do little better in defending criminalist Dan Gregonis's mis-reading of the blood on the A-41 sample, saying all he did "was change the label" to the correct reading months after misidentifying it.

Regarding Negus's criticism of Deputy Dale Sharp not taping his hospital interviews with Josh and developing the information about three Mexican men rather than three white men being the attackers, Kottmeier said, "You almost get the impression from listening to the defense argue that Deputy Sharp goes upstairs to the CAT scan room to get Josh's story straight in some form or fashion. Is that consistent with the gentle man that you saw here testify"?

Moving on to Detective Hector O'Campo, who denied ever questioning Josh about the attack until June 14, Kottmeier said, "Do you think [ICU nurse] Linda Headley or Dr. Howell would have allowed Hector O'Campo to begin questioning Josh the first day that he [O'Campo] comes in contact with him? And did Hector O'Campo look like the type of person who would do that"?

This was tantamount to the district attorney calling both the registered nurse and Josh's grandmother liars because both had testified that O'Campo questioned Josh about the attack during his first three days in ICU.

The district attorney intentionally distorting the trial record should have brought an objection from the defense, but it did not. Nor would it when Kottmeier asserted that O'Campo's written report of the June 14 interview with Josh jibed with the notes that staff psychologist Dr. Hoyle made of Josh's responses. In O'Campo's report, no mention was made of multiple assailants, but Dr. Hoyle noted Josh making numerous references to them.

Kottmeier would persist in misrepresenting the trial record when he said, "Josh told the same basic story, a story that you, ladies and gentlemen, got a chance to hear, the story that shows that there was just one attacker: Kevin Cooper with a hatchet in one hand and a knife in another."

Conspicuously missing in the district attorney's efforts to vouch for investigative personnel was any mention of the discredited Detective Steve Moran.

Kottmeier's final flourish was to say, "Ladies and gentlemen of the jury, four dead victims, and even Josh Ryen, depend on you to apply the evidence, the law as his Honor, Judge Garner, will give you and come up with a verdict.

"And for those innocent victims, I submit to you that the law and the evidence means that Kevin Cooper is guilty."

CHAPTER FORTY-ONE

Guilty

The trial that began on October 23, 1984, would go to the jury in mid-afternoon of Friday, February 8, 1985 after Judge Garner issued the instructions. Among them was the admonition to show "no pity for the defendant," and its corollary to hold "no bias against the defendant because he has been charged with these crimes." He told the jurors not to be swayed by sentiment, public opinion or public feeling. To the jurors, there was little doubt what the public sentiment was concerning Kevin Cooper. Just outside the courtroom on January 24, jurors were exposed to signs reading "Die Cooper!" and "Kevin Cooper must be hanged," the *Los Angeles Times* reported. Questioned that morning about the graffiti by the judge, none of the jurors said it would influence his or her decision.

In other instructions, the judge told them to disregard anything stricken from the record; and to not feel bound to accept expert opinion as conclusive, telling them if they found something an expert said to be unreasonable, to disregard it.

The jury had heard testimony from 141 witnesses and observed 788 exhibits being introduced.

On Monday, February 11, the jury foreperson, Frank Nugent, asked that the trial testimony of criminalist Daniel Gregonis be read in the jury room. The only other request for a read back was for the two taped interviews with Josh Ryen.

Two days later Nugent sent a note to the judge, informing him that one of the jurors, Shirley LaPage, had brought up Cooper's arrest for the burglary charges in Los Angeles. Inadvertently, Public Defender Negus had included an exhibit that referenced those arrests when he turned over the rest of the defense exhibits to the court the previous week.

The judge summoned Mrs. LaPage for an in-chambers session with Kochis and Negus where the juror said one of the other jurors had quoted from the exhibit, a transcript from a preliminary hearing that concluded in January of 1983, detailing that Cooper had indicated he was suffering from "headaches and hallucinations." Mrs. LaPage said this caused another juror to say, "I think we should take this into consideration," and another juror to respond, "No, I don't think so."

Mrs. LaPage quoted herself then saying, "Yes, I believe that, you know, that I knew personally that there was supposed to have been a mental problem with Mr. Cooper."

At that point, she said, the foreperson stopped the discussion and said they should not consider it. She said the foreperson then proceeded to poll the jurors, asking them if any of this information would interfere with their judgment. Each juror, in turn, said it would not.

The judge then sent Mrs. LaPage back to the jury room.

Judge Garner told Kochis and Negus his reaction to what Mrs. LaPage had just told them was to strike the exhibit from the record and to tell the jurors" to disregard it totally."

"I don't think that will help," Negus said. "I mean, I think we should have a mistrial."

To Negus, the jury learning about Cooper's claiming to be suffering from hallucinations would give them reason to rationalize away his total lack of motive in murdering two innocent adults, two children, and attempting to murder a third child.

The judge, either missing Negus's point entirely or simply not wanting the trial to blow up at this late date, asked Negus what was prejudicial about the jury knowing that Cooper had been convicted of two burglaries.

NEGUS: WHAT'S PREJUDICIAL IS THE DETAILS OF THE BURGLARY
AND THE—THE EVIDENCE OF MENTAL INSTABILITY. MR. COOPER DOES
NOT, IN FACT, HAVE MENTAL INSTABILITY. HAD THE PROSECUTION

TRIED TO BRING THAT IN, I WOULD HAVE REBUTTED WITH EVIDENCE
OF PSYCHIATRISTS WHO HAVE EXAMINED MR. COOPER AND SAY HE HAS
NO MENTAL INSTABILITY WHATSOEVER.

JUDGE GARNER: WE CAN EASILY CURE IT BY TELLING THE JURORS
THAT IT CAME IN BY INADVERTENCE AND MISTAKE. NO. 1, IT WAS
WITHDRAWN FROM EVIDENCE, THEY ARE TO DISREGARD ANYTHING. NO.
2, BOTH SIDES AGREE AND THEY CAN ACCEPT IT AS BEING CONCLU-
SIVELY PROVED THAT THE DEFENDANT HAS NO MENTAL INSTABILITY
PERIOD. MR. KOCHIS, CAN'T YOU AGREE TO THAT?

KOCHIS: NO, I CAN'T AGREE TO THAT.

JUDGE GARNER: THINK ABOUT IT.

KOCHIS: I'M THINKING ABOUT IT. I CAN'T AGREE TO SOMETHING
AS BLANKET AS THAT.

JUDGE GARNER: HOW CAN IT HURT YOU? A MISTRIAL CAN HURT YOU.

NEGUS: THE REASON IT HURTS THEM IS BECAUSE THEY HAVE IM-
PLIED THAT MR. COOPER HAS A MENTAL INSTABILITY BECAUSE THAT
SUPPLIES THEM A MISSING MOTIVE WHICH THEY DON'T HAVE. THAT'S
WHY IT'S PREJUDICIAL; IT SUPPLIES A MISSING MOTIVE WHICH THEY
DON'T HAVE.

The judge said his solution was to strongly admonish the jurors to disregard the information in the exhibit and to poll the individual jurors "to see if any of them have any trouble doing that and go from there."

Negus said he did not think an admonition would cure the problem, particularly considering all the prejudicial pre-trial publicity the jurors had been exposed to about his client.

In open court, with the gallery and media excluded, Judge Garner told the jurors that the exhibit in question was entered into evidence by mistake and is now withdrawn. "I order it stricken from the record. I instruct you strongly to disregard it and anything contained in it. Strike it from your mind, no longer discuss it nor consider it in weighing the evidence on either side of an issue in this trial."

To assess the prejudicial impact on the jurors, Judge Garner decided he would interview each one separately in chambers with Kochis and

Negus present. During several of these interviews, Negus's suspicion that negative pre-trial publicity about Cooper would end up permeating the jury deliberations was confirmed. Such confirmation should have led the judge to declare a mistrial then and there. The judge had no one to blame for this all-but-inevitable development than himself. It was his refusal to move the trial to downtown Los Angeles, Oakland, or Sacramento that was now producing the exact result Negus had argued that it would during his change of venue motion back in October of 1984.

The matter of the exhibit from Cooper's preliminary hearing in Los Angeles in January of 1983 came up when juror Rita Lister interjected it into the jury's deliberations by reading eight or nine pages from it. The mention of Cooper having hallucinations occasioned Mrs. Lister, according to other jurors interviewed by the judge, to say that she knew Cooper was an escaped mental patient or that he was at least a former mental patient. Juror Shirley LaPage told her fellow jurors she knew from reading pre-trial newspaper accounts that Cooper had been some sort of mental patient in Pennsyvlania.

In chambers, Mrs. LaPage told the judge that a year-and-a-half ago she had read in newspapers that Cooper was some sort of mental patient in Pennsylvania. Jetalyn Doxey, an older black juror, told the judge that she commented to the other jurors that due to the "brutalities of murders one would think that a person who did this might have been a crazy person." Asked if she could disregard the information about the defendant's mental state, Mrs. Doxey said she could, adding, "I would hope this trial wouldn't stop on that account. I didn't do this to stop a trial. I just thought it should be known."

Prior to Mrs. Doxey's interview, juror Catherine Lopez told the judge she could put the contents of the exhibit out of her mind but doubted if Mrs. Doxey could. She said the exhibit read about Cooper claiming hallucinations, plus juror Rita Lister saying during deliberations that Cooper was an escaped mental patient "bothered me."

Juror William Woods told the judge after Mrs. Doxey was interviewed that he was concerned that Mrs. Doxey could not put aside the information about Cooper's mental condition.

After the judge had polled all the jurors, he asked for comments.

NEGUS: JUST I WOULD NOTE THAT ACCORDING TO MRS. DOXEY THAT
THERE WAS AT LEAST MENTION MADE OF [COOPER] BEING A FORMER
MENTAL PATIENT, IF NOT AN ESCAPED MENTAL PATIENT, SO APPAR-
ENTLY THAT HAS COME UP. I THINK THAT AGAIN ACCENTUATES THE
NEED FOR A MISTRIAL.
JUDGE GARNER: OKAY. COUNSEL, AGAIN I DO NOT SEE THE GRAVAMEN
OF THE SITUATION. I THINK IT IS HARMLESS BEYOND A REASONABLE
DOUBT…THE MOTION FOR MISTRIAL WILL REMAIN DENIED.

On February 19, 1985, after just over a week of deliberations, the jury found Kevin Cooper guilty of four counts of first-degree murder, one count of attempted first-degree murder and one count of escaping from prison.

Unlike some juries that take an initial poll to determine the leanings of the various jurors, this jury sifted through the evidence for over a week before reaching its verdict on its first vote. Taking this much time to consider the evidence indicated that one or more of the jurors was not convinced beyond a reasonable doubt that Cooper had committed the crimes. In post-trial interviews, this division was underscored. On the one hand, juror Shirley LaPage said, "It was just one of those things where there was so much there it couldn't have been a coincidence. It all just came together too well." On the other hand, two of the jurors expressed a different take to the reporters, saying the prosecution had "barely enough evidence" and that Cooper would not have been convicted "if there had been one less piece of evidence."

In juror interviews conducted in 2000 by a private investigator working for Cooper's defense team at the time, the two jurors who did speak to the investigator said the number one piece of evidence against Cooper was the hatchet from the hideout house being found down the road from the Ryens' house with blood on it. One juror said, "…the defense could never explain how a hatchet taken from the Lease house was identical to a hatchet found near the [Ryens' home] scene."

That juror also said the shoeprint on the spa was damaging to the defense because it was her understanding that the shoe that made that print was "given only to state prisoners."

Asked about the bloody coveralls the sheriff's department destroyed, the juror said she had "no recollection of coveralls."

Shown a photograph of Jessica Ryen's hand clutching a number of long blond hairs, the juror said she could not explain how those hairs "could have come from anybody other than another assailant."

The other juror interviewed told the investigator that the thing that convinced her of Cooper's guilt was his "cocky" demeanor on the witness stand. "He [Cooper] referred to stealing things and other immoral acts and because he had such a nonchalant attitude about committing these immoral acts, it convinced me he committed the murders."

CHAPTER FORTY-TWO

Death

In death-penalty cases, the penalty phase takes on a special importance to the convicted. It is a separate trial in its own right with its own set of rules. With the issue of guilt no longer on the table, the jury would consider only two options: a sentence of death or one of life without the possibility of parole. At the time, executions in California were conducted in the gas chamber at San Quentin Prison.

It is not uncommon, even for indigent defendants such as Kevin Cooper, to have another public defender handle the penalty phase. In fact, it is highly recommended by the American Bar Association that separate defense counsel represent the convicted during the penalty phase. There are two good reasons for this: The trial lawyer has already lost the case and his defense has been rejected by the jury; new counsel, not strapped with the stigma of losing the case, may be able to present the jury with a new perspective.

The ABA also recommends that there be adequate spacing between the guilt phase and the penalty phase for the defense to prepare for this crucial stage. For one thing, the extra time allows the jury a cooling off period. For another, it allows defense counsel to concentrate for the first time on the penalty phase—to develop the mitigating circumstances that would persuade the jury not to impose the death penalty.

The time granted between the guilt phase and the penalty phase varies from state to state and even from judge to judge within a state, but it is quite common for there to be a period of two weeks or even a month between the two phases. In Cooper's case, where the jury was not sequestered, there was no need not to wait at least two weeks. Judge Garner gave no indication that he was in any rush to open the penalty phase.

David Negus, on the other hand, was eager to be rid of this case, informing the judge in-chambers immediately after the guilty verdict was handed down that he wanted the penalty phase to start the next day, a Wednesday, or wait until only Monday. Assistant D.A. John Kochis said he had witnesses flying in from Pennsylvania and they would not be available to testify until Thursday. Negus said that was fine with him as long as "we don't have to work Friday," telling the judge he had taken on some other cases in Ontario and needed to be there Friday. The judge set the penalty phase to begin Thursday and to recess until Monday.

While the jury had been in deliberations on the guilt phase, Negus had returned to the public defender's law offices in Ontario to begin involving himself in new cases. Considering the monumental implications of the penalty phase to Kevin Cooper, Negus's behavior was bordering on, if not crossing, the definition of "ineffective counsel." He did not dispel that notion when he told the judge the witnesses he would call on Cooper's behalf would take no more than an hour or so. In fact, these witnesses would only take less than a half hour.

The essence of the penalty phase is a competition between aggravating and mitigating circumstances. Do the aggravating circumstances the prosecution presents outweigh the mitigating circumstances the defense advances?

As a person convicted of multiple murders, including the murders of two children and the attempted murder of a third child, the aggravating circumstances of these crimes carried enormous weight. Unless Clarence Darrow returned from the grave to plea for his life, Cooper was doomed.

Nonetheless, the prosecution wanted one more shot at showing the jury that Cooper was unworthy of any sympathy. Lori Stahl, the young woman Cooper allegedly kidnapped in Pennsylvania the night he escaped from the state mental hospital, was called to testify on Thursday, February 14. Before she was sworn in, Negus agreed to stipulate that his client kidnapped and raped her. Normally, a stipulation would obviate the need for hearing a witness's testimony, but in this instance the prosecution wanted the jury to know the details.

Stahl, who was seventeen-years-old at the time of her abduction, testified that when she rang the doorbell of the house Cooper was robbing, he tricked her into entering the house by telling her that her friend was upstairs. Once inside, Cooper hit her on the side of her face with a camera, grabbed the back of her hair and then forced her to her car in the driveway. He pushed her in through the drive's side to the passenger side with her head down.

She said that during the forty-five minute drive to Frick Park in Pittsburgh, he told her he would kill her. He parked the car in a secluded part of the park and told her to take her pants and underwear off. He forced her out of the car by pulling her hair. Once outside, she said she kneed him in the groin and he then hit her in the face with a screwdriver.

She begged him not to harm her. He grabbed her hair and forced her to the ground, face down, holding the screwdriver toward the back of her neck so that she could feel the tip. She was crying. He took his pants off and got on top of her "and entered me from behind into the vagina."

She said he pushed up his pants and jumped into the car, telling her, "I should kill you." He threw her blue jeans out by the entrance to the park where she found them. She ran to the nearest house, where the people called the police. She was taken to the hospital for an examination.

She said she never got a good look at her assailant.

Walter Lorenz, a criminalist from Allegheny County, testified next. From the vaginal swab taken from Stahl at the hospital and from semen on her blue jeans, he tested sperm samples. He said the tests matched Cooper's serological profile.

On Monday, Negus took his turn to put on witnesses. Cooper's adoptive father, Melvin Cooper, went first. He said he still loved his son and "I really think that he didn't do this." He asked the jury for compassion, "I would hope that maybe through all the grace of the Almighty God that the truth will come out and we will find out that Kevin don't (sic) do this."

In succession, Negus called upon Cooper's godfather, Calvin O'Neal, his godmother, Gloria O'Neal, his sister, Sandra Cooper Thomas, and finally his adoptive mother, Esther Cooper. Mrs. Cooper said she has been talking by phone with her son three or four times a week since his arrest. During those conversations she learned that she was a grandmother; Kevin had fathered a son who was now one-and-half years old. She quoted her son saying, "Please, help take care of Dietrich, Mommy."

As a boy, Kevin was always bringing stray animals home—dogs and rabbits—she said. As an adult, he was "great with kids."

Negus asked her if she still loved Kevin. "I love Kevin, yes. I love Kevin. I have always loved Kevin. I will always love Kevin," she responded.

Did she have anything she wanted to say to the jury, Negus asked.

"Just please have mercy on my child, that is all I am asking," she said. "Save my child's life, please." The *Los Angeles Times* reported that her plea brought her son and two female jurors to tears.

District Attorney Kottmeier began his penalty phase argument by stating that Cooper's parents and godparents were as much victims of his crimes "as are the survivors in this particular case, and the relatives whose lives were touched by Mr. Cooper's deadly actions."

Kottmeier told the jury that deciding the penalty comes down to balancing the aggravating and mitigating circumstances involved and he wanted them to focus on these three aggravating circumstances: Cooper's abduction and rape of Lori Stahl, his felony conviction for two burglaries in Los Angeles, and the brutality of the Ryen/Hughes murders, particularly the murdering of children. "To attack children requires a special coldness, a complete abandonment of those human values all of us hold dear, that causes us to respect the rights of the other individuals. No one is safe in their own bed."

The district attorney concluded his argument by stating, "The only appropriate verdict in this case is death."

It was now Negus's turn to make a final plea to the jury to spare his client's life. "I am here this afternoon to ask you not to execute my friend,

Kevin Cooper," he began. "You have already decided by your decision last Thursday that Kevin Cooper will die in prison in California. But I am asking you not to vote to execute him."

Negus said that under normal circumstances a person convicted of capital crimes would ask the jury for mercy to avoid the gas chamber, "but Kevin Cooper cannot do that. He won't do that. He told you before that he didn't commit the crime, and he maintains his innocence."

He said the reason not to impose the death penalty was "lingering doubt," adding, "I don't believe you'll be able to say that you know beyond all possible doubt that Kevin Cooper is the person that committed the crime."

This was a dicey approach to take considering the jury had found Cooper guilty on all charges beyond a reasonable doubt. It was an invitation for each juror to take umbrage and develop a mindset that said, "How dare you question the verdict?"

Could the jurors really be sure that "Josh Ryen was mistaken in the emergency room" when he communicated that the assailants were three white men? Considering the improper collection of evidence at the crime scene, could they know beyond a reasonable doubt that one person committed these crimes?

Negus said the evidence presented by the prosecution "has substantial gaps in it," and does not allow "that degree of positiveness which a civilized society would require in order to execute you."

He told them the brave thing to do, not because of mercy or leniency, would be to sentence Cooper to life imprisonment.

In an attempt to counter the district attorney's depiction of Cooper's not possessing any human values, Negus took the jury back to the previous Tuesday when the jury's verdict was announced in court. "Kevin turned to both Ron [Forbush] and myself and shook our hands to thank us for fighting for him. I have been a public defender for almost eleven years now…the kind of response that Kevin Cooper has shown to me over this year and a half that I have been sitting next to him day after day in court, is the response of one friend to another. It is not the kind of response of somebody who is outside the pale of civilized society, as Mr. Kottmeier has suggested."

He concluded by reminding the jury that his client has always maintained his innocence. "I would suggest to you that the state of the evidence is such that you cannot be sure that he's not innocent, and for that reason I ask you not to kill my friend, Kevin Cooper."

Judge Garner then proceeded to instruct the jury on the penalty phase guidelines. Unlike the guilt phase, the jury was now free to consider "pity, sympathy, or mercy for the defendant. However, you must not be swayed by mere conjecture, passion, prejudice, or public feeling."

Because Cooper's previous conviction for burglary in Los Angeles and his alleged kidnapping and rape of Lori Stahl were aggravating factors, the judge instructed the jury that they must be convinced beyond a reasonable doubt that he committed those crimes. In the instance of the Pennsylvania crimes, the judge stated that the defendant had not been convicted of those and therefore is presumed to be innocent.

In chambers, Negus asked the judge for permission to return to Ontario if the jury did not reach a verdict by Tuesday afternoon. Negus's insistence on being in Ontario would soon prove disastrous for Cooper.

On Wednesday, the judge received a note from the foreperson, Frank Nugent, that read, "A question, informative in nature, has been raised pertaining to the sentencing procedure if the jury cannot unanimously agree on a penalty verdict." After two days of deliberations, the jury was in deadlock.

By phone, Judge Garner read the note to Negus and Kochis, soliciting their comments on how he should respond. Kochis said he would prefer for the judge to inform the jury if they did not reach a unanimous verdict that the law provides for the impaneling of another jury. This was an extraordinary request, not just because impaneling a new jury would be tantamount to holding a new trial even though the new jury would only be considering sentencing, but because it would place extreme pressure on the jurors to reach a verdict or be unceremoniously dismissed.

Judge Garner recognized the coercive impact of what Kochis was suggesting, saying giving the jury such an ultimatum would be "verboten" under the sentencing laws.

Negus said he would prefer for the judge to tell the jurors if they cannot reach a verdict to just tell the judge when they considered they were hopelessly deadlocked.

The judge said he thought both Negus and Kochis should return to San Diego at once because "we might well have a mistrial this afternoon." Neither attorney wanted to make the two-hour trip and neither did. Judge Garner finally decided to advise the jury, considering the duration of the trial and the length of deliberations, to retire for the day and continue its deliberations tomorrow.

A day and a half would pass before the jury foreperson sent Judge Garner another note. This one arrived at 11:25 a.m. Again by phone, the judge read the note to Negus and Kochis. It stated, "Your Honor, with regret it seems that we are unable to arrive at a verdict." The judge said the word "seems" was underlined. He told both attorneys he thought they should return to San Diego. He then read them a reply he intended to send to the jurors: "In response to your note about your possible inability to agree on penalty, it will take us until 2 p.m. to get everybody together. We must therefore call you into open court at that time. Please inform the bailiff whether you desire to continue deliberating or to adjourn until 2 p.m."

The judge should have declared a mistrial upon receipt of the second note from the foreperson stating the jury was deadlocked. His allowing them the option of having up to two and a half more hours to deliberate was exactly the type of coercive impact the judge just two days before had termed "verboten."

After caucusing with fellow jurors, Nugent informed the judge that the jury would continue deliberations "even if it takes us through the lunch hour." Cooper's immediate fate was now compressed into the two hours set aside for the lunch break.

When court reconvened at 2 p.m., the jury foreperson informed the judge that a unanimous verdict had been reached. The verdict read, "We, the jury, in the above entitled cause, determine that the penalty shall be death."

Had Negus remained in San Diego and been there that morning when the jury foreperson informed the judge that the jury was deadlocked, a mistrial would have been declared on the penalty phase. Kevin Cooper would not have been sentenced to death. Over the next two or three months it would have taken for a new jury to be impaneled, Negus might have taken the opportunity to interview Diana Roper and Anthony Wisely and find out who at least two of the white men were that Josh saw in his house the night his family and best friend were murdered.

CHAPTER FORTY-THREE

Sentencing

Sentencing for Kevin Cooper was held in Superior Court in San Diego on May 15, 1985, with Judge Garner presiding. The judge opened the proceedings by asking Cooper if he wanted to address the court. Public Defender Negus told the judge that he had advised his client not to make a statement, but that he knew what he "wished to—would have said."

"I am not sure I will consider it the same way coming from you," the judge replied.

The head-strong defense attorney who had single-handedly thrown away Cooper's chances for an acquittal by not reading the discovery pertaining to Lee Furrow's coveralls—and insisting that they be tested for the presence of the victims' blood—was not about to give up control now. "Whatever, we will take our risk," he blithely stated, as if it involved any risk to him. He said all his client wanted to say was "to maintain that he did not do the crime."

As the judge would immediately demonstrate, it did not matter what Cooper had to say, although hearing a defendant profess his innocence in a sincere, heartfelt manner would have at least allowed him, at last, to have his say in his own words.

In upholding the sentence of death, the judge said, "…the court is satisfied beyond a reasonable doubt, all reasonable doubt, that the defendant, Kevin Cooper, is the one who entered the Ryen home and committed the various murders, and that he is thus guilty beyond a reasonable doubt."

He then enumerated various points that persuaded him of Cooper's guilt: Cooper was in the hideout house until at least 8:30 p.m. on the night of the murders; the hatchet used in the attack was from the hideout house; tobacco in the Ryens' station wagon proved Cooper was the one who stole it; he changed his plans about going to Los Angeles to avoid detection of a far more serious crime than escape from prison.

The judge said Cooper not being culpable "simply strains my imagination." He could not picture, in the few hours between the time Cooper said he left the hideout house and when the murders occurred, how other perpetrators could have gained access to the hideout house, stolen the hatchet, gone up to the Ryen house and committed the crimes, then returned to the hideout to clean up before departing.

Over the course of the trial, Judge Garner had not just been sitting there passively making rulings and preserving order. He was developing theories of his own that implicated Cooper and Cooper alone even if he had to disregard conflicting testimony to do so. It was established at trial that Kathy Bilbia, the last person to live in the Lease house before Cooper holed up there, had used bleach to clean the shower and that bleach has a positive reaction for Luminol testing. Despite that testimony, the "blood" in the Lease house shower was proof to the judge that someone involved in the murders went back to clean up afterwards. "A stranger or strangers to the scene, coming after 8:30 at night, I suggest would not have felt so secure that they would go back and calmly take showers and cleanup before making their escape after committing such heinous crimes.

"But to the defendant, however, who had used that as a secure haven for several days and made his home there, knew that it was not occupied by that time, and that it would be a safe place, that he was in no particular rush, logic tells me that there is no question but what he was the one that did it."

These type of deductions had freed the judge to now to be "absolutely" certain there was no credible evidence linking anybody else to the crimes and to "have no doubt about the defendant's guilt."

Before issuing the sentence, the judge invited statements from family or relatives. Mary Ann Hughes and Dr. Mary Howell spoke.

Mrs. Hughes said that if Cooper's escape from CIM had been made public, she would have kept her son home that night. "If Kevin Cooper is put to death some other little boy is going to get to live longer than eleven and a half years," she said.

Dr. Howell said she had a lot of questions for Cooper, but the main one was "why would he kill her family in that fashion"? With Rose Bird the chief justice of the California Supreme Court, Cooper's case would not be heard until "the year 2010," she said. If Dr. Howell had her way, the judge would sentence him to life without parole "and specifically with no special protection and no special privileges, that I would like to see him be one of the prisoners and let the prisoners take care of him. Thank you."

The judge then invited comment from anyone on behalf of the defendant. Only one person would step forward. For the first time someone was about to say precisely what Public Defender Negus should have said in his opening and closing arguments to the jury:

I AM REVEREND BRADFORD AND I WANT TO SAY SOMETHING ON BEHALF OF KEVIN COOPER, THE DEFENSE. I FEEL LIKE THAT HE IS INNOCENT. I BELIEVE THAT THERE ARE OTHER PEOPLE WHO HAVE COMMITTED THIS CRIME. I BELIEVE THAT THE INVESTIGATION WASN'T HANDLED PROPERLY, AND I FEEL LIKE THAT IF IT WOULD HAVE BEEN HANDLED PROPERLY, I BELIEVE THAT THE PEOPLE WHO PERPETRATED THIS CRIME WOULD BE—IT WOULD HAVE BEEN BROUGHT OUT WHO ACTU-ALLY COMMITTED THE CRIME.

I FEEL LIKE THAT HE HAPPENED TO BE IN THE WRONG PLACE AT THE WRONG TIME. THIS EVIDENCE THAT CONNECTED HIM WITH THE CRIME, I DON'T SEE WHERE IT CONNECTED HIM WITH THE CRIME, AND I FEEL LIKE THAT JUSTICE HASN'T BEEN SERVED, WITH ALL DUE RESPECT FOR THE FAMILY, AND I CERTAINLY DO FEEL SORRY FOR THEM, BUT I DON'T BELIEVE THAT KEVIN COOPER IS THE MURDERER.

I DON'T SEE HOW ONE PERSON COULD GO IN A HOME AND KILL ALL THESE PEOPLE SINGLE-HANDED WITH ALL THESE DIFFERENT WEAPONS. IT IS NOT EVEN POSSIBLE.

SO, I FEEL LIKE AN INJUSTICE IS BEING DONE TO HIM, AND WHO HAVE DONE THE CRIME I FEEL LIKE THEY SHOULD BE THE ONE, THEY SHOULD RECEIVE THE PENALTY WORTHY OF THE CRIME. BUT I DON'T FEEL THAT HE DID IT.

THAT'S ALL I HAVE TO SAY ABOUT IT.

Judge Garner then sentenced Kevin Cooper to die in the gas chamber. In the event that the death verdict was modified at some later date, the judge also sentenced him to four life sentences to be served consecutively.

Throughout the trial and in his many in-chambers sessions with Judge Garner, Cooper's decorum had been exemplary, a fact the judge took into account in his final awkward words: "Mr. Cooper, I thank you at least for your forbearance during the trial of any outbursts and restraint from any untoward action."

CHAPTER FORTY-FOUR

Early Appeals

B*ecause they have been sentenced to be executed,* the appeal process for death row inmates typically drags on for over twenty years and does not really cease until the condemned person's conviction is overturned, reduced to a lesser punishment, or, far more frequently, the prisoner either dies in prison or is executed. A surprisingly large number of death row inmates decline the appeals open to them because they find that life on death row is no life at all. An Amnesty International study released in 2000 reported that since the U.S. Supreme Court ruled in 1973 to reinstate the death penalty, ninety of the seven-hundred-twenty-two convicted murderers executed in the United States hastened their own executions by opting to forego any future appeals.

Kevin Cooper, who professed his innocence from the time of his arrest in late July of 1983, has been asserting it in appeal after appeal since his conviction in February of 1985. As an indigent death row inmate, Cooper was entitled to a court-appointed counsel to challenge his conviction by direct appeal to the California Supreme Court.

Attorney Mark Cutler was appointed to represent Cooper in this automatic state appeal and briefing ensued. Years passed due to the backlog of cases before the court. However, in May 1991, the California Supreme Court denied Cooper's numerous appellate claims, noting there was "overwhelming evidence" to convict him. One of the justices, Allen Broussard, wrote a dissent in which Justice Stanley Mosk concurred.

Justice Broussard's dissent was based on two factors. The first was the trial judge's failure to instruct the jury on a charge of second-degree murder.

He wrote that Cooper's trial attorney could not waive that right. The second dealt with the jury misconduct regarding extra-record information resulting from the discussions jurors had over the non-admitted exhibit Cooper's trial attorney, Public Defender David Negus, had inadvertently supplied the jury. The exhibit revealed Cooper's complaining of experiencing headaches and hallucinations during court proceedings involving his burglaries in Los Angeles. This discussion included at least one juror's professing personal knowledge that Cooper was an "escaped mental patient." This was tantamount, as Negus unsuccessfully argued to the trial judge in seeking a mistrial, of supplying the other jurors with the missing motive for the murders.

Following the rejection of his state appeal, Cooper's court-appointed counsel, Mark Cutler, filed a petition for writ of certiorari with the U.S. Supreme Court, asking the court to review the state court's decision. The high court, without comment, denied the petition in December of 1991. Cutler was then appointed executive director of the Central California Appellate Program and ceased representing Cooper in state matters (although he technically remained counsel of record for several years thereafter because the California Supreme Court failed to appoint new counsel to represent Cooper).

After losing his state appeal, Cooper's best hope for relief would be in filing a habeas corpus petition in federal district court. A habeas petition seeks a new trial or other redress from a state court conviction on the basis that such conviction or sentencing violated the U.S. Constitution.

In 1991, in an attempt to gauge the frequency with which federal judges found errors in appeals of death-penalty cases and as a result set aside the sentence and/or ordered new trials, then Senator Joe Biden, as chair of the Senate Judiciary Committee, commissioned Professor James S. Liebman of the Columbia Law School to do a comprehensive study of the issue.

Over the next nine years, Professor Liebman tracked 5,767 and sixty-seven death sentences adjudicated through the full, three-stage review process—direct appeal, state post-conviction hearings, and federal habeas corpus review—during the period 1973 through 1995.

Liebman reported that sixty-eight percent of the convictions in capital cases were "seriously flawed." He found that 1,885 death sentences, some forty-one percent, were reversed on direct state appeal due to serious error made at trial. Five-hundred-ninety-nine of the cases that survived appeal in state courts were accepted for the first time as habeas petitions in federal district courts. In those cases, 237, or 40 percent, were reversed because of serious error.

The two major causes of serious error in capital cases, according to Liebman's findings, were "egregiously incompetent defense lawyering" and "prosecutorial suppression of evidence that the defendant is innocent or does not deserve the death penalty."

The study Professor Liebman published concluded that "nationally, over the 1973-1995 period, the overall error-rate in our capital punishment system was sixty-eight percent." In two of the states with the most executions, Texas and Florida, the study found the error rate to be fifty-two percent in Texas and seventy-three percent in Florida.

The vast majority of the reversals led the state to retry the defendant. Of those who were retried, eight-two percent were not re-sentenced to death and seven percent were found actually innocent and set free, according to James E. Coleman Jr., chair of the American Bar Association's Section of Individual Rights and Responsibility, in testimony he gave to a U.S. House Subcommittee on Crime in 2000.

Although no one could have predicted it at the time of his original conviction, Cooper had little more than a ten-year window of opportunity to file a federal habeas petition before Congress enacted the Anti-Terrorism and Effective Death Penalty Act (ADEPA) in 1996, which severely restricted the bringing of and relief afforded under habeas petitions.

On March 24, 1992, Cooper, as an indigent death row inmate facing an execution date, requested appointment of federal habeas counsel and a stay of execution from the United States District Court, Southern District. Nine months later, the court appointed Charles D. Maurer Jr. as Cooper's counsel. Maurer, a highly regarded trial lawyer, was the managing partner of Maurer, Higginbotham & Harris, a mid-sized San Francisco law firm.

The task of representing Cooper in his habeas appeal was enormous. In addition to over fifteen-thousand pages of pre-trial and trial transcripts, the files from his trial lawyer consisted of sixteen large boxes of witness statements, police reports, and other evidentiary material from his case. In examining this enormous record and after looking over the evidence locker in San Diego pertaining to Cooper's case, Maurer determined that any effective representation of Cooper would call for a full-scale reinvestigation of the case. "I just found too many loose ends in going over this material," Maurer said in a 2011 interview. "The evidence locker in San Diego was in a cage in the basement of the courthouse. There was no order to it, no legends, just boxes and bags of documents from the trial. It was in total disarray. Just trying to put everything together, sort it out, was an extremely difficult, monumental task."

Maurer, who had handled over one-hundred capital cases, found the Cooper appeal "the most complicated criminal case I've ever seen. After spending an entire day interviewing Cooper at San Quentin, Maurer could not believe that the "disarming, cordial, sensitive, gentle guy" was in any way capable of committing the terrible Chino Hills murders. "Kevin is a very charming guy. You can sit down and talk to him and have a cup of coffee. I never saw any dark side to him. I very much wanted to represent him in his appeal."

After spending over one-hundred hours on the case, Maurer went to the federal judge in charge of the case, U.S. District Court Judge Marilyn Huff, and made his first request for compensation. "I asked the district court for $50,000 to $60,000 in fees to cover my own time and to hire experts to conduct the reinvestigation, but the court granted me less than a third of what I requested. I realized from that point on, as a practical matter, that the court wasn't going to pay for any investigation.

Maurer had wanted to hire an investigator to go to Pennsylvania to look into the charges pending against Cooper there and he wanted to hire various forensic experts to examine the blood and cigarette evidence the prosecution used against Cooper at trial. In effect, he wanted a complete reinvestigation of the state's case against Cooper. This investigation he had in mind would have cost the state hundreds of thousands of dollars in reimbursements.

After Judge Huff refused to pay his initial invoice, "I gave up the idea of Pennsylvania and hiring experts. I knew I was going to have to allocate my resources very carefully," Maurer said.

Not long after his appointment, Maurer's personal circumstances changed radically. He had just relocated from San Francisco to San Diego to open a satellite office for his law firm when he became embroiled in a prolonged custody battle with his estranged wife over the couple's two children, ages five and seven. After obtaining custody of the two children, he resigned from his law firm to set up his own private practice so that he could be available for significantly increased parental duties. These changes made it impossible for him to represent Cooper effectively and he began asking the court to relieve him of his assignment. He filed his first motion for dismissal in July of 1994.

Despite the fact that Maurer was no longer actively involved in representing Cooper and asking to be relieved, Judge Huff repeatedly denied his requests to be released from the case even though Maurer by this time had ceased doing any legal work for Cooper. As a result, Maurer remained Cooper's of record as his execution date of November 26, 1994 closed in.

On July 7, 1994, Judge Huff issued an order informing Maurer that unless some sort of habeas corpus petition was filed on Cooper's behalf that no stay of execution would be granted.

To satisfy this order, Maurer enlisted the assistance of Jeannie Sternberg, the staff attorney for the California Appellate Project, a non-profit based in San Francisco that offers legal resources to lawyers representing death row inmates. Under severe deadline pressure, Sternberg put together a boiler plate habeas corpus petition that Maurer filed with the district court on August 8, 1994. This led Judge Huff to grant Cooper a temporary stay of execution.

On June 2, 1995, Judge Huff appointed William McGuigan and Robert Amidon as Cooper's substitute counsel in federal court. On February 21, 1996, the two attorneys were also appointed to be Cooper's counsel in the

California Supreme Court. In the end, however, McGuigan and Amidon's efforts came too late, as Judge Huff would only grant a short continuance to allow for the preparation and filing of both state and federal petitions for habeas corpus. Ultimately, the California Supreme Court rejected Cooper's state habeas petition on February 19, 1997, and Judge Huff followed suit, denying Cooper's federal habeas claims on August 25, 1997, sixteen months after ADEPA took effect.

The Anti-Terrorism and Effective Death-Penalty Act was part of Speaker of the House Newt Gingrich's "Contract with America" that swept Republicans into control of Congress following the 1996 elections. The measure—an emasculation of federal habeas corpus—passed with broad bipartisan support: The U.S. Senate approved the bill 91-8-1 and the U.S. House by a margin of 293-133-7. President Bill Clinton, a former constitutional law professor, signed the bill into law on April 24, 1996. He would soon be in a tight re-election campaign against Republican Senator Bob Dole of Kansas, who resigned as the longest tenured majority leader of the U.S. Senate to seek the presidency.

Supporters of ADEPA used the pretext of Timothy McVeigh's bombing of the Alfred P. Murrah Federal Building in Oklahoma City on April 19, 1995 as the rationale to quit pussyfooting with terrorists and murderers. The real catalyst for the new law were state judges, attorney generals, and state prosecutors who, behind the scenes, raised the state right's flag with their senators and representatives in Congress, telling them it was long past time that "activist" federal judges stopped meddling in state court decisions and overturning forty percent of the death sentences handed down.

For death row petitioners, ADEPA was a draconian measure, limiting the power of federal judges to grant habeas relief to two narrow circumstances: The petitioner had to show either that his or her conviction and/or sentencing was "contrary to, or involved an unreasonable application of clearly established federal law as determined by the U.S. Supreme Court," or "his conviction and/or sentencing was based on an unreasonable determination of the facts in light of the evidence presented in state court proceedings."

Two other aspects of ADEPA further constricted a death row petitioner's access to habeas relief. The law imposed a one-year statute of limitations for filing a habeas corpus petition, measured from the time when post-conviction state court consideration of the case ended; and the act made it more difficult to present claims that had not been presented to the post-conviction state court due to attorney error or incompetence. Both of these restrictions would greatly reduce the number of habeas petitions filed on behalf of death row inmates.

For death row inmates, ADEPA was a disaster. The act did nothing to improve the trial representation capital defendants were assigned by the court nor did it in any manner proscribe that district attorneys and prosecutors not suppress evidence favorable to the defendant.

In the first twenty years after the passage of ADEPA, the number of successful habeas petitions filed by death-row inmates plummeted to twelve percent, according to David Dow, a law professor at the University of Houston, who published a study on the stunning reversal.

Regarding the two major reasons capital cases are flawed—ineffective counsel and suppression of evidence by the prosecution—Cooper had strong claims to make in both those areas. His trial attorney ignored the single most important piece of evidence that would have established Cooper's innocence—the bloody coveralls belonging to convicted murderer Lee Furrow. In terms of suppression of evidence by law enforcement, the destruction of Furrow's coveralls precluded Cooper's defense from establishing his innocence. So did the sheriff's department not producing the bloody blue shirt found not far from the Canyon Corral Bar that Cooper's appellate attorneys would for the first time become aware of in 2004.

A Date with Death

On May 21, 1985, Cooper entered his four-foot by nine-foot cell on death row at San Quentin a bitter man, outraged at what he knew to be a trumped-up conviction. After two years of wallowing in self-pity and being totally isolated from family and friends, he realized that if he did not change himself for the better "I would surely die a violent death in here," he wrote about his adjustment to life on death row. "Over a period of two years, I started to change from the angry man that I was into the person I am today."

"I guess the bottom line is this: We all have to make real life decisions at one time or another in our lives," he wrote in his clemency petition to the governor. "I decided to live and not to die just because I was sentenced to die. Because if I did not make the decision to live, I would be making the decision to die—a decision that I as an innocent man could not do."

One of the first positive steps he took was to get a copy of the *Oakland Tribune* and write a letter to each of several hundred churches that advertised in the newspaper. Only one response came back. Pastor Jacquelyn Jackson of the Cellar Christian Ministries Fellowship told Cooper he would be a welcome member of her community. Over the years, Pastor Jackson provided spiritual advice and counseling and brought other members of her community to visit him.

When available, Cooper signed up for education programs, taking classes in literacy and art that greatly expanded his ability to communicate. Some of his writings and art work are available on a web site dedicated to his case: www.savekevincooper.org.

Eighteen years after Cooper entered death row, San Diego Superior Court Judge William H. Kennedy directed the warden at San Quentin to execute Kevin Cooper on, at 12:01 a.m. on February 10, 2004, by lethal injection, a method of execution the state had adopted to replace the gas chamber in1994. In the courtroom as Judge Kennedy signed Cooper's death warrant were Josh Ryen, the lone survivor of the 1983 massacre at his home, and Bill and Mary Ann Hughes, the parents of eleven-year-old victim Chris Hughes.

It was the fourth time a Superior Court judge had set an execution date for Cooper. His previous execution dates in 1985, 1991, and 1996 were rendered moot due to the state and federal district court appeals still open to him. Now, only three avenues of relief stood between him and death by lethal injection. The first would be an appeal for clemency to newly installed Governor Arnold Schwarzenegger, an avowed supporter of the death penalty. Failing clemency, his next option would be to petition the U.S. Court of Appeals for the Ninth Circuit for permission to file a new habeas corpus petition. If denied, he could file a writ of certiorari with the U.S. Supreme Court.

By 2003, Cooper was one of 650 inmates on San Quentin's death row, the largest in the Western Hemisphere and the largest in the nation by over 250 condemned men. Despite its size, only two inmates have been executed at San Quentin since the state resumed capital punishment in 1992. Both were performed by lethal injection inside the prison's 230-square-foot gas chamber surrounded by three separate viewing areas: one for the family of the victim, one for the media, and one for the family or loved ones of the man to die.

San Quentin's property sprawls over 432 acres of prime real estate overlooking the north side of San Francisco Bay. Its massive prison buildings consume 275 acres and house over five-thousand convicted felons.

Cooper's clemency petition was sent to Governor Schwarzenegger on January 9, 2004 by David T. Alexander, an attorney with Orrick, Herrington & Sutcliffe, a major international law firm headquartered in San Francisco. Thanks to Alexander's belief in Cooper's total innocence, Orrick had taken up Cooper's case pro bono in September of 2003. Alexander had been approached by the Northern California Innocence Project to represent Cooper.

The petition urged the governor to consider matters far beyond those available to any other decision-maker, stating that his "power to look at the totality of circumstances gives you a power and perspective held by no one else. The jury did not hear and could not consider important issues or evidence. By contrast, you have the ability and complete discretion to consider all relevant facts and circumstances."

The argument for clemency focused on ten major points:

1.) The investigation was seriously mismanaged. Once the investigators zeroed in on Cooper as the lone perpetrator, law enforcement systematically ignored evidence that pointed to three young white males as the assailants.

2.) Law enforcement intentionally destroyed evidence that implicated other assailants.

3.) The crime scene was literally destroyed, preventing Cooper from reconstructing it and demonstrating that the prosecution's single-perpetrator theory was implausible.

4.) The sheer magnitude of the violence and the number of different weapons used in the crime cast doubt on Cooper as sole-perpetrator theory.

5.) The notion that a single person used several weapons on several victims over an unknown but very brief period of time is, on its face, counterintuitive.

6.) The notion that a single perpetrator would switch weapons once or twice for no discernible need or reason lacks anchor in logic or common sense.

7.) The prosecution argued to the jury that Cooper murdered to aid his escape without ever explaining how murdering four people would facilitate a quiet escape.

8.) The need to obtain a car to escape does not provide a motive to murder innocent people or explain the level of brutality exhibited in the Ryen/Hughes murders. Nor does it explain why the victims were severely mutilated, including the infliction of post-mortem wounds.

9.) If escape was the motive, no one can explain why money, guns and other valuables in plain view were left untouched.

10.) The courts have denied Cooper testing that could show that law enforcement planted evidence against him to convict him as well as DNA testing that could exonerate him.

The petition referenced that several of the victims had blond or light brown hair in their hands that could not have come from Cooper and that Cooper's attempts to have those hairs subjected to DNA testing had been aggressively opposed by the attorney general and denied by the courts.

"Such testing might determine that they [the hairs] can be matched with any person in the DNA database, possibly with [Lee] Furrow or [Kenneth] Koon [suspects identified to law enforcement as the possible perpetrators]. Even if no match were obtained, DNA testing of the hair could prove that the clutched hair belonged to persons other than the victims, thereby lending further support to the fact that multiple assailants, not Mr. Cooper, were responsible."

The petition did not sidestep the fact that recent DNA testing conducted by the U.S. Justice Department Lab in Berkeley at the insistence of Cooper—over objections from the prosecution—on the bloody tan T-shirt found discarded near a bar a mile or so from the Ryens' home implicated Cooper. The petition pointed out that the original tests of the shirt found only blood consistent with Doug Ryen on it. Now, over ten years later, it showed Cooper's blood as well. When Cooper sought to have the T-shirt tested for the presence of EDTA, a preservative used to maintain blood in a test tube, to prove that his blood had been planted on the T-shirt, the government prevailed in stopping the test.

If the governor declined to grant Cooper clemency and spare his life, the petition requested that he grant a reprieve and direct that his defense be allowed to conduct further testing.

Aside from clemency or a reprieve to allow further testing, the purpose of the petition was to win a clemency hearing so that Cooper's attorneys could address the governor directly on Cooper's behalf.

Some of the letters requesting Governor Schwarzenegger grant Cooper clemency came from some surprising sources. Six of the jurors who voted to convict and sentence him to death asked the governor to halt Cooper's execution so that more investigation into the case could be done.

Lillian Shaffer, Peggy Ryen's half sister, also wrote to the governor: "Kevin Cooper is to be executed next week and I would like to go on record in saying that I do not believe he was the killer of my family and the Hughes boy. I am in disagreement with the other members of the family who want him dead. Please give more time for fact-finding. Along with others who are questioning the jury's verdict, I find some of the information disturbing. There should be justice, but please let it be true."

In a clemency letter written by Dr. Lorna Forbes, the psychiatrist who treated Josh, she informed the governor that it was "only after extended contact with the police who were convinced Mr. Cooper was the assailant, and a bombardment of media reports flashing Mr. Cooper's picture and naming him as the attacker, that Josh decided that he did not know who did it."

Dr. Forbes then quoted from her December 1983 interview with Josh to illustrate that point:

DR. FORBES: OKAY. AND AS FAR AS YOU ARE CAN REMEMBER, THE THING THAT YOU DON'T REMEMBER HOW YOU TOLD THEM THAT THERE WERE THREE AT ALL WHEN YOU TALKED TO [DETECTIVE] O'CAMPO?

JOSH: I'M NOT, I DON'T REMEMBER. WHAT WAS THE QUESTION?

DR. FORBES: YEAH, I JUST SAID HOW YOU TOLD THEM.

JOSH: OH, I REALLY THOUGHT IT WAS THEM [THREE MEXICANS], BUT AFTER A WHILE I SAW ON TELEVISION THAT IT WAS COOPER.

In the meantime, the *San Francisco Chronicle* ran an editorial calling on the governor to grant Cooper clemency and for its readers to keep calling, faxing and emailing the governor until he complied.

The Terminator was not swayed. On January 30, 2004, he denied clemency and for the first time since California had reinstated the death penalty in 1992, a California governor denied a death row inmate an open hearing, stating in a prepared release, "I have carefully weighed the claims presented in Kevin Cooper's plea for clemency. The state and federal courts have reviewed this case for more than eighteen years. Evidence establishing his guilt is overwhelming, and his conversion to faith and his mentoring of others, while commendable, do not diminish the cruelty and destruction he has inflicted on so many. His is not a case for clemency."

Cooper was now only eleven days from execution.

With his clemency petition denied and the odds strongly against any judicial relief, Cooper released a written statement on January 29, entitled, "This is Not My Execution." He may have entered San Quentin under-educated and inarticulate in any formal sense, but he would not be leaving it that way. He was by now well-read and well-versed in social and justice issues and quite capable of speaking in sharp, cogent sentences not only for himself but for others as well:

I, KEVIN COOPER, AM WRITING THIS FROM DEATH ROW AT SAN QUENTIN PRISON. I AM SCHEDULED TO BE THE NEXT BLACK MAN EXECUTED BY THE STATE OF CALIFORNIA ON FEBRUARY 10, 2004.

WHILE I AM AN INNOCENT MAN ABOUT TO BE MURDERED BY THIS STATE, I REALIZE THAT INNOCENCE MAKES NO DIFFERENCE TO THE PEOPLE WHO CONTROL THE CRIMINAL JUSTICE SYSTEM, INCLUDING THIS PRISON. THIS IS THE SAME SYSTEM THAT HAS HISTORICALLY AND SYSTEMATICALLY EXECUTED MEN, WOMEN, AND CHILDREN WHO LOOK JUST LIKE ME, IF ONLY BECAUSE THEY CAN.

WHILE IT IS MY LIFE THAT WILL BE TAKEN, AND MY BODY FILLED WITH POISON, I WILL NOT SAY THAT THIS IS MY EXECUTION! THAT'S BECAUSE IT IS NOT; IT IS JUST A CONTINUATION OF THE HISTORIC SYSTEM OF CAPITAL PUNISHMENT THAT ALL POOR PEOPLE ALL OVER THIS WORLD HAVE AND ARE SUBJECTED TO.

TO PERSONALIZE THIS CRIME AGAINST HUMANITY AS "MY EXECU-TION" WOULD BE TO IGNORE THE UNIVERSAL PLIGHT, STRUGGLE AND MURDER OF POOR PEOPLE ALL OVER THIS PLANET WE CALL EARTH. THIS I CANNOT AND WILL NOT DO!

IF I MUST BE MURDERED BY THE STATE, THEN I WILL DO SO WITH
MY DIGNITY INTACT. THIS GUILT THAT THE CRIMINAL JUSTICE SYSTEM
HAS PUT ON ME WILL BE QUESTIONED BY ANYONE AND EVERYONE WHO
FINDS OUT THE WHOLE TRUTH OF THIS CASE.

On January 31, 2004 a signature ad criticizing Governor Schwarzenegger's refusal to grant clemency ran in the San Jose Mercury News and the West Coast edition of *The New York Times*. It was signed by, among others, Danny Glover, Janeane Garofalo, Michael Farrell, Noam Chomsky, Howard Zinn, the executive board of the International Longshore and Warehouse Workers Union Local 10, Jesse Jackson Sr., some members of the California legislature, and nine members of the European Parliament. The president of Austria, Kurt Waldheim, expressed his disappointment in his former countryman for denying Cooper's petition.

Later that day, at the First Congregational Church of Berkeley, the University of California Chapter of the Campaign to End the Death Penalty drew a packed audience to hear an array of anti-death penalty speakers: Shujaa Graham, who was exonerated from California's death row in 1981; Darrel Mexers from Murder Victims' Families for Reconciliation; indomitable civil rights attorney Lynne Stewart, and actor Danny Glover.

A week before Cooper's scheduled execution, an anti-capital punishment news conference was held at the Catholic church in Santa Monica where Schwarzenegger and his family attend services. Jesse Jackson, accompanied by the church's pastor and more than twenty religious leaders from various denominations, participated. Also that day, two-hundred people rallied in front of the State Building in San Francisco and one-hundred-fifty at the Capitol Building in Sacramento to protest capital punishment. In Santa Cruz, Angela Davis addressed over four-hundred people, decrying state executions. Smaller rallies were held in Fresno, Riverside, and at the gates of San Quentin.

CHAPTER FORTY-SIX

Stay of Execution

Faced with the unlikely prospect of Governor Schwarzenegger granting clemency, a team of attorneys at Orrick, Herrington & Sutcliffe, led by David Alexander, frantically went to work drafting a successor petition for a writ of habeas corpus and a stay of execution to file with the U.S. Ninth Circuit Court of Appeals once the denial of clemency was made final.

The task before them was daunting as Cooper's execution date rapidly approached. The odds against Cooper's attorneys prevailing at the Ninth Circuit were extremely high if not astronomical due to the legal hurdles involved. Because Cooper had been convicted of a capital crime, the burden of proof had shifted one-hundred-eighty degrees to the defense. For the Ninth Circuit to grant Cooper a stay of execution and a successor habeas petition, his attorneys must now advance evidence that is so "clear and convincing" that no reasonable fact-finder would have found him guilty if this evidence had been known to the trial jury.

Two days before his scheduled execution date, Cooper's attorneys at Orrick filed Cooper's request for a successive habeas petition and a stay of execution. That same day, a three-judge panel of that court denied the petition in a two-to-one decision, invoking the severe restrictions of the Anti-Terrorism and Effective Death Penalty Act in issuing its ruling. In the majority were Circuit Judges Pamela Ann Rymer and Ronald M. Gould. Judge James R. Browning, for whom the Ninth Circuit Court of Appeal Courthouse in San Francisco is named, dissented.

262 J. Patrick O'Connor

The petition asserted that the state had violated Cooper's constitutional rights by withholding from the defense the information supplied by CIM Warden Midge Carroll that Pro-Keds were not a special-issued prison shoe. It also contended that the state had manufactured evidence against Cooper in respect to a blood spot of his found at the Ryens' home, his blood on the tan T-shirt, and the cigarette butts of his in the Ryens' stolen station wagon. New testing of those three items, the petition argued, would prove state tampering and exonerate Cooper. The petition also asked for DNA testing of the hairs found clutched in Jessica Ryen's fingers and strands of hair that adhered to other victims' bodies, arguing that such testing could substantiate the presence of an assailant other than Cooper. In addition, Cooper's petition contained the newly acquired declaration of Christine Slonaker who swore she saw two young white, blond males splattered with blood at a bar near the Ryens' house the night of the murders, both wearing tennis shoes.

Judge Rymer, writing for the majority, saw no merit in granting either a new habeas corpus petition or a stay so that any additional testing could be conducted. Using the stringent time restrictions imposed on federal courts as a result of the passage of the Anti-Terrorism and Effective Death Penalty Act, she wrote:

...THIS APPLICATION TURNS ON FACTS THAT HAVE LONG SINCE BEEN KNOWN AND THAT HAVE ALREADY BEEN PRESENTED AND RESOLVED ADVERSELY TO COOPER IN STATE COURT EVIDENTIARY HEARINGS, PROCEEDINGS BEFORE THE CALIFORNIA SUPREME COURT ON DIRECT AND COLLATERAL REVIEW, IN HIS ORIGINAL HABEAS PETITION IN FEDERAL COURT, AND IN CONNECTION WITH HIS APPLICATIONS TO THIS COURT TO FILE SECOND OR SUCCESSIVE PETITIONS. TO THE EXTENT THAT THE CLAIMS ARE FORMULATED DIFFERENTLY IN THE PETITION HE NOW ASKS TO FILE, THEY ARE NEVERTHELESS BASED ON FACTS THAT WERE AVAILABLE AND COULD PREVIOUSLY HAVE BEEN DISCOVERED WITH THE EXERCISE OF DUE DILIGENCE. FOR THIS REASON, COOPER FAILS TO MAKE THE SHOWING THAT THE ANTI-TERRORISM AND EFFECTIVE DEATH PENALTY ACT OF 1996 REQUIRES FOR APPROVAL OF HIS APPLICATION.

IN ADDITION, COOPER'S PETITION DOES NOT SET FORTH FACTS
THAT ARE SUFFICIENT TO SHOW BY CLEAR AND CONVINCING EVIDENCE
THAT, IN LIGHT OF THE EVIDENCE AS A WHOLE, NO REASONABLE FACT
FINDER WOULD HAVE FOUND HIM GUILTY OF THE OFFENSES CHARGED.
THE FEW ITEMS OF EVIDENCE UPON WHICH COOPER NOW RELIES THAT
WERE NOT BEFORE THE JURY HAVE LITTLE OR NO PROBATIVE VALUE AND
FALL SHORT OF SHOWING THAT IT IS MORE LIKELY THAN NOT THAT NO
REASONABLE JUROR WOULD HAVE CONVICTED HIM

COOPER HAS MADE NO SHOWING OF ACTUAL INNOCENCE, NOR HAS HE
SHOWN THAT IT WOULD BE MANIFESTLY UNJUST FOR THE COURTS TO
DECLINE TO REVISIT THE SAME ISSUES AGAIN. ACCORDINGLY, WE DENY
THE APPLICATION TO FILE THIS SUCCESSIVE PETITION. GIVEN THIS
DECISION, THERE IS NO BASIS FOR GRANTING A STAY.

Contrary to what was stated in the majority opinion, the declaration of
Christine Slonaker was probative, i.e., it tended to prove that it was likely
that assailants other than Cooper were responsible for the murders. Had
Sloanaker's testimony been heard at trial, there was a strong possibility that
the jury would have given it credence and connected her description of the
white "blond" men with the blond or light brown clump of hair clutched in
Jessica Ryen's fingers.

The same can be said of the prosecution's withholding information
exculpatory to Cooper provided by the warden of the California Institute
for Men, Midge Carroll. She had informed one of the lead detectives prior
to trial that the Pro-Keds Dude tennis shoes the prosecution used as the
centerpiece of its evidentiary case against Cooper were not prison-issue and
were available for sale throughout California in retail outlets such as Sears.
Had the defense had access to the warden's report, it could have exposed
the fraudulent testimony the state used to tie Cooper to the murder scene
through its claim that the tennis shoes were prison-issue.

In an extraordinary development following the two-to-one decision to
deny Cooper a successive habeas petition and a stay of execution, Judge
Browning attached his eighty-three-paragraph dissent to the majority
decision and on his own circulated his dissent to the other judges of the

court in an effort to get an en banc majority of the court to grant Cooper's habeas petition and stay his execution. En banc reversals are extremely rare, but Judge Browning enticed eleven of the thirteen judges to turn his dissent into a majority ruling the next day, just eight hours before Cooper's scheduled execution.

What appears to have influence the favorable en banc ruling more than anything else was the *Brady* violation involving the prosecution's withholding of Warden Carroll's report about the Pro-Keds Dude tennis shoes not being prison-issue. The *Brady* violation opened the door for the Ninth Circuit to direct the Federal District Court in Southern California to allow testing of the tan T-shirt to determine if state agents had planted Cooper's blood on it and to test the hairs found in Jessica Ryen's fingers to see if they implicated other perpetrators.

Court-ordered stays of execution were rare before California halted executions in 1967 and had never occurred in the years since the state resumed executions in 1992.

News of the stay of execution did not reach Cooper until 6:15 p.m., while he was in the visitor room with his pastor, Jacqueline Jackson, Jesse Jackson Sr., and several friends. As he heard that news from Jeannie Sternberg, the deputy director of the Habeas Corpus Resource Center, he was also informed that two hours earlier California Attorney General Bill Lockyer had filed an appeal with the U.S. Supreme Court to reverse the en banc decision. This had the effect of keeping the prison's pre-execution protocol in full gear for a 12:01 a.m. execution.

After Jesse Jackson said a prayer for him and his friends, prison guards told the visitors to leave. Six guards then took Cooper to a holding cell where his handcuffs were removed and he was ordered to undress. Guards stripped-searched him and gave him a new set of prison clothes to wear. He was then re-cuffed and escorted on his "dead man walking" trip to the waiting room cell adjacent to the death chamber and handed over to an eight-man unit of death-chamber guards.

Cooper was told to place his back against the back wall of the cell and was then surrounded by all of the guards. The leader of the squad asked him if there was going to be any trouble when they removed his handcuffs. Cooper told him no. When his handcuffs were removed, he was told to undress. The room was very cold as Cooper stood barefoot and naked awaiting another strip-search. This one would be conducted with a flashlight shining into his mouth and anus.

He was given another set of clothing to put on and then taken a few feet to a much smaller cell that contained only a toilet, a mattress, and a pillow. About a half an hour later his pastor was allowed to visit with him from a cell at a slight angle from his. She began reading scripture passages to him.

A warden's representative came by to ask him if he wanted a last meal. He had been fasting since the Friday before, and told him no. He also refused the offer of water. Asked if he wanted to make a final statement, he declined.

Guards checked his arms, looking for prominent veins.

Jeannie Sternberg called to tell him she was with him in spirit and she would call him again when she heard something from the U.S. Supreme Court.

His pastor continued reading scripture aloud to him.

Outside the gates of San Quentin that evening, six-hundred people gathered to hold a candlelight vigil to protest Cooper's execution.

At 8:15 p.m. Attorney Jeannie Sternberg called Cooper to inform him the U.S. Supreme Court had upheld his stay. Instead of first telling his pastor the good news, he told the squad of death-chamber guards that he meant them no disrespect but they would not be doing their job that night. In a radio interview the next week, Cooper said the guards "did not react at all. They were as cold as that room that I was in. I was a nonhuman. I was just part of their job." Cooper had come within three hours and forty-five minutes of being executed.

In an interview with radio station KPFA-FM's "Flashpoints" program eight days later Cooper said he had "no confidence" in the U.S. Supreme Court upholding his stay of execution but that when he heard the court had left his stay intact "I just felt life coming back into my body."

CHAPTER FORTY-SEVEN

U.S. District Court Judge Marilyn L. Huff

When the *en banc Ninth Circuit Court of Appeals* stayed Cooper's execution on February 3, 2004, it ordered the U.S. District Court for Southern California to hold evidentiary hearings to test Cooper's claims that his blood had been planted on the tan T-shirt and to order mitochondrial DNA testing of the blond or light brown hairs clutched in Jessica Ryen's hands to determine if those hairs excluded all the victims. If they did, those hairs would prove Cooper's innocence. If the testing of the tan T-shirt showed high levels of the preservative EDTA, it would prove that someone had planted Cooper's own blood on the shirt. Such tampering would call into question the state's entire evidentiary case against Cooper and be grounds for a reversal of his conviction or at least grounds for a new trial. For Cooper, the importance of the testing was enormous.

In remanding Cooper's case to the district court, the Ninth Circuit Court was allowing Cooper the extremely rare opportunity of having not only the testing he wanted done performed but also the opportunity to bring any other claims before the district court in the form of a successive habeas corpus petition.

For Cooper and his attorneys, though, there was a major catch involved that, in essence, doomed his chances of relief in district court. Because U.S. District Court Judge Marilyn L. Huff had presided over Cooper's first habeas corpus appeal, denying it in 1997, as well as denying his second habeas petition in 1998—the second without conducting any evidentiary hearings—she would, because she was still active, be the federal judge in charge of presiding at the evidentiary hearings and testing ordered by the Ninth Circuit.

Anne Hawkins, the staff attorney for the Habeas Corpus Research Center, said in 2010 interview that she was not aware of one federal district judge who had ever granted relief to a death row petitioner in a successor habeas petition if that judge had denied the original habeas petition. Located in San Francisco, the purpose of the Habeas Corpus Research Center is to provide timely, high-quality legal representation for indigent petitioners in death penalty habeas corpus proceedings before the Supreme Court of California and the federal courts.

Judge Huff was appointed to the district court by President George H.W. Bush in 1991. Born in Ann Arbor, Michigan in 1951, she graduated from Calvin College in Grand Rapids, Michigan in 1972. She took her law degree at the University of Michigan, graduating in 1976. From there she signed on with a major San Diego law firm, Gray, Ames & Faye, and made partner there in 1983. Her specialty was representing major media clients in civil litigations.

A petite woman with blond hair and an engaging smile, she has piled up her share of sharp critics from the attorneys who appear in her courtroom. Norm Hile of the Orrick law firm, who represented Cooper at the evidentiary hearings Judge Huff conducted in 2004-2005, said about her in a 2010 interview, "She smiles at everybody like she's being the most wonderful den mother and then proceeds to deny every motion for discovery I made. She's really quite impossible. Her design was to make a record that she could use to rule against us. The last day of arguments was when Josh Ryen got to give his statement. That day she orally ruled against us from the bench and then a month later sent out her written denial. She was writing her denial as she went along. She'd take three or four days off between sessions to do that."

Mild mannered, soft-spoken and affable, Hile said his experiences with Judge Huff often left him feeling like "I was in court in the Deep South. You're from out of town and you get railroaded like in *My Cousin Vinny*."

Hile, who graduated from Yale in 1967 and Columbia Law School in 1973, is partner-in-chief of Orrick's Sacramento office. He is a specialist in business and government litigation with extensive experience in intellectual property, securities, antitrust, and environmental litigation. Because he had won a new penalty phase trial for James Karis during a federal habeas corpus proceeding, Orrick asked him to take over as lead counsel for Cooper right after the Ninth Circuit Court of Appeals stayed Cooper's execution in February of 2004 and granted his successive habeas corpus petition in federal district court. David Alexander, now in his own private practice, assisted Hile in his preparation for the evidentiary hearings conducted by Judge Huff.

An Internet site called "The Robing Room" (www.therobingroom.com) is a forum that rates federal judges on a scale of one to ten by taking written comments from practicing attorneys. Judge Huff's rating in December of 2010 was 3.9 based on postings from 2006 through 2010. A year ago, her rating was 4.1, but two one-star ratings posted in 2010 dropped it further.

In checking "Robing Room" ratings for the other fourteen judges on the U.S. District Court for Southern California, only James Lorenz had a rating (3.9) as low as Judge Huff's. In comments, Judge Lorenz was characterized as arbitrary and ill-tempered. Two judges, Irma Gonzalez and Michael Annelo, garnered ratings of 9.0. Their fairness, knowledge of the law, and courtroom courtesy were lauded. Judge Dana Sabraw was rated 8.6, Judge Jeffrey Miller 8.3, and Judge Thomas Whelan 8.2. None of the other judges were rated below 5.0.

Of all the judges in her federal district, Judge Huff also pulled in the most comments, sixteen. The judge with the second highest number of comments was Larry Burns, who had nine and a rating of 6.8.

Building up animus with practicing attorneys will eventually limit a judge's career, but federal judges are appointed for life and may only be removed if impeached by the U.S. House of Representatives and convicted in the U.S. Senate. In December of 2010, U.S. District Court Thomas Porteous became only the eighth judge so removed. His crime was taking numerous cash bribes from lawyers and bail bondsmen.

The reactions to Judge Huff expressed on "Robing Room" are extremely harsh. The most recent comment posted stated, "The judge never stops being a lawyer...She believes that the federal court is reserved for big corporations and feels sorry for herself that she has a heavy case load. The worst judge in San Diego and a contrast to many of the other judges on the federal bench."

The most persistent complaints against Judge Huff over the last five years have been her perceived bias and her lack of basic knowledge about the law, flaws that can form a lethal combination. "The judge has no understanding of evidence. Once she picks a side, heaven help you if you are on the wrong side," a posting in 2008 read.

"The hard fact is that Judge Huff clearly appeared to lack understanding of the subject matter and the evidence supporting it...In my opinion she exhibits a strong bias in favor of this particular plaintiff," another attorney wrote, commenting on a copyright case he had before her. "Regrettably, I believe she has a marginal understanding of the issues in these type of cases."

Another civil litigation attorney wrote in 2007 that Judge Huff was weak on evidence, adding, "She appears to decide early which attorneys/parties she likes and exhibits clear bias. Makes up her mind before all the evidence is in...She is the worst judge in the district by far."

That sentiment was stated in different ways by several other attorneys. One called her "the absolute worst judge on this otherwise good bench." Another wrote, "She is pathetic. The fact that she is on the bench means we need to look closer at how judges are nominated." A third stated in commenting on her "obvious bias" that "This judge makes one wish federal judges were not appointed for life."

The problems Kevin Cooper's appeal attorneys would encounter with Judge Huff when she presided at his habeas hearing in 2004-2005 would be the same experienced by a lawyer in a case the judge heard in 2008. "Had her for a complex civil case against the U.S. Attorney General's Office. [She] gave the AG's Office every break in the book while hammering my case under the exact same circumstances. Never want to litigate in her court again."

CHAPTER FORTY-EIGHT

Evidentiary Hearings

The evidentiary hearings opened on April 2, 2004 in federal court in San Diego. Over the course of the next year, the hearings would be held periodically for several days at a time as the court dealt with the various claims in Cooper's habeas corpus petition.

At the center of Kevin Cooper's claim of innocence was that he was framed, not by overzealous investigators and prosecutors, but by an array of unconscionable San Bernardino County sheriff's deputies, detectives, and crime lab personnel and county prosecutors who would stop at nothing to hang the Chino Hills murders on him. In a host of state and federal appeals, he had asserted that the investigators planted incriminating evidence against him at the vacant house where he stayed for two days, at the crime scene, and in the Ryens' station wagon; that sheriff's deputies intentionally destroyed evidence that proved his innocence and implicated other assailants; that the crime lab conspired to rig its test results and later planted his blood on a key piece of evidence. Pre-trial, prosecutors withheld crucial evidence favorable to his defense and, at trial, used unreliable snitch testimony and patently false testimony to convict him.

All of these claims would be in play during the evidentiary hearings.

The first matter Judge Huff took up was designing a protocol for the testing of the tan T-shirt to determine if Cooper's blood on it contained high levels of EDTA. The Ninth Circuit had specifically ordered the court to have such testing performed. As one of the judges of the Ninth Circuit stated in voting to stay Cooper's execution and grant him a successive habeas corpus hearing, the testing of the T-shirt for EDTA would either exonerate Cooper or prove he "was guilty as sin."

EDTA is anti-clotting substance used in blood labs to preserve blood in vials, to prevent it from coagulating and breaking down. If tests conducted showed high levels of EDTA on the blood attributed to Cooper on the T-shirt, it would establish tampering. If tampering were established, it would call into question all the forensic evidence the prosecution used to link Cooper to the crime scene. Cooper, after nineteen years of asserting his innocence from death row, would be vindicated. At a minimum, the district court would have had to order a new trial or exonerate him outright.

Judge Huff was not going to let that happen.

Experts from both the defense and the state gave the judge a tutorial on EDTA testing. It was actually quite a simple matter to do the testing properly, they explained. An expert criminalist from each side would examine the tan T-shirt for blood stains that were not tested in 2002, select the most obvious ones, and send those to an independent laboratory for EDTA analysis. For the purposes of establishing controls, some cuttings from the shirt that appeared to contain no blood would be tested as well. In addition, the lab would retest the stain found to contain Cooper's blood in 2002 for the presence of EDTA. This stain was labeled "6G."

On June 4, 2004, Cooper's attorneys filed their proposed protocol for testing the tan T-shirt. They also requested the judge to allow testing of not only EDTA but two other blood preservatives known to have been used on Cooper's blood sample and to do the same tests on the blood spot labeled "A-41."

The judge denied any further testing of A-41, accepting the state's declaration that the sample had been exhausted. When Cooper's attorney, Norm Hile, asked the judge to allow his expert to view the canister containing A-41, the request was denied. The judge really had no legal basis for denying this request. Denying it was, in fact, an abuse of her discretion because it was patently unfair not to give Cooper's experts the opportunity to see for themselves what the state claimed. The judge, in a completely arbitrary ruling, also would not permit the testing of the tan T-shirt for the two other preservatives the defense wanted included in the testing.

Nearly four months into the hearings, Deputy Attorney General Holly Wilkens, who represented the state at the hearings, informed the court for the first time that the stains from the tan T-shirt that had been DNA tested in 2002 were prepared using a buffer containing EDTA—a process that precluded any further EDTA testing on those stains. This caused Hile to request that his expert, Dr. Peter DeForest, and the state's expert, Stephen Myers, be allowed to examine the shirt to select new stains for EDTA testing. Dr. DeForest told the judge that it was essential for him and the state's expert to examine the shirt in person to select new areas to be sampled, including control areas.

Judge Huff demonstrated extreme bias against the defense when she ruled that only the state's expert could view the shirt for the purpose of determining what remained of the stain, labeled "6G," the only stain on the shirt that contained only Cooper's DNA, according to the 2002 DNA test results, for further EDTA testing. Other stains were known to contain the DNA of Doug Ryen.

On August 13, 2004, Wilkens corrected her earlier depiction of 6G by informing the court that a portion of 6G remained that had not been subjected to a buffer containing EDTA. Two weeks later Judge Huff issued her EDTA testing order, establishing a protocol for testing only 6G for the presence of EDTA.

In response to the new protocol issued by Judge Huff, Dr. DeForest wrote a letter to the judge on September 3 saying he was "concerned with the protocol being designed before any examination of the T-shirt."

I FEEL THIS PROTOCOL IS FLAWED…IT WILL NOT BE POSSIBLE TO OBTAIN ANY MEANINGFUL QUANTITATIVE RESULTS USING IT. FURTHER-MORE, MORE GENERALLY, I FEEL THAT IT IS NOT POSSIBLE TO DESIGN SUCH A PROTOCOL A PRIORI. THIS PROBLEM NEEDS TO BE APPROACHED

IN A SUCCESSION OF STAGES WHERE A CAREFUL ASSESSMENT IS CONDUCTED AT THE CONCLUSION OF EACH STAGE. IN OTHER WORDS, A FLEXIBLE PROCEDURE IS CALLED FOR WITH PERIODIC EVALUATIONS.

WHATEVER IS DONE NEEDS TO BE BASED ON SCIENTIFIC CONSENSUS. ONCE I HAVE EXAMINED THE SHIRT, I AM WILLING TO DESIGN AN APPROACH FOR REVIEW BY ANOTHER SCIENTIST OR DEVELOP ONE IN CONJUNCTION WITH A CRIMINALIST REPRESENTING THE PROSECUTION. AS I HAVE BEEN TRYING TO EXPLAIN FOR SOME TIME NOW, THERE NEEDS TO BE A CAREFUL ASSESSMENT OF THE SHIRT FOLLOWED BY A SCIENTIFIC CONSENSUS OF THE PRE-EXTRACTION SAMPLING. THE PROBLEM IS NOT A TRIVIAL ONE.

ALTHOUGH I AM VERY BUSY, I AM INTERESTED IN THIS CASE. THE EDTA OR ANTI-CLOTTING AGENT QUESTION IS NOT GOING TO GO AWAY. THIS IS A CASE THAT COULD HAVE IMPORTANT RAMIFICATIONS FOR FUTURE CASES. IT IS IMPORTANT THAT IT BE DONE RIGHT. FOR THAT REASON, DESPITE MY BUSY SCHEDULE, I WOULD LIKE TO CONTINUE TO ASSIST. HOWEVER, UNLESS I HAVE THE FREEDOM AND FLEXIBILITY TO DESIGN THE SAMPLING PROTOCOL, IN CONJUNCTION WITH A CRIMINALIST REPRESENTING [THE STATE], I DO NOT WISH TO CONTINUE.

Judge Huff seized the opportunity to terminate Dr. DeForest's participation in the testing. No one from the defense would ever be allowed to see and inspect the tan T-shirt. Discounting Dr. DeForest's advice in its entirety, Judge Huff proceeded to assign the handling of the T-shirt to Dr. Lewis Maddox of Orchid Cellmark, a highly regarded private DNA testing lab headquartered in Germantown, Maryland. She ordered Dr. Maddox to prepare three identical sets of vials from the 6G stain, control samples from the T-shirt area around 6G, and separate positive and negative controls from a different T-shirt.

Norm Hile, to no avail, persisted in objecting to any further testing of 6G before his expert had been allowed to view the shirt.

Before the shirt was shipped to the Orchid lab, Wilkens notified the court that 6G, contrary to what she had told the court earlier, was no longer available for testing because it had been consumed in previous testing. She now suggested, based on information from the state's criminalist, Stephen Myers, who had examined the T-shirt, that the area of the shirt between stains 6I and 6J was the most likely to contain Cooper's blood.

In a matter of a few weeks, Wilkens had gone from saying the previous testing of 6G had used a buffer containing ETDA that rendered further testing if for EDTA useless, to saying a portion of 6G that had not been subjected to the EDTA buffer was still available, to saying all of 6G had been consumed.

The state claiming the 6G stain was consumed after first informing the court that a portion of it remained was highly suspicious and reminiscent of the hijinks surrounding the San Bernardino County Sheriff's Department Lab's "consumption" of the A-41 blood spot only to have it keep reappearing when needed and disappearing when not.

The 6G stain was the conclusive knockout punch the state used to dash Cooper's post-conviction appeals and persuade a judge to set his execution date. Whether or not any other blood stain areas of the T-shirt would have EDTA was an unknown, but if any stain was likely to, it was 6G. One of the primary reasons the en banc Ninth Circuit remanded Cooper's case to district court was to determine if 6G contained elevated levels of EDTA and answer Cooper's charge of the state planting his blood on the T-shirt.

Once again, Hile asked the judge that "an expert of his be allowed to inspect the T-shirt and be part of the selection and preparation process for the anticoagulant testing."

Incredibly, the judge denied the defense any access to the T-shirt and instead ordered Dr. Maddox and the state's expert, Myers, to select and prepare samples for testing over the defense's strong objections. The samples they would select would be sent to Drs. Kevin Ballard, the defense's expert, and Gary Siuzdak, the state's expert, for double-blind EDTA testing.

On October 15, 2004, Wilkens presented a declaration from her criminalist expert, Stephen Myers, addressing the prior consumption of 6G. Myers averred the state had provided inaccurate information about the status of 6G because he "had failed to fully research [his] notes and photographs prior to representing to the district court the condition of that portion of the stain" regarding 6G. Myers further revealed, without explaining why, that the cutting used to conduct presumptive testing was performed on 6G after it had already been DNA tested and he had not preserved the cuttings.

It made no sense to perform any presumptive blood testing of the 6G stain because it was known to be Cooper's blood. Presumptive blood testing is only called for when there is uncertainty about the composition of a stain—to ensure that the stain is actually blood and not some other substance. Presumptive testing uses up part of the sample and it was most likely this totally unnecessary testing performed by Myers that exhausted what remained of 6G, if, in fact, it was exhausted. It would not take a cynic to conclude that if 6G was exhausted, it was to deny Cooper his best opportunity to prove the state planted his blood on the T-shirt.

Although Myers had suggested to the court that the area of the shirt between 6I and 6J would be the next most likely to contain Cooper's blood, Dr. Maddox chose to sample the area of the shirt between 6J and 6K without doing any presumptive testing to determine if the area actually contained blood. He simply "eyeballed" the shirt and selected what he thought most likely to contain blood. To Cooper's experts, Marc Taylor and Elizabeth Johnson, it was "inexplicable" why such presumptive testing was not done of the stain Dr. Maddox selected for testing. There would be no point in testing a stain that was not a blood stain.

Dr. Maddox used the same technique to select control samples from the shirt. From other portions of the T-shirt that appeared to him not to be stained, he prepared extracts from five control samples without revealing how these areas were deemed suitable controls. He then prepared three extracts from a newer control T-shirt, one with EDTA contamination, one with no EDTA contamination, and one left blank. The samples were then sent in three sets of tubes to Drs. Ballard and Siuzdak to conduct double-blind testing.

Both Drs. Ballard and Siuzdak correctly determined which of the three samples taken from the new T-shirt had been contaminated by EDTA, both found lower levels of EDTA in the uncontaminated control sample and no EDTA in the blank control sample.

On the samples taken from the tan T-shirt, Dr. Ballard found elevated levels of EDTA on the sample taken from the area between 6I and 6K, as well as on the control sample taken from above 6I when compared with the non-EDTA contaminated samples taken from the new T-shirt. Dr. Siuzdak, likewise, found an elevated concentration of EDTA in the region surrounding stains 6I, 6J, and 6K—stains that DNA testing in 2002 concluded were from Cooper and Doug Ryen. Just as Dr. Ballard had, Dr. Siuzdak found elevated levels of EDTA in the second control sample that was taken from the tan T-shirt directly above 6I. In addition, Dr. Siuzdak confirmed Dr. Ballard's finding that the concentration of EDTA was lower for the fifth control sample, the sample taken from a different region of the tan T-shirt that was not close to any of the stains previously determined by the state Department of Justice tests conducted in 2002 to contain Cooper's blood.

Dr. Siuzdak found the highest level of EDTA in the sample taken from the stain between 6J and 6K, a smoking-gun type finding that confirmed Cooper's tampering theory. On October 5, 2004, he sent his tests results to Judge Huff.

Just over three weeks later, Dr. Siuzdak sent a facsimile to the district court, informing Judge Huff that he was withdrawing his report, now claiming EDTA contamination in his lab while he performed the tests. He made no attempt to explain how his results that matched Dr. Ballard's had been compromised.

As part of the testing protocol designed by Judge Huff in September, Drs. Ballard and Siuzdak were to document their testing procedures and preserve all raw data until further order by the district court. Norm Hile requested access to Dr. Siuzdak's testing protocols, relevant documents, and raw data from his bench notes to determine if the belated contamination claim Dr. Siuzdak had made would hold up to expert scrutiny. It was a more than fair request considering that the state's own expert had detected the elevated EDTA levels on the sample from the tan T-shirt.

Judge Huff ordered Dr. Siuzdak only to produce his testing protocol, but disallowed the defense from seeing his raw data, thus cutting off any investigation into the nature of the contamination alleged by Dr. Siuzdak. Without the raw data, the defense had no way of determining if the contamination Dr. Siuzdak claimed was valid.

Judge Huff dispensed with any further EDTA testing by ruling that the EDTA testing of the tan T-shirt conducted was not conclusive and that EDTA testing in general was an unproven science and of no value. She was wrong on both counts: both Drs. Ballard and Suizdak found high levels on EDTA on the samples tested from the tan T-shirt and EDTA testing is a proven science.

Hair Testing

The extreme bias against Cooper that Judge Huff displayed with impunity throughout the evidentiary hearings was at its most obvious when it came to the mitochondrial DNA testing of the hairs clutched in various victims' hands ordered by the en banc Ninth Circuit. When a portion of those hairs had been tested in 2002, they were found to have no antigen roots, denoting that the hairs had fallen out rather than been yanked out during the assault. Those hairs, the tests showed, were either from the victims themselves or were dog hairs.

There could be no purpose in retesting those hairs. Over half or more of the hairs in the victims' hands or adhered to their bodies had not been tested in 2002 and may well have contained antigen roots. If the mitochondrial testing of those hairs resulted in a DNA that excluded all the victims and Cooper, there would be proof positive that someone other than Cooper was a perpetrator. This could have led the court to order testing of hair samples from potential suspects Lee Furrow and Kenneth Koon. (Through his attorney, Furrow had already informed the California Attorney's Office that he would not be submitting any hair samples for possible testing. Koon informed the office that if a hair samples was requested, he would comply.)

Inexplicably, Judge Huff ordered testing of the hairs already tested.

"As a result, the mitochondrial DNA testing was pre-determined to have a negative result before it began," Norm Hile said.

The testing that Judge Huff did order of the already tested hairs led to an astonishing discovery. When a swatch of Cooper's blood was tested by Dr. Terry Melton at her lab in College Station, Pennsylvania, she found the sample was contaminated with the DNA of at least one other person. The blood sample sent to the lab was taken from the vial of blood drawn from Cooper in the San Bernardino County Sheriff's Crime Lab shortly after Cooper was arrested in 1983. The vial was labeled "VV-2." Blood from that vial had been the basis for all blood testing involving Cooper before and after trial. VV-2 was what criminalist Daniel Gregonis used in his testing, and it was used again as the basis for 2002 DNA testing as well.

Dr. Melton's finding strongly suggested—if not confirmed—the very tampering claim Cooper's attorneys had been arguing about the state planting his blood on the tan T-shirt and on the blood spot from the Ry- ens' home known as "A-41." The presence of someone else's DNA on the swatch taken from VV-2 was hard evidence that some of Cooper's blood had been removed and later replaced by another person's blood to make the vial appear to be full.

Norm Hile immediately asked for discovery and testing of the swatch to determine when and how it had become contaminated, telling the court it was "extremely alarming and mandate[d] further inquiry." Clearly this was discovery of monumental importance to Cooper's tampering claims and should have been aggressively pursued by the district court. Instead, Judge Huff denied all requests to investigate the contamination, accepting the state's claim that the VV-2 swatch had been consumed and ignoring the importance of testing the remaining blood from the VV-2 vial itself.

Judge Huff's denying Cooper's requests for discovery and accepting at face value the unproven assertions of the state's attorneys infected every aspect of the evidentiary hearings.

The defense wanted to depose and later take testimony at the hear- ings from criminalist Daniel Gregonis regarding his testing and handling of A-41, the only serological link to Cooper from the crime scene the prosecution had. The defense knew that Gregonis had testified falsely at the preliminary hearing about his testing of A-41, had altered his lab notes to match A-41 to Cooper's blood profile, and had lied in 1999 about not opening the package containing A-41 when he had removed it from the crime lab for a day. He was a ripe target for the defense to probe on numerous issues, starting with how VV-2 had come to contain the DNA of not only Cooper but also at least one other person. Judge Huff denied the defense discovery and refused to allow the defense to call Gregonis to testify.

Blue Shirt

During the evidentiary hearings, the defense learned for the first time about a blue shirt that had been found the day after the murders were discovered not far from the Canyon Corral Bar. In trying to disprove that any sheriff deputies had entered the Canyon Coral Bar on the night of the murders, the state turned over police logs that revealed a "blue shirt with possible blood on it" had been spotted by a citizen, Laurel Epler, and collected by Deputy Scott Field on June 6. The police log stated, "Evidence picked up." The next day, the tan T-shirt would be found not far away on the other side of the road leading away from the bar. It, too, would be collected by Deputy Field.

The defense proceeded to contact Epler, who now lived in Florida. She confirmed what the log said. As a defense witness at the evidentiary hearings conducted by Judge Huff, Epler testified that she recalled seeing the shirt at the side of the road from her car, and confirmed the location it was found and that she had called the sheriff's office about it.

There are numerous pieces of evidence that point to Cooper's innocence—the couple who reported seeing three or four white men driving rapidly away from the direction of the Ryens' home in a white station wagon around midnight of the night of the murders; Josh's original statements in the emergency room about his attackers being three or four white men; Josh's statements in his hospital room on two separate occasions when he saw Cooper's picture on TV as the suspect and told the deputy guarding him "that's not the one who did it"; and on another day when Cooper's picture appeared and his grandmother asked him if Cooper was one of his attackers and he told her no; Cooper's utter lack of motive to kill innocent adults and children to aid his escape; the number of weapons involved; the improbability of a lone assailant being able to overwhelm two able-bodied adults and three children, one of whom made it outside the house before her mother was murdered; the three strange men in the Canyon Corral Bar the night of the murders, two with blood on their clothing —but the bloody blue shirt is among the most convincing because when combined with the tan T-shirt later found near the crime scene with Doug Ryen's blood on it, it is evidence of at least two perpetrators.

Shirley Killian, the manager of the Canyon Corral Bar, bolstered the evidentiary importance of the blue shirt when she testified at the 2004 hearing that one of the three strange men in the bar the might of the murders was possibly wearing a blue shirt.

The fact that the sheriff's recovery of the blue shirt was never revealed to Cooper's trial attorney constituted a major *Brady* violation—the prosecution's withholding exculpatory evidence from the defense—and as such was grounds for Judge Huff to order a new trial. To Cooper's defense team, it did not seem possible that the state could wiggle its way out of this major violation.

John Kochis, one of Cooper's two prosecutors at his original trial, made a point of attending the open sessions of the evidentiary hearings, often conferring with Deputy Attorney General Holly Wilkens as she represented the state's interest. By now Kochis was chief deputy district attorney for San Bernardino County. Ensuring that Cooper's conviction went undisturbed was a vested interest of his and of paramount importance to him. His role in the Cooper conviction remained the signal achievement of his long career in the District Attorney's Office.

Kochis would play the key role in enabling Judge Huff to avoid finding a *Brady* violation regarding the prosecution's non-disclosure of the blue shirt to the defense. He testified at the evidentiary hearing that the prosecution was blameless because it had turned over the police logs that referenced the blue shirt as part of the discovery submitted to Cooper's trial attorney, David Negus. According to Kochis, regardless of whether the prosecution failed to disclose the existence of the blue shirt to the defense, since the defense supposedly had knowledge of it by reading the logs, the prosecution should not be penalized for failing to do what was its duty: preserve the blue shirt and disclose it to the defense.

When he heard Kochis's excuse, Norm Hile checked the trial counsel files that Orrick had inherited when the law firm took over the case in 2003. There was no such reference in the logs. Hile then phoned David Negus to ask him if he recalled receiving any discovery that included police logs identifying a blue shirt. Negus told him he did not. Hile then obtained a declaration under penalty of perjury from Negus, and asked the judge to allow Negus to testify at the hearings to disprove what Kochis was claiming. The judge refused to allow Negus to testify.

Hile then requested that Kochis be required to produce a copy of the actual discovery page Kochis claimed the prosecution had turned over to Negus. It was known that when the prosecution turned over discovery to the defense pre-trial, it had stamped each page with a separate number. One set of discovery had gone to the defense and a duplicate set had remained with the prosecution. The police log document Kochis brought to the evidentiary hearing had no page markings, so Hile requested the judge to order the state to produce the copy of the police log from the prosecution's discovery file. Judge Huff denied this request, and never required the state to show a marked copy of the police log.

She also denied Cooper's motion for discovery as to the whereabouts of other documents that the sheriff's department should have retained regarding the blue shirt. These included the property tag that, under sheriff's department procedures, should have been attached to the blue shirt when it was recovered, and under sheriff's department protocol, should have been retained even if the shirt was not. She also denied Hile's request that the prosecution produce the evidence logs showing how the blue shirt was processed at the sheriff's department and what subsequently happened to the blue shirt. These would have been items such as entries in logs and, like the disposition report regarding the destruction of the bloody coveralls, any subsequent handling of the blue shirt. Judge Huff also denied Cooper's motions for evidentiary hearings to explore what happened to the blue shirt and why it was not turned over to the defense. To this day, the prosecution has never had to explain what happened to this shirt or why it cannot produce the property tag for the shirt.

In her ruling at the end of the hearings, Judge Huff dismissed the existence of the blue shirt and denied the defense's *Brady* claim, concluding, without any possible factual basis other than the testimony of Chief Deputy D.A. Kochis, that "the 'blue shirt' reported on June 6, 1983 was "most likely" the tan T-shirt at issue in this case as testified by Mr. Kochis." She noted that since Deputy Field and Sergeant Billy Arthur were both deceased, no one was available to clarify the issue of the blue shirt. The fact that the blue shirt was found on a different day and in a different location than the tan T-shirt did not appear to trouble the judge. Neither did the fact that Laurel Epler was alive and told the court she remembered calling in the blue shirt and that the police logs proved exactly that.

Pro-Keds Dude

Back in 2004, just hours before Cooper's scheduled execution, Judge Robert Browning of the Ninth Circuit Court of Appeals had persuaded an en banc Ninth to stay Cooper's execution and grant him the successor habeas petition that Judge Huff was now conducting. A potential *Brady* violation involving the prosecution's withholding from the defense information supplied by the warden of the California Institute for Men, Midge Carroll, was the primary reason the en banc Ninth voted in Cooper's favor. Now the issue was before Judge Huff to weigh.

There was no dispute that the prosecution had made the claim that Cooper escaped in a pair of Pro-Keds Dude tennis shoes a centerpiece of its evidentiary case against Cooper. The question the en banc Ninth wanted the district court to resolve was whether the prosecution had violated the *Brady* rule by not informing the defense about what the prison warden had communicated to one of the top homicide detectives about the shoes.

Midge Carroll, now retired from CIM, testified at the hearing that she called either the lead detective, Sergeant Arthur, or his top assistant to inform homicide that there were no special-issued tennis shoes at the prison and that all the shoes in use at the prison were available at retail. She made her first call and actually spoke with one of the two detectives during pre-trial hearings held months before the trial commenced. When she read newspaper accounts of the prosecution persisting in alleging that the Pro-Keds were prison-issue shoes at subsequent pre-trial hearings, she made other calls to homicide to correct the mistake, but none of those calls were returned.

To rebut former Warden Carroll, the state called Deputy Derrick Pacifico to testify. Pacifico, who was not a member of the sheriff's department in 1983 or 1984, testified he had reviewed the sheriff's department files for the period 1983-84 and had not found any phone message slips showing that the warden had called.

When Norm Hile requested the court allow him to examine the sheriff's files that Pacifico had reviewed, Judge Huff denied him.

Back in 1997, when Judge Huff was assigned Cooper's original habeas petition, she ordered his appeal lawyers to turn over to the Attorney General's Office the entire defense file from his trial because one of the claims being made on Cooper's behalf was ineffective assistance of counsel by his trial attorney, David Negus. In that file was a phone slip indicating that Warden Carroll had called Negus pre-trial.

In her ruling, Judge Huff dispensed with this *Brady* claim by ruling that Deputy Pacifico's testimony disproved the former warden's testimony and that the phone slip was evidence that Cooper's trial attorney actually knew that Pro-Keds Dude tennis shoes were available at retail outlets and through catalogue sales. Judge Huff refused to allow Negus to testify at the hearing or to enter his affidavit stating that he had called the warden seeking some prison documents related to Cooper and that the issue of the tennis shoes had never been discussed.

Canyon Corral Bar

The defense claim that someone other than Cooper was responsible for the Chino Hills murders was supported at the hearings by the testimony of three patrons of the Canyon Corral Bar the night of the murders. In 2004 when Christine Slonaker read news accounts of Cooper's pending execution, she contacted the Orrick law firm to report that she and two friends were in the Canyon Corral Bar the night of the Chino Hills murders and that she observed two white men, acting obnoxiously, with blood on them. She could not remember the name of one of the women with her, but she provided the defense with the name of the other woman, Mary Wolfe, who now lived in Missouri. Slonaker and Wolfe, although friends many years ago, had not spoken to each other in eight years.

Contacted by an attorney from Orrick, Wolfe confirmed that she recalled seeing the men. Both Slonaker and Wolfe agreed to provide affidavits and to appear at the evidentiary hearings being conducted by Judge Huff.

Slonaker testified that the events of that night remained fresh in her mind because, as she stated, "It isn't too often you run into people that have blood all over their clothes." She recalled seeing only two men. She described them to the court as "falling all over each other and kind of out of it." She said the men were "blond-haired, kind of Caucasian, probably in their twenties, maybe twenty-five to thirty years old, possibly, and extremely delusional." She said one of the men was wearing a tan or white T-shirt, jeans, and tennis shoes; the second man was wearing coveralls and tennis shoes.

When she first saw the men they were standing behind the bar, right in front of her. She said they were acting "strange," not making sense, and speaking "gibberish." The other woman with Slonaker and Wolfe was wearing a low-cut, red, white and blue blouse that accentuated her cleavage.

Slonaker said that when the two men noticed her friend, they walked around the bar and approached the table where the three women were seated. As the men began "hitting" on her friend, Slonaker noticed that one of them had "blood all over him," on his arms, face, shirt, and shoes. She testified that when she told him he was covered in blood that he acted surprised and then his behavior changed.

Wolfe's testimony corroborated Slonaker's descriptions of the men and their drunken behavior, saying they were "very intoxicated. She noticed three men, noting that the third man was "pretty quiet and standoffish."

She said the men "were stumbling, slurring their words." She described one of the men as wearing a light tan or white T-shirt and jeans, and said the other two were wearing coveralls; all three wore tennis shoes. She said the man in the T-shirt had spots of blood on his shirt and a bit of blood on his face. She said one of the men in coveralls also had blood on him.

Lance Stark, a regular patron of the Canyon Corral Bar, buttressed Slonaker and Wolfe's testimony. He testified he saw "a couple of loud mouths" being rude to some women at the bar. Like Wolfe, he described the third man in the group as quiet. He said he did not get close enough to the men to determine if the smudges on them were mud or blood, but he could not rule out them being blood. He testified that he recalled one of the women telling one of the men that he had something on him.

Stark also testified that not long after he had been interviewed by a defense investigator prior to appearing for the defense at the evidentiary hearing on July 23, 2004, a man in an all white, unmarked Ford Crown Victoria that had a computer screen extending from the dashboard approached him to tell him it would be in his best interest not to talk about the Cooper case. Stark was duly concerned. When Norm Hile approached Stark about testifying at the evidentiary hearing, he told Hile, "Well, I'm not sure if I should talk to you because I was told not to."

An investigator for the defense, Joe Soldis, checked the parking lot of the San Bernardino Sheriff's Department headquarters and saw a number of unmarked, all white Ford Crown Victoria cars in the parking lot. Soldis, a no-nonsense, former police officer, confirmed that same day with a woman employee of the Automotive Division of the San Bernardino Vehicle Maintenance Unit that the Sheriff's Department had unmarked all white Ford Crown Victoria cars with computers in them.

Based on Soldis's findings, Norm Hile filed a motion requesting the court to issue subpoenas to identify the person or persons responsible for the witness intimidation tactic exerted on Stark.

On the grounds that such an inquiry would be "too speculative," Judge Huff, in her inimical fashion, denied to issue any subpoenas and refused any further exploration of the intimidation of Stark.

In Cooper's Certificate of Appealability filed with the Ninth Circuit Court after the evidentiary hearings concluded, the defense stated:

THE EFFORT TO INTIMIDATE A WITNESS BY WORDS THAT BOTH IN THEIR SUBSTANCE AND THEIR MANNER (PULLING UP VERY BRIEFLY TO MAKE THE THREAT AND THEN DRIVING OFF) IS AN EXTREMELY GRAVE MATTER. OUR SYSTEM OF JUSTICE CANNOT IGNORE SUCH A BLATANT ACT UNLESS AND UNTIL IT HAS MADE A THOROUGH EFFORT TO INVESTIGATE IT, ESPECIALLY IN THE CONTEXT OF THIS CAPITAL HABEAS CORPUS PROCEEDING.

THE DISTRICT COURT REFUSED ANY FURTHER EXPLORATION OF THE INTIMIDATION OF MR. STARK BECAUSE IT DEEMED IT TOO SPECULA-TIVE. THE OBJECTION OF THE SPECULATION BEGS THE VERY QUESTION TO BE INVESTIGATED. WHO WAS THE PERSON AND WHO ALSO WAS INVOLVED? SOMEONE OR SOME PERSONS HAVING ALL THE APPEARANCE OF BEING ASSOCIATED WITH LAW ENFORCEMENT WERE HIGHLY MOTIVATED TO TRACK DOWN MR. STARK, DRIVE OUT TO LAKE ELSINORE, WHICH IS NOT HIS RESIDENCE, AND THREATEN HIM. A SIMPLE INQUIRY TO THE SAN BERNARDINO SHERIFF'S DEPARTMENT WAS ALL THAT WAS REQUESTED. THE INEXPLICABLE DENIAL OF THIS SIMPLE, NON-BURDENSOME RE-QUEST SAYS MUCH ABOUT THE DISTRICT COURT'S APPROACH TO THESE PROCEEDINGS.

Additional corroboration of Slonaker and Wolfe's testimony came from an unlikely source, former San Bernardino Sheriff's Department Detective Tim Wilson. He testified at the evidentiary hearings that within a week or two of the murders he was informed that the three men in the Canyon Corral Bar had blood on their clothing. He said he may have heard this "listening in on briefings" among law enforcement personnel. He did not learn about it from Slonaker, Wolfe or Stark because none of them ever spoke with law enforcement.

Wilson testified that he thought what he had heard was significant enough to convey it to his superior, Sergeant Billy Arthur, the lead inves-tigator.

In saying he reported this information to Sergeant Arthur, Wilson was exposing another probable *Brady* violation. The information that Wilson supplied Arthur is precisely the type, even if it is hearsay, that the prosecution is compelled under the discovery rules to turn over to the defense pre-trial.

If Cooper's trial attorney, David Negus, had information about the men in the bar having blood on them, he may have made the effort to further investigate. If he did, it is likely that his investigation would have uncovered a great deal more detail about the three men, namely that they had approached three women in the bar. This would have led the defense to Slonaker, Wolfe, their friend in the red, white and blue shirt, Stark, and possibly other bar patrons who observed the unruly, blood-spotted men. Such information, coupled with the destroyed blood-splattered coveralls and the bloody tan T-shirt, would have been a game changer at Cooper's trial. Negus's theory of other perpetrators would have become the five-hundred-pound gorilla in the courtroom.

For Judge Huff, the testimony of Slonaker, Wolfe, and Stark failed to establish Cooper's actual innocence. In her ruling denying Cooper habeas relief, she wrote, "None of the Canyon Corral Bar witnesses are (sic) able to refute the physical evidence linking petitioner to the crime. The blood from the crime scene, A-41, recovered at around 12:25 a.m. on June 6, 1983 came from an African American individual, and post-conviction DNA tests confirmed that it was petitioner's blood (1 in 310 million). None of the bar witnesses describe an inebriated African American individual with blood. As such, the evidence from the bar does not undermine petitioner's guilt."

Bottom line from Judge Huff: Cooper is guilty, get over it.

Josh Ryen

In Cooper's successor habeas petition was a claim that the prosecution manipulated the testimony of young Josh Ryen. By the time the jury was shown two videotaped interviews of Josh at Cooper's trial, he had gone from saying his attackers were three white men to saying he only saw only a single "shadow on the wall."

While convalescing at Loma Linda University Hospital he had two occasions to see a mug shot of Cooper on the television in his room. Each time, once to a reserve deputy and later to his grandmother, he said Cooper was not involved. During the summer of 1983, while Josh was staying in New Jersey, living with his uncle and aunt, he saw a newspaper account of Cooper's arrest. "Are you sure they have the right guy"? he asked his uncle, Dick Ryen.

Judge Huff denied all discovery the defense asked for into this claim, refusing to allow the defense to put various hospital personnel on as witnesses. She also denied the defense the opportunity to interview, depose or obtain testimony from Josh Ryen.

Near the close of the evidentiary hearings in April of 2005, Judge Huff invited Josh Ryen, by now a thirty-year-old man, to make an unsworn statement to the court. She had already denied the defense's repeated requests to allow discovery concerning Josh's memory and his testimony at trial, and she would not allow the defense to cross-examine him now. Josh made the following statement:

THE FIRST TIME I MET KEVIN COOPER, I WAS EIGHT YEARS OLD AND HE SLIT MY THROAT. HE HIT ME WITH A HATCHET AND PUT A HOLE IN MY SKULL. HE STABBED ME TWICE, WHICH BROKE MY RIBS AND COLLAPSED ONE LUNG...

I DON'T WANT TO BE HERE. I CAME BECAUSE I OWE IT TO MY FAMILY, WHO CAN'T SPEAK FOR THEMSELVES. BUT BY COMING I AM ACKNOWLEDGING AND VALIDATING THE EXISTENCE OF KEVIN COOPER, WHO SHOULD HAVE BEEN BLOTTED FROM THE FACE OF THE EARTH A LONG TIME AGO. BY COMING HERE IT SHOWS THAT HE STILL CONTROLS ME. I WILL BE FREE, MY LIFE WILL START THE DAY KEVIN COOPER DIES. I WANT TO BE RID OF HIM, BUT HE WON'T GO AWAY...

THE COURTS SAY THERE ISN'T ANY HARM WHEN KEVIN COOPER GETS ANOTHER STAY AND ANOTHER HEARING. THIS JUST SHOWS THEY DON'T

CARE ABOUT ME, BECAUSE EVERY TIME HE GETS ANOTHER DELAY I AM HARMED AND HAVE TO RELIVE THE MURDERS ALL OVER AGAIN. EVERY TIME KEVIN COOPER OPENS HIS MOUTH, EVERYONE WANTS TO KNOW WHAT I THINK, WHAT I HAVE TO SAY, HOW I'M FEELING, AND THE WHOLE NIGHTMARE FLOODS ALL OVER ME AGAIN. THE BARBECUE, ME BEGGING TO LET CHRIS SPEND THE NIGHT, ME IN MY BED, CHRIS ON THE FLOOR BESIDE ME. MY MOTHER SCREAMS. CHRIS GONE, DARK HOUSE, HALLWAY, BUSHY HAIR, EVERYTHING BLACK, MOM CUT TO PIECES, SATURATED IN BLOOD, THE NAUSEATING SMELL OF BLOOD...

HELICOPTERS GIVE ME FLASHBACKS OF THE LIFE FLIGHT AND MY INCREDIBLE HULKS BEING CUT OFF BY PARAMEDICS. BUSHY HAIR REMINDS ME OF THE KILLER. SILENCE REMINDS ME OF THE QUIET BEFORE THE SCREAMS. COOPER IS EVERYWHERE. THERE IS NO ESCAPE FROM HIM...

KEVIN COOPER HAS MOVIE STARS AND JESSE JACKSON HOLDING RALLIES FOR HIM, PEOPLE CARRYING SIGNS, LIGHTING CANDLES, SAYING PRAYERS. TO THEM AND YOU I SAY:

I WAS EIGHT WHEN HE SLIT MY THROAT,
IT WAS DARK AND I COULDN'T SEE.
THROUGH THE NIGHT AND DAY I LAID THERE,
TRYING TO GET UP AND FLEE.
HE KILLED MY MOTHER, FATHER, SISTER, FRIEND,
AND STARTED STALKING ME.
I TRY TO RUN AND FLEE FROM HIM BUT CANNOT GET
AWAY.
WHILE HE DEMANDS PETITIONS AND CLAIMS, SOME
FRESH ABSURDITY.
JUSTICE HAS NO EAR FOR ME NOR CARES ABOUT MY
PLIGHT,
WHILE CROWDS PRAY FOR THE KILLER AND LIGHT CANDLES
IN THE NIGHT.
TO THOSE WHO LONG FOR JUSTICE AND LOVE TRUTH
WHICH SETS MEN FREE, WHEN YOU PRAY YOUR
PRAYERS TONIGHT, PLEASE REMEMBER ME.

Josh's two references to "bushy hair" in his witness impact statement were disingenuous on several levels. For one thing, they showed that over the intervening years he was still locked in on the mug shot the media ran of Cooper in an Afro. It was indisputable from trial testimony that when Cooper escaped from the California Institute of Men his hair was in tight braids, just as it was that his hair was in cornrows when he checked into the hotel in Tijuana the day the murders were discovered. On another level, the "bushy hair" references underlined what the young, frightened boy had told his psychiatrist, Dr. Lorna Forbes, in trying to explain to her how he had moved away from saying his attackers were three Mexican men to now only recalling seeing "a big puff of hair" in his parents' bedroom. As he told her in 1984, "Oh, I really thought it was them [three Mexican men], but after a while I saw on television that it was Cooper."

"Judge Huff allowing Josh to make an impact statement was totally gratuitous," Hile said. "What is the reason for doing that when considering a petition of innocence other than to provoke sympathy for the victims and make the execution of Cooper more palatable?"

At the close of the hearings, Judge Huff broke with tradition by announcing she was denying all claims asserted in Cooper's habeas petition. Normally, a federal district judge, if for no other reason than for demonstrating the pretense of judicial consideration, does not reveal the ultimate ruling until months after concluding evidentiary hearings.

On May 31, 2005, she issued a one-hundred-fifty-nine page ruling denying Cooper's habeas petition, attaching pictures of the attractive Ryen family and one of a smiling Chris Hughes to the final page of her ruling. There was no judicial reason to attach the photos. The ruling stated:

PETITIONER IS ON DEATH ROW BECAUSE HE IS THE PERSON WHO BRUTALLY CHOSE TO SLAUGHTER A FATHER, A MOTHER, AND TWO CHILDREN IN THE SANCTITY OF THE RYEN HOME, AND LEAVE ANOTHER CHILD BARELY CLINGING TO LIFE. THE POST-CONVICTION DNA TESTING HAS CONFIRMED PETITIONER'S GUILT, AND THE COURT REJECTS PETITIONER'S CLAIMS ON THE MERITS. AFTER HAVING CONDUCTED MITOCHONDRIAL DNA AND EDTA TESTING, REVIEWED THE PARTIES'

PAPERS, HEARD TESTIMONY FROM FORTY-TWO EXPERT WITNESSES, RE-
VIEWED NUMEROUS EXHIBITS, CONSIDERED THE PRIOR RECORD, AND
LISTENED TO THE PARTIES' ORAL ARGUMENTS, THE Court DENIES
Petitioner's PETITION...ON ALL GROUNDS.

At the end of her written ruling, Judge Huff took the unusual step of declaring she would not agree to certify any of Cooper's claims for appeal to the Ninth Circuit Court of Appeals. This was tantamount to rubbing salt in the wound because the rules governing the filing of a certificate of appealability require the petitioner to first file with the district court. It is only after the district court denies certifying any of the claims presented in the certificate of appealability that the petitioner is allowed to proceed to the appeal court. Cooper's attorney dutifully did file certificate with the district court, and Judge Huff quickly denied it.

CHAPTER FORTY-NINE

Oral Arguments

On *October 3, 2005,* Cooper's attorneys at Orrick filed a certificate of appealability with the Ninth Circuit Court of Appeals, requesting the court to certify eight separate claims Judge Huff had denied and refused to certify for further appeal. A month later, the Ninth Circuit agreed to certify all claims and informed Cooper's attorneys that the court considered the certificate of appealability to be its opening brief on appeal.

The Ninth then invited the California Attorney General's Office to respond. The attorney general filed a brief in opposition and attorneys at Orrick filed a reply brief. This set the stage for a three-judge panel of the Ninth to hold oral arguments on the claims certified for appeal.

Because Judges Pamela Rymer, James Browning, and Ronald Gould had heard Cooper's stay of execution appeal in 2004 – denying it two-to-one with Judge Browning dissenting – they would have been the three judges to hear this appeal, but Judge Browning's advanced age led the chief judge to replace him with Judge Margaret McKeown. It was Judge Browning's eleventh- hour efforts to rally other judges on the Ninth to grant Cooper a stay of execution and grant his habeas petition that landed the case in Judge Huff's courtroom.

Judge Rymer, who wrote the denial of Cooper's habeas petition and stay of execution in 2004, was appointed to the Ninth Circuit Court of Appeals by President George H.W. Bush in 1989. In 1964 she was director of research and analysis for the Goldwater for President Committee.

Both Judges Gould and McKeown were appointed to the Ninth Circuit by President Clinton; Judge Gould in 1999 and Judge McKeown 1998.

Two days before oral arguments were set to begin in San Francisco on January 9, 2007, Judge Rymer, in her role as presiding judge for the oral arguments, informed counsel for both sides that the arguments would be conducted by video conference. It would be the first time in the history of the Ninth Circuit Court that oral arguments were to be heard without any of the three judges present in person.

Norm Hile of Orrick, representing Cooper, drove down from Sacramento and Holly Wilkens of the California Attorney General's Office, representing the state, flew in from San Diego.

Oral arguments have a hidebound tradition of their own and serve a unique and distinct purpose in the justice system. By the time three appellate judges are ready to conduct oral arguments, they have received and reviewed hundreds of pages of briefs from opposing counsel. They know what the briefs state. What they want opposing counsel to do is to narrow the issues the judges must decide and to answer questions for which they seek clarification. Opposing counsel do not actually give presentations per se; they engage in a spirited debate with the three judges.

Judge Rymer's decision to conduct the arguments by video conference undermined the entire importance of the proceedings. The message she sent was that she was too busy to give Cooper's request for yet another successive habeas petition the attention it deserved. If that particular day had been inconvenient for her or one of the other judges to be present in San Francisco, it would have been a simple matter to reschedule the arguments.

With Judge Rymer in chambers in Pasadena, Judge Gould in chambers in Seattle, and Judge McKeown in chambers in San Diego, the plan was to show the three judges on a large TV screen divided into four sections that was set up below the courtroom's bench: one section for each judge and one section for the counsel who had the floor.

Interest in the proceedings caused the large ceremonial courtroom at the James R. Browning U.S. Courthouse to be packed with more than one-hundred observers; to accommodate the overflow, a separate video feed was piped into the courthouse's cafeteria.

As the clerk got everyone in position and the TV screen came on, only two judges were visible. The feed from Judge Rymer's chambers malfunctioned, leaving her to participate by disembodied voice via her cell phone.

The awkward proceedings and technical glitches left Cooper's attorney Norm Hile, feeling "somewhat disoriented" having "to argue to a TV set. It certainly felt strange and not appropriate in a death penalty case. It just felt like we weren't getting due process. They [the judges] weren't really paying attention."

Argument via videoconference, particularly when Judge Rymer could not be seen, "denies lawyers the nonverbal cues they get from the judges when the judges and the attorneys are assembled in the same location," Professor Arthur Hellman of the University of Pittsburgh told a reporter from the *Los Angeles Times* who called the legal scholar for comment on the Cooper proceedings.

Videoconferencing oral arguments is a trend that Duke University law professor Erwin Chemerinsky also finds "disturbing" for the same reason. "The interaction among the participants is just different when everyone is there, as opposed to when some or all are present electronically," he told the *Los Angeles Times*.

The Ninth Circuit Court chief judge at the time, Mary M. Schroder, told the *L.A. Times*, "I was at the courthouse in San Francisco on Tuesday, and I was very surprised and concerned when I learned all three judges were on video," something Judge Rymer did not run by her for approval. "I don't think this is going to happen again," she said.

For Cooper, though, it did happen and the results of the oral arguments were more than predictable; they seemed foreordained.

On December 4, 2007, a three-judge panel of the Ninth Circuit unanimously upheld Judge Huff's denial of Kevin Cooper's request for a successor habeas corpus. Judge McKeown's concurrence read more like a dissent. She found merit in a number of Cooper's claims but felt restrained by the provisions of the Anti-Death Penalty and Terrorism Act.

I CONCUR IN THE OPINION BUT AM TROUBLED THAT WE CANNOT, IN KEVIN COOPER'S WORDS, RESOLVE THE QUESTIONS OF HIS GUILT "ONCE AND FOR ALL…"

SIGNIFICANT EVIDENCE BEARING ON COOPER'S CULPABILITY HAS BEEN LOST, DESTROYED OR LEFT UNPURSUED, INCLUDING, FOR EXAMPLE, BLOOD-COVERED COVERALLS BELONGING TO A POTENTIAL SUSPECT WHO WAS A CONVICTED MURDERER, AND A BLOODY T-SHIRT, DISCOVERED ALONG THE ROAD NEAR THE CRIME SCENE. THE MANAGING CRIMINALIST IN CHARGE OF THE EVIDENCE USED TO ESTABLISH COOPER'S GUILT AT TRIAL WAS, AS IT TURNS OUT, A HEROIN ADDICT, AND WAS FIRED FOR STEALING DRUGS SEIZED BY THE POLICE. COUNTLESS OTHER ALLEGED PROBLEMS WITH THE HANDLING OF EVIDENCE AND THE INTEGRITY OF THE FORENSIC TESTING AND INVESTIGATION UNDERMINE CONFIDENCE IN THE EVIDENCE...

DESPITE THE PRESENCE OF SERIOUS QUESTIONS AS TO THE INTEGRITY OF THE INVESTIGATION AND EVIDENCE SUPPORTING THE CONVICTION, WE ARE CONSTRAINED BY THE REQUIREMENTS OF THE ANTI-DEATH PENALTY AND EFFECTIVE TERRORISM ACT OF 1996…

IN LIGHT OF THIS DEMANDING STATUTORY BARRIER, I AGREE THAT COOPER HAS FAILED TO QUALIFY FOR RELIEF…

THE HABEAS PROCESS DOES NOT ACCOUNT FOR LINGERING DOUBT OR NEW EVIDENCE THAT CANNOT LEAP THE CLEAR AND CONVINCING HURDLE OF AEDPA. INSTEAD, WE ARE LEFT WITH A SITUATION IN WHICH CONFIDENCE IN THE BLOOD SAMPLE [A-41] IS MURKY AT BEST, AND LOST [THE BLUE SHIRT], DESTROYED [FURROW'S COVERALLS], OR TAMPERED EVIDENCE [THE TAN T-SHIRT] CANNOT BE FACTORED INTO THE FINAL ANALYSIS OF DOUBT. THE RESULT IS WHOLLY DISCOMFORTING, BUT ONE THAT THE LAW DEMANDS.

CHAPTER FIFTY

Judge Fletcher's Dissent

Twelve days after the three-judge panel of the Ninth Circuit Court upheld Judge Huff's denial of Cooper's habeas petition, Cooper's attorneys filed a petition for rehearing and a suggestion for rehearing en banc with the Ninth Circuit Court of Appeals. The fact that the petition was filed so soon after the release of the ruling was in compliance with the federal rules of appellate procedure that mandate such a filing within fourteen days.

En banc requests are rejected ninety-five percent of the time, and usually within a month or so of their filing. But this one seemed to take on a life of its own. Month after month passed with no response from the Ninth Circuit. The delay bespoke how divided the appeal court had become over the Cooper case.

A vote of the active, non-recused judges of the circuit court decides en banc requests. To prevail, a petitioner must garner a majority of the votes. In this case, that meant fourteen affirmative votes among the twenty-seven judges voting. The judges cast their ballots in secret. The circuit court only reveals whether the request passed or failed. It withholds divulging how any particular judge voted.

On March 25, 2009, then California Attorney General Jerry Brown tried to break the exceptionally long, unprecedented impasse by petitioning the court for its decision. On May 11, 2009, after almost a year and a half of delay, the Ninth denied to hear Cooper's petition en banc. Although the Ninth did not release the final vote tally, the vote to deny Cooper's petition was apparently razor thin, failing by one or two of the fourteen required.

That same day, Ninth Circuit Court Judge William Fletcher filed his meticulously detailed one-hundred-three-page dissent. Four judges signed it. Three other judges wrote supporting dissents. In all, eleven judges dissented. Only Judge Pamela Ann Rymer, the presiding judge at Cooper's oral arguments, wrote a concurrence of the denial.

Judge Fletcher began his dissent, "The State of California may be about to execute an innocent man."

To Judge Fletcher, the primary reason for remanding the case to federal district court was to conduct EDTA testing of the tan T-shirt to determine if Cooper's blood had been planted on it and to perform mitochondrial DNA testing of the hairs clutched in Jessica Ryen's hands.

Back in May of 2001, Cooper and the State of California entered into an agreement to conduct joint nuclear DNA testing on various pieces of evidence, using a recently developed ProFiler DNA test on each item. The state had strongly objected to Cooper's request to have new DNA testing done on any of the forensic evidence the prosecution used to win his conviction, but the California General Assembly passed a law allowing death row inmates access to such tests earlier that year. Cooper, in fact, became the first death row inmate to utilize the new law.

Cooper and the state agreed to have the Department of Justice Lab run the ProFiler tests on a hand-rolled cigarette butt, a Viceroy cigarette butt, a hatchet, hairs recovered from the victims' hands, a tan T-shirt, a blood-stained chip labeled "A-41," and a bloody button. All of the items except for the tan T-shirt and the hairs found in the victims' hands were entered into evidence at Cooper's trial by the prosecution and used to convict him.

When the report summarizing the findings of the DNA tests was released in September of 2002, it stated that there was "strong evidence" that Cooper's DNA was located on the bloodstain labeled "A-41," the three blood smears taken from the tan T-shirt, and both the Viceroy and the hand-rolled cigarette butts.

The most startling finding was the presence of Cooper's DNA on the tan T-shirt. When the San Bernardino County Sheriff's Department lab had tested it in 1983 the results showed that all the blood on it was consistent with only Doug Ryen's serological profile. At Cooper's trial, his attorney, not the prosecution, entered the tan T-shirt into evidence as part of its claim that someone other than Cooper was responsible for the attack at the Ryens' house. The shirt was clearly not prison-issued and no one at the Lease house where Cooper holed up had ever seen it before. The bartender at the Canyon Corral Bar had testified that one of the three men who entered the bar on the night of the murders had worn a T-shirt similar to it.

Cooper's blood now being detected on the tan T-shirt proved to Cooper and his attorneys that someone had planted his blood on the shirt. The EDTA testing ordered by the en banc Ninth Circuit Court for the federal district court to supervise was supposed to be the defense's opportunity to prove gross tampering.

To Judge Fletcher, Judge Huff's handling of the EDTA and hair tests undermined any opportunity the defense had to establish Cooper's innocence.

"There's no way to say this politely," Judge Fletcher wrote in his dissent. "The district court failed to provide Cooper a fair hearing and flouted our direction to perform the two tests."

In a separate dissent written by Judge Kim McLane Wardlaw, she stated that "[T]hrough a series of errors accurately described by Judge Fletcher in his dissent, the district court precluded Cooper from having his last day in court."

On the first page of his dissent, Judge Fletcher began to detail just how Judge Huff went about scuttling Cooper's opportunity to for anything resembling a fair evidentiary hearing:

...THE DISTRICT COURT IMPEDED AND OBSTRUCTED COOPER'S ATTORNEYS AT EVERY TURN AS THEY SOUGHT TO DEVELOP THE RECORD. THE COURT IMPOSED UNREASONABLE CONDITIONS ON THE TESTING THE EN BANC COURT DIRECTED; REFUSED DISCOVERY THAT SHOULD HAVE BEEN AVAILABLE AS A MATTER OF COURSE; LIMITED TESTS THAT SHOULD NOT HAVE BEEN LIMITED; AND FOUND FACTS UNREASONABLY, BASED ON A TRUNCATED AND DISTORTED RECORD.

THE MOST EGREGIOUS, BUT BY NO MEANS THE ONLY EXAMPLE, IS THE TESTING OF COOPER'S BLOOD ON THE T-SHIRT FOR THE PRESENCE OF EDTA...THE DISTRICT COURT SO INTERFERED WITH THE DESIGN OF THE TESTING PROTOCOL THAT ONE OF COOPER'S SCIENTIFIC EXPERTS REFUSED TO PARTICIPATE IN THE TESTING. THE DISTRICT COURT ALLOWED A STATE-DESIGNATED REPRESENTATIVE TO HELP CHOOSE THE SAMPLES TO BE TESTED FROM THE T-SHIRT. THE COURT REFUSED TO ALLOW COOPER'S SCIENTIFIC EXPERT TO PARTICIPATE IN THE CHOICE OF SAMPLES. INDEED, THE COURT REFUSED TO ALLOW COOPER'S EXPERTS TO EVEN SEE THE T-SHIRT.

THE STATE-DESIGNATED LAB OBTAINED A TEST RESULT SHOWING AN EXTREMELY HIGH LEVEL OF EDTA IN THE SAMPLE THAT WAS SUPPOSED TO CONTAIN COOPER'S BLOOD. IF THAT TEST RESULT WAS VALID, IT SHOWED THAT COOPER'S BLOOD HAD BEEN PLANTED ON THE T-SHIRT, JUST AS COOPER MAINTAINED.

A CAREFUL ANALYSIS OF THE EVIDENCE BEFORE THE DISTRICT COURT STRONGLY SUGGESTS THAT THE RESULT OBTAINED BY THE STATE-DESIGNATED LAB WAS VALID. HOWEVER, THE COURT ALLOWED THE STATE-DESIGNATED LAB TO WITHDRAW THE TEST RESULT ON THE GROUND OF CLAIMED CONTAMINATION IN THE LAB. THE COURT REFUSED TO ALLOW ANY INQUIRY INTO THE ALLEGED CONTAMINATION. THE COURT REFUSED TO ALLOW COOPER'S EXPERTS TO REVIEW THE BENCH NOTES OF THE STATE-DESIGNATED LAB. THE COURT THEN REFUSED TO ALLOW FURTHER TESTING OF THE T-SHIRT, EVEN THOUGH SUCH TESTING WAS FEASIBLE.

Judge Fletcher clearly stated his suspicion that state agents framed Cooper at trial and continued to do as he fought to prove his innocence. "There is a strong likelihood that the results of the blood tests performed on A-41, presented at trial, were false evidence," he wrote. "There is also a strong likelihood that state actors tampered with A-41 to ensure that it would generate inculpatory results when Cooper's post-conviction DNA testing was conducted in 2002."

He pointed out that A-41 "has had a disturbing pattern of being 'consumed' in the testing, and then reappearing in a form that could be subjected to further testing." He detailed how criminalist "Gregonis had initially used so much of the limited sample (or so he said) that when the parties finally did joint testing, they were forced to place the remaining flakes of white paint in a liquid solvent to dissolve any remaining blood. The sample was so small that their test results were largely inconclusive. All the chips that had had any traces on blood on them were discarded."

Judge Fletcher then recounted how A-41 would make one final appearance to damn Cooper.

IN AUGUST 1999, GREGONIS CHECKED A-41 OUT OF THE EVIDENCE STORAGE ROOM FOR ONE DAY. WHEN COOPER'S POST-CONVICTION DNA TESTING TOOK PLACE IN 2002, A "BLOODSTAINED PAINT CHIP" AND "BLOOD DUST" HAD INEXPLICABLY, AND CONVENIENTLY, APPEARED IN THE A-41 CANISTER. THE BLOOD ON THAT CHIP WAS TESTED, AND COOPER'S DNA WAS FOUND.

THE APPEARANCE OF A BLOOD-STAINED CHIP IN 2002 IS, TO SAY THE LEAST, SURPRISING, GIVEN THAT GREGONIS HAD TESTIFIED AT TRIAL THAT IN THE OCTOBER 1984 TESTING OF A-41 THEY HAD PROCESSED AND DISCARDED ALL THE PAINT CHIPS WITH BLOOD ON THEM.

IN THE 2004-2005 HABEAS PROCEEDING, COOPER REQUESTED EDTA TESTING OF A-41. WITHOUT TAKING EVIDENCE ON THE FEASIBILITY OF TESTING ANY REMAINING A-41 FOR THE PRESENCE OF EDTA, THE DISTRICT COURT REJECTED COOPER'S REQUEST.

As for the other pieces of evidence the prosecution used to win Cooper's conviction – the shoe prints from the Pro-Keds, the cigarette and tobacco from the Ryens' station wagon, the hatchet sheath and button from the bedroom Cooper used – Judge Fletcher was equally dubious, considering it highly likely that they too had been planted to frame Cooper.

In the summary of his dissent, Judge Fletcher stated:

THE EN BANC [OF THE NINTH CIRCUIT] PANEL GRANTED PERMISSION
TO FILE A SECOND OR SUCCESSIVE APPLICATION FOR HABEAS CORPUS
BASED ON A PRIMA FACIE SHOWING THAT THE STATE VIOLATED *BRADY*
IN NOT PROVIDING TO COOPER WARDEN MIDGE CARROLL'S INFORMATION
ABOUT THE TENNIS SHOES ISSUED BY THE PRISON. NOW, AFTER THE
2004-2005 DISTRICT COURT HEARING, WE KNOW THAT THERE WERE
NUMEROUS *BRADY* VIOLATIONS. FIRST, THE STATE VIOLATED *BRADY*
BY NOT PROVIDING WARDEN CARROLL'S INFORMATION.

SECOND, THE STATE VIOLATED *BRADY* BY NOT PROVIDING A COPY OF
THE DISPOSITION REPORT WITH DEPUTY SCHRECKENGOST'S INITIALS
ON IT, AND BY NOT PRESERVING AND MAKING AVAILABLE LEE FURROW'S
BLOODY COVERALLS.

THIRD, THE STATE VIOLATED *BRADY* BY NOT PROVIDING A COPY
OF THE SBCSD DAILY LOGS SHOWING [CITIZEN LAURA] EPLER'S CALL
REPORTING THAT SHE HAD FOUND A BLUE SHIRT, AND BY NOT PRESERV-
ING AND MAKING THE SHIRT AVAILABLE.

GIVEN THE WEAKNESS OF THE EVIDENCE AGAINST COOPER, IF THE
STATE HAD GIVEN COOPER'S ATTORNEYS THIS EXCULPATORY EVIDENCE
IT IS HIGHLY UNLIKELY THAT COOPER WOULD HAVE BEEN CONVICTED.
THUS, BASED ON THE STATE'S *BRADY* VIOLATIONS, COOPER WOULD BE
ABLE TO MAKE A SHOWING OF ACTUAL INNOCENCE…

In his conclusion, Judge Fletcher referenced the horrible murders
inflicted on the Ryens and Chris Hughes, the traumatized life Josh Ryen
has lived, and the grief of the Hughes's family. He then ended his dissent
by writing:

…THE CRIMINAL JUSTICE SYSTEM HAS MADE THEIR NIGHTMARE EVEN
WORSE.

SAN BERNARDINO COUNTY SHERIFF'S DEPARTMENT INVESTIGATORS
WERE CONFRONTED WITH A HORRIFYING MULTIPLE MURDER, FAR WORSE
THAN ANY THAT HAD PREVIOUSLY OCCURRED IN THE COUNTY. THEY HAD
AN OBVIOUS SUSPECT, AS ESCAPED PRISONER WHO HAD STAYED FOR TWO
DAYS AT A HOUSE 125 YARDS AWAY FROM THE MURDER VICTIMS. THEY

WERE UNDER HEAVY PRESSURE FROM THE NEWS MEDIA FROM THE VERY
FIRST MOMENT OF THEIR INVESTIGATION. THEY DREW WHAT SEEMED,
AT THE BEGINNING, A SENSIBLE CONCLUSION — THAT KEVIN COOPER,
THE ESCAPED PRISONER, WAS A MURDERER…

ONCE SBCSD INVESTIGATORS DREW THAT CONCLUSION, THEY MANIPU-
LATED AND PLANTED EVIDENCE IN ORDER TO CONVICT COOPER. IN THE
COURSE OF THEIR INVESTIGATION, THEY DISCOUNTED, DISREGARDED,
AND DISCARDED EVIDENCE POINTING TO OTHER KILLERS. THEIR
DECISION TO CLOSE THEIR EYES EARLY IN THE INVESTIGATION TO
THE POSSIBILITY THAT SOMEONE OTHER THAN KEVIN COOPER MIGHT BE
GUILTY HAS LED US TO THE SITUATION IN WHICH WE FIND OURSELVES
TODAY.

UNFORTUNATELY, THE DISTRICT COURT MADE THINGS WORSE. AFTER
OUR EN BANC PANEL GRANTED COOPER PERMISSION TO FILE A SECOND
HABEAS APPLICATION, THE DISTRICT COURT OBSTRUCTED AND IMPEDED
COOPER AND HIS LAWYERS IN ALMOST EVERY WAY IMAGINABLE.

KEVIN COOPER HAS NOW BEEN ON DEATH ROW FOR NEARLY HALF
OF HIS LIFE. IN MY OPINION, HE IS PROBABLY INNOCENT OF THE
CRIMES FOR WHICH THE STATE OF CALIFORNIA IS ABOUT TO EXECUTE
HIM. IF HE IS INNOCENT, THE REAL KILLERS HAVE ESCAPED. THEY
MAY KILL AGAIN. THEY MAY ALREADY HAVE DONE SO.

WE OWE IT TO THE VICTIMS OF THIS HORRIBLE CRIME, TO KEVIN
COOPER, AND TO OURSELVES TO GET THIS ONE RIGHT. WE SHOULD
HAVE TAKEN THIS CASE EN BANC AND ORDERED THE DISTRICT JUDGE
TO GIVE COOPER THE FAIR HEARING HE HAS NEVER HAD.

In a concurrence to Judge Fletcher's dissent, Judge Stephen Reinhardt wrote that the judicial failures his colleague enumerated were not "solely those of the district court. Our own handling of the matter…leaves much to be desired and is a cause of considerable regret. There is no purpose, however, to looking backward at this point. What matters is that we have an obligation to afford Kevin Cooper a full and fair judicial hearing, and that once again we fail. By denying en banc review, we add to the prior systemic judicial malfunctions, and this time, we do under a cloak of secrecy."

Judge Reinhardt wanted, as he has in the past, for the en banc vote to be public so that the public would know where each of the twenty-seven judges stood. Other than the votes against granting Cooper another habeas petition cast by Judges Rymer, McKeown, and Gould, it is not known who else voted that way. Four judges, Harry Pregerson, Reinhardt, Richard Paez, and Johnnie Rawlinson, signed Fletcher's dissent. In addition, Judges Reinhardt wrote a separate dissent. So did Judges Kim Wardlaw and Raymond Fisher. Judge Wardlaw's dissent was signed by Judges Pregerson, Reinhardt, Sidney Thomas, and Marsha Berzon. Judge Fisher's dissent was signed by Chief Judge Alex Kozinski, Judges Pregerson, Susan Graber, and Berzon. In all, eleven judges were on record for Cooper. Of those, all but Chief Judge Kozinski, who was appointed in 1985 by President Reagan, had been appointed by Democrat presidents.

According to Judge Reinhardt, the vote was actually closer that the known eleven dissents would indicate and that making the vote public would show that. Making the vote public would allow not just the public, but also the legal community, fellow judges, and those who appoint judges to better gauge "our performance on the bench." He said public disclosure was particularly important in a case like this one where a man's life is at stake.

"Kevin Cooper may or may not be guilty, but serious flaws in our legal system have been exposed. Whether to go en banc or not is a matter of judicial discretion. An en banc review by our court would surely do no harm. Nor would revealing the names of those who agree and disagree with affording this capital defendant a final protection before sending him on his way to execution by the state," the judge ended his concurrence.

At Gonzaga University School of Law on April 12, 2010, Judge Fletcher delivered the inaugural Justin L. Quackenbush lecture on the subject of the death penalty, holding that the problems with the administration of it are widespread and endemic rather than merely regional or local. To illustrate he cited the Kevin Cooper case, stating "The case I am about to describe is horrible in many ways. The murders were horrible. Kevin Cooper, the man now sitting on death row, may well be – and in my view probably is – innocent. And he is on death row because the San Bernardino Sheriff's Department framed him."

Judge Fletcher, a Rhodes Scholar who roomed with Bill Clinton at Oxford University, said what happened in the Cooper case "is a familiar story. It is by no means the usual story. But it happens often enough to be familiar. The police are under heavy pressure to solve a high profile crime. They know, or think they know, who did the crime. And they plant evidence to help their case along."

CHAPTER FIFTY-ONE

Kevin Cooper's Future

With all of his appeals exhausted and the State of California intent on resuming executions, Kevin Cooper's future is in grave doubt.

Clearly the best hope for Cooper would be for a court to order new testing of both the A-41 blood sample from the Ryens' house, the tan T-shirt, the hairs on the victims that have never been tested, and to get to the cause of the contamination in the vial of Cooper's blood that is known to contain the DNA of at least one other person.

In a state court filing, Orrick lawyers took that step, asking Superior Court Judge Kenneth K. So to allow more sophisticated nuclear DNA testing of A-41, the tan T-shirt, and the vial of Cooper's blood. The filing also requested testing of any sweat residue on the T-shirt, particularly in the armpit areas, to see if that DNA excluded Cooper. The filing stated that such tests were still needed because Judge Huff had sabotaged the testing of the tan T-shirt and had refused to allow any testing of A-41 or the vial of Cooper's blood.

On January 14, 2011, Judge So denied Cooper's request for any further testing. In issuing his ruling, the judge echoed Judge Huff, writing that the evidence of Cooper's guilt was such that there "is no practical significance from performing additional nuclear DNA testing on the requested items..."

If his lawyers at Orrick are unable to come up with any new grounds upon which to base yet another request for a federal habeas petition and an execution date is set, Cooper's next best hope for survival would rest with Governor Jerry Brown in the form of a clemency petition.

308 J. PATRICK O'CONNOR

"Unless he [Cooper] can present new evidence and can show under AEDPA (the Anti-Terrorism and Effective Death Penalty Act) that he could not have discovered through the exercise of due diligence, Kevin will be executed when California resumes executions," Norm Hile said in a 2011 interview. "In other words, even if new evidence comes to light that proves he is innocent, or that he was framed, he could be denied habeas corpus relief if the courts think he should have discovered it earlier. Moreover, he must convince the court by 'clear and convincing evidence that, but for constitutional error, no reasonable fact finder would have found him guilty.'"

Despite these imposing legal hurdles, Hile said Orrick was committed to continue to "investigate every lead and witness we can, hoping to find someone to come forward with new evidence of innocence or prosecution misconduct. To that end, we've retained a private investigator to re-examine all evidentiary leads. Short of new evidence, the only remaining avenue Kevin has is through the clemency petition to the governor."

There are four other death row inmates, who like Cooper, have exhausted all of their appeals. Execution dates for two of those inmates were set: one in February of 2006 and the next not until September of 2010. Both were halted due to legal challenges in federal court over the administration of the so-called "three-drug cocktail" the state intended to use in the executions. Lawyers for the inmates argued successfully that the use of the three-drug cocktail constituted "cruel and unusual punishment" and as such was a violation of the U.S. Constitution's Eighth Amendment that specifically prohibits that.

The controversy over the lethal injection protocol continued well into 2012 and showed no signs of reaching a swift resolution. U.S. District Court Judge Jeremy Fogel had set June of 2011 for an evidentiary hearing into the challenge, but on March 28, 2011 the lawyers for the death-row inmates and the state filed a joint stipulation with the court postponing that hearing until November of 2011. A year later, government lawyers agreed to another postponement that will push any court resolution of the issue off until 2013.

Several months before this postponement, Judge Fogel, after five years at the center of the lethal injection controversy, accepted appointment as director of the Federal Judicial Center in Washington, D.C., effective September 1, 2011. U.S. District Judge Richard Seeborg picks up where Fogel left off. A former federal prosecutor and magistrate judge in San Jose, Judge Seeborg was appointed to a federal judgeship by President Obama in 2009. In reporting on Judge Fogel's reassignment, the *San Jose Mercury News* said, "The [lethal injection] case is expected to be on hold through the end of this year, as state prison officials work to put a new execution team in place at San Quentin and lawyers finish the wrangling over remaining issues to be resolved in a hearing."

With the Morales and Brown court challenges effectively halting California's legal right to conduct executions using the three-drug cocktail, it will now be up to Judge Seeborg to determine if the state's next execution protocol complies with constitutional mandates forbidding cruel and unusual punishment. The U.S. Supreme Court ruled in 2008 that the three-drug cocktail in and of itself was not unconstitutional. What has made the challenges to it such a roadblock to the California Department of Corrections and Rehabilitation is the administering of it by untrained, non-medically certified personnel. It remains doubtful any certified medical practitioner would agree to participate in taking the life of a human being. The question that obtains is will the state be able to put together an execution team that can qualify as competent without any medical personnel involved.

If, and when, Judge Seeborg rules to allow state executions to resume in California, execution dates for Cooper and the other four inmates would be set. There is no way to know what order those five inmates would be scheduled for execution, but in the past the governor, attorney general, and state district attorneys have used the date of conviction as a way to establish the pecking order. If that practice were followed, Cooper would be fourth in line.

If an execution date were set for Cooper, his lawyers at Orrick would submit a wide-ranging clemency petition to Governor Jerry Brown. Clemency, in the United States, is the final fail-safe for correcting miscarriages of justice that occurred, but went uncorrected, in the judicial process.

The clemency power in the United States derives from the English establishment of the "Royal Pardon," whereby kings and queens of England from time to time forgave crimes against the Crown. The pardoning tradition was carried over to the American colonies and vested in the royal governors.

Article II Section 2 of the U.S. Constitution provides that the president of the United States "shall have the power to grant reprieves and pardons for offenses against the United States, except for impeachment. The president may only pardon those convicted of federal crimes. Likewise, the various states have constructed assorted processes for the granting of clemency with regard to state law crimes.

The California Constitution vests the power to grant clemency solely with the governor unless the petitioner is a two-time felon, as Kevin Cooper is. For Governor Brown to grant clemency in Cooper's case he would need to obtain a majority approval of the justices on the California Supreme Court – that would mean approval from four of the seven justices.

Clemency is comprised of three executive options: A pardon, a reprieve, and a commutation. A pardon legally absolves a person of his conviction and sentence; a reprieve stays a sentence for a short period of time; a commutation is a reduction in sentence. These options vest the governor with wide discretion to craft a just result. For example, a governor of California may grant a "conditional pardon" that orders the state to either retry the petitioner within a certain time period or set the petitioner free.

Before Governor Schwarzenegger left office, Norm Hile of Orrick sent the governor a letter dated November 23, 2010 asking him to commute Cooper's sentence to life in prison without the possibility of parole in recognition of the large amount of evidence that had surfaced since Schwarzengger's 2004 clemency denial. "As one of your final acts as governor, you have the opportunity to commute the death sentence of Kevin Cooper and thereby prevent a grave injustice. Mr. Cooper is condemned to death based on a trial that violated almost every notion of our state's and country's sense of justice," Hile wrote.

Andrea Lynn Hoch, the governor's legal affairs secretary, responded by asking Hile to file a formal clemency petition, which he did on December 17, 2010.

The clemency petition that Hile filed on behalf of Cooper noted several striking developments that had come to light in the interim, including:

• That the San Bernardino County Sheriff's Department recovered a blue shirt with blood on it near the crime scene the day after the murders were discovered in 1983, but that shirt was never disclosed to the defense, and it now is missing;

• That blood taken from Cooper after he was arrested, and which was used to convict him, was contaminated with the DNA of another person;

• That three witnesses the prosecution never interviewed, who came forward in 2004, saw three white men the night of the murders in a bar near the crime scene and two of the men had blood on them;

• That Midge Carroll, the warden of the prison from which Cooper escaped, testified in 2004 that prosecutors presented false evidence at Cooper's trial regarding the origin of tennis shoes the prosecution claimed could have only come from that prison.

• That a sheriff's deputy lied at Mr. Cooper's trial in 1983 when he testified that he acted on his own when he destroyed the bloody coveralls turned in by a woman who said her boyfriend, a convicted murderer, had come home in them the night of the Chino Hills murders.

Hile's clemency request to the outgoing governor was the subject of numerous media reports in the weeks leading up to the governor's leaving office on January 2, 2011. Nicholas D. Kristof in *The New York Times* and Allen Desrhowitz and David Rivkin in the *Los Angeles Times* wrote impassioned Op-Ed columns in support. In addition, the *LA Times, San Francisco Chronicle* and *Sacramento Bee* published editorials calling on the governor to act to spare Cooper's life.

On his final day in office, the governor, through his legal affairs secretary, wrote to Hile:

At this time there is no execution date set for inmate Cooper. A request for clemency is an extraordinary request and requires serious consideration. In this case, the clemency application raises many evidentiary concerns which deserve a thorough and careful review of voluminous records. Such an extraordinary request needs more than two weeks of attention.

Accordingly, Governor Schwarzenegger will not act on this clemency application. The clemency filings and exhibits will remain in the Governor's Office for consideration by Governor-elect Brown.

The letter from the Governor's Office, even if it did nothing to improve Cooper's current status, represented a tectonic shift in attitude toward Cooper's case. Governor Schwarzenegger had moved from his "unequivocal" belief in Cooper's guilt in 2004 to now stating that Cooper's clemency application "raises many evidentiary concerns which deserve a thorough and careful review of voluminous records."

With Governor Brown now in office, the full range of clemency options available to a petitioner such as Cooper is back on the table: an outright pardon, a conditional pardon or a commutation of sentence. In addition to all the new evidence indicating Cooper's innocence contained in his last clemency petition to Governor Schwarzenegger, there is the unprecedented division among the judges of the Ninth Circuit Court of Appeals that speaks to the unfairness of the judicial proceedings that failed to exonerate Cooper. Clemency is called the final "fail-safe" remedy to correct precisely this type of error.

Governor Brown, just as his father, Governor Pat Brown before him, has shown a strong aversion to the death penalty. During Jerry Brown's first term as governor, the California Legislature re-enacted the death penalty in 1977 over Brown's veto. His appointment of Rose Bird as chief justice of the California Supreme Court that year accomplished what his veto failed to do: With Chief Justice Bird and several other like-minded justices Brown appointed, the California Supreme Court vacated all sixty-one death sentences brought to the court on appeal. For her blatant opposition to the death penalty, Rose Bird became the most controversial chief justice in state history and during her time in office the most controversial politician in the state. She survived several spirited efforts to recall her, but was ousted by voters in 1986, along with two other Brown appointed-justices, after Governor George Deukmejian, a Republican, led an aggressive pro-death-penalty campaign against her. Rose Bird and the other two justices, Cruz Reynoso and Joseph Grodin, were the only justices ever turned out of office by California voters.

When Jerry Brown was first elected governor in 1975, he was, at age thirty-seven, the sixth youngest governor in California history, winning election just eight years after his father left the office. From the start, the former Jesuit seminarian and Yale Law School graduate began fashioning his own legacy. Rather than move into the newly constructed Governor's Mansion in Sacramento, he rented a small, sparsely furnished apartment in downtown, not far from the Capitol and slept on the floor. Instead of being driven around in a chauffeured limousine, he drove a Plymouth sedan. More buzz engulfed him when he began dating rock star Linda Ronstadt. An off-hand remark she made during an interview in *Rolling Stone,* led *Chicago Sun-Times* columnist Mike Royko to dub him "Governor Moonbeam."

When Brown defeated former eBay executive Meg Whitman in November of 2010 to win back the governor's office, he was, at seventy-two, the oldest person ever elected governor in the state's history.

The previous four years he had served as the state's attorney general. During the campaign for that office, he pledged to uphold all the state's laws, including the death penalty. It would be Attorney General Brown who would try to break the impasse at the Ninth Circuit Court of Appeals when Kevin Cooper's request for a successive habeas corpus petition was being considered en banc; and it would be Attorney General Brown who moved to resume capital punishment in 2006 with the execution of Albert Greenwood Brown.

During his eight years as governor, 1975-1983, there were no executions in California and thus no capital clemency petitions filed for him to consider. Based on his appointment of Rose Bird as chief justice and his vetoing the death penalty statute the State Legislature enacted in 1977, it would be fair to speculate that Governor Brown, no longer constrained by the requirements of being the state's attorney general and chief law enforcement officer, would be open to the possibility of clemency, particularly in a case such as Kevin Cooper's.

In an editorial board interview at the *Sacramento Bee* in late September of 2010, Brown told the editors that he would "prefer a society that didn't have to use the death penalty." But the Associated Press reported that Brown, as a 1992 Democratic presidential candidate, said he was "morally opposed" to state executions, though he also said it was an issue for states to decide.

Two aspects of the clemency petition for Cooper could be quite compelling for Governor Brown to consider. The first is the extraordinary number of Ninth Circuit Court of Appeal judges who are on record in the form of dissents saying the justice system had violated Cooper's constitutional rights and that he may well be innocent. The second is that Cooper has proclaimed his innocence from the day he was arrested. Contrary to popular belief, only a minuscule number of death row inmates in the United States claim actual innocence. One of the last to do so in California was Caryl Chessman, who was executed in 1960 while Brown's father was governor.

One subtle factor working in Cooper's favor is California's schizophrenic relationship with the death penalty since the U.S. Supreme Court ruled in 1976 that it may be constitutionally applied. Although California has by far the most inmates on death row – just over seven hundred men and fourteen women at the end of 2011 – it has only executed thirteen death row inmates – all men – since the state reenacted the death penalty in 1977. In that interim, seventy-two condemned inmates died in prison, twelve by suicide; several were murdered in the prison yard reserved for death row inmates. An article published in 2006 by Professors Carol and Jordan Steiker categorized all death penalty states as falling into two categories – executing states and symbolic states. Symbolic states retain the death penalty, but largely refrain from using it. Texas was a prime example of an executing state while California, dating from 1977 clearly fell into the symbolic category.

For a bellwether state such as California to still be classified as a death-penalty state is an anomaly. In March of 2011, Illinois became the sixteenth state to abolish the practice when Governor Pat Quinn signed the bill the state legislature passed earlier in the year. At a news conference at the Capitol in Springfield, Governor Quinn said signing the bill was the most difficult decision he had to make as governor but that he had concluded "…after looking at all the evidence I have received, that it is impossible to create a perfect system – one that is free of all mistakes."

Shari Silberstein, the executive director of the anti-capital punishment group called Equal Justice USA, saw the Illinois abolition as "…a real turning point in the conversation about the death penalty in the United States."

Another phenomenon is in the works that may moot Cooper's execution. Various anti-death penalty groups in California, including Death Penalty Focus that is led by activist Mike Farrell of "M*A*S*H*" fame, are planning to place an anti-death-penalty initiative on the ballot in 2012. If that initiative were to pass, all death row inmates' sentences would be commuted to life without the possibility of parole.

California began state executions in 1893 when Jose Gabriel was hanged at San Quentin. From then until 1972, when the California Supreme Court ruled the death penalty to be a violation of the state's constitution prohibiting "cruel and unusual punishment," the machinery of death worked with regularity: nearly eight hundred men and four women were executed.

That same year, the U.S. Supreme Court ruled in *Furman v. Georgia* that the death penalty violated the "cruel and unusual punishment" provision of the Eighth and Fourteenth Amendments of the U. S. Constitution. In a five-to-four ruling, the court found the imposition of the death penalty on William Henry Furman was arbitrary and capricious and no doubt tinged with racism. (Furman, a black man, was convicted of accidentally shooting to death a member of a white household while he was in the process of burglarizing the home.)

The 1972 California Supreme Court ruling overturning the death penalty commuted the sentences of one-hundred-seven death row inmates to life sentences with the possibility of parole. Charles Manson and Sirhan Sirhan were among those spared the gas chamber.

Over the next four years, sixty-eight more convicted men were sent to death row at San Quentin. In 1976, the California Supreme Court ruled again that the death penalty was unconstitutional, commuting all of those sentences to life without the possibility of parole.

Later in 1976, the U.S. Supreme Court ruled in a case entitled *Gregg v. Georgia* that the death penalty in and of itself is not a violation of the Eighth Amendment if safeguards were put in place as has been by the Georgia Legislature. Georgia's new statute provided for a penalty phase at the trial that allowed the defense to present mitigating circumstances in an attempt to persuade the jury not to condemn the convicted defendant to death. Also included in the new statute were automatic state appeals. Justice Potter Stewart, writing for the seven-to-two majority, stated capital punishment did not violate the Eighth Amendment as long as the punishment was "proportional to the severity of the crime." In its new statute, Georgia had eliminated all crimes but murder as reason to impose the death penalty.

The next year, the California Legislature re-enacted the death penalty. Like Georgia's revised law, the statute allowed for the introduction of mitigating circumstances during the penalty phase of the trial; it was amended later that same year to include the sentence of life without the possibility of parole in capital cases.

Fifteen years would elapse before California carried out its next execution in San Quentin's gas chamber. During the hiatus, two death row inmates were exonerated by the courts and set free: Jerry Bigelow in 1988, after eight years; and Patrick Croy in 1990, after eleven years. (In 1996, Troy Lee Jones became the last man to be exonerated from California's death row, after serving fourteen years.)

In 1994, the California Supreme Court ruled the gas chamber was "cruel and unusual punishment," establishing lethal injection as the only means of execution.

In 1996, William Bonin, dubbed "The Freeway Killer," by *Orange County Register* reporter J.J. Maloney, was the first to die by lethal injection. Ten years would pass before California executed Clarence Ray Allen, the gang leader for whom Lee Furrow murdered seventeen-year-old Mary Sue Kitts in 1974 to prevent her from testifying against him. Allen would be the last to be executed in California, leaving more than 700 awaiting execution, including "The Night Stalker," Richard Ramirez; "Dating Game Killer" Rodney Alcala; serial killer Randy Kraft; and pregnant-wife murderer Scott Peterson.

What placed all those executions on hold was a ruling by U.S. District Court Judge Jeremy D. Fogel, staying the execution of Michael Morales in February of 2006. (Morales admitted to the brutal rape and murder of seventeen-year-old Terri Winchell in 1981, claiming he was high on PCB at the time.) Morales's attorneys, the high-powered Kenneth W. Starr and David A. Senior of McBreen & Senior, argued that the lethal injection procedures deployed by the state violated the Eighth Amendment's proscription against "cruel and unusual punishment."

A week before the scheduled execution, Judge Fogel ruled that the state would have to modify its lethal injection procedures, accepting the defense claim that the three-drug cocktail used could cause excruciating pain to the condemned man.

The lethal injection protocol consists of three separate dosages. The first is the barbiturate, sodium thiopental, that functions as an anesthetic. The next drug is pancuronium bromide; it acts to paralyze the muscle system and stop the person from breathing. The last drug is a dose of potassium chloride that stops the heart. The combination of the three drugs causes an anesthetic overdose, resulting in death by respiratory and cardiac arrest.

The problem with the three-drug cocktail, which is used in almost all of the thirty-four states that impose the death penalty, is that if an insufficient amount of the sodium thiopental is administered, the condemned person may reawaken during the eleven or more minutes it takes for death to occur. While awake, the condemned person would experience wrenching pain from having his breathing and heart stopped.

In an attempt to remedy this possibility, Judge Fogel ordered the state to have two anesthesiologists in the death chamber to advise the execution team and to intervene by administering additional barbiturates if Morales were to awaken during the execution or appeared to be experiencing pain.

The state complied by enlisting two unidentified anesthesiologists. Just hours before the scheduled execution, both of the anesthesiologists backed out, citing ethical grounds. In a written statement released the next day, the two doctors said, "Any such intervention would clearly be unethical."

"I don't know of any other case where a physician has sat through and ordered an increased drip of whatever," said Richard Dieter, director of the Death Penalty Information Center. "That seems to be participation in the execution."

The American Society of Anesthesiologists issued a statement praising California doctors for refusing to take part in the execution. "To the credit of the state's medical community, California was unable to come up with alternate anesthesiologists to participate in the grisly procedure."

Undeterred and determined to execute Morales that day before his execution order lapsed at midnight, the state returned to Judge Fogel's courtroom later that day and obtained his permission to execute Morales at 7:30 p.m. The judge stipulated that Morales be given just one drug, five grams of sodium thiopental, a lethal overdose of the anesthetic.

To avoid the problem of not having an anesthesiologist on hand to supervise the execution, the judge ordered that the anesthesia be directly administered in the death chamber straight into Morales's veins by a "licensed medical professional." Because no one had ever been executed in this fashion, it was not known how long it would take for the overdose to kill Morales, but estimates gauged the process would take up to forty-five minutes or four times as long as the three-drug cocktail.

The death protocol the judge set up was macabre. The judge ruled that the medical professional administering the injection could wear "appropriate clothing to protect their (sic) anonymity." As the World Socialist Web Site reported, "One can envision, according to this scenario, a masked or hooded doctor approaching the condemned prisoner with the loaded syringe."

Two hours before the scheduled execution, a deputy attorney general informed Judge Fogel that the execution had been cancelled. A spokesperson for San Quentin said the state "was not able to find any medical professional willing to inject medication intravenously, ending the life of a human being."

Following the stay of Morales's execution, Judge Fogel ruled to suspend executions in California, effectively imposing a moratorium on executions until the state developed an effective death protocol and made extensive improvements to the poorly lighted, cramped, and antiquated death chamber that had formerly housed the gas chamber. The assignment to develop the new execution protocol and improve the death chamber was turned over to the California Department of Corrections and Rehabilitation. As a matter of course, the state's Office of Administrative Law would have to sign off on the new protocol before it could become effective. A state court also ruled that the protocol developed by the department would be subject to public review and comment before becoming effective.

Improving the death chamber was something the department was capable of accomplishing. At an expense of $853,000 a new "execution center" was constructed at San Quentin – one hundred yards from the gas chamber – that contains eleven white, cinder block rooms. The death center included a viewing room for up to thirty officials and media to witness future executions through glass windows. Separate viewing rooms were provided for the family of the victim(s) and the family of the condemned inmate. A secluded holding cell for the inmate to spend his last six hours alive in was constructed just off the death chamber that contains a phone and a flat-screen television, without cable TV. A small room next to the holding cell was provided for the inmate's attorney or spiritual adviser.

The death chamber itself is Spartan, although it is both brighter and much roomier than the gas chamber. At over two-hundred square feet, it is more than four times the size of the old death dungeon. Hexagonal in shape, it contains only a gurney covered with a green vinyl sheet overlaid with five black nylon straps that have metal clasps. A large Elgin clock ticks away above the gurney.

Behind the death chamber is a control center where the masked execution team concocts the lethal cocktail that will be sent through tubes into the death chamber through two holes in the wall on either side of the gurney.

With the new death center clearly ready to pass muster, the California Department of Corrections and Rehabilitation proposed new lethal injection procedures in early 2010. The proposed protocol, which continued to contain the three drug-cocktail, generated twenty thousand comments from the public, the great majority of which were negative. In addition, the proposed new procedures were rejected by The California Office of Administrative Law on the basis that several passages were unclear. The function of the Administrative Law Office is to ensure that agency regulations are clear, necessary, legally valid, and available to the public. The office is responsible for reviewing administrative regulations proposed by over two-hundred state agencies for compliance with the standards set forth in California's Administrative Procedure Act, for transmitting these regulations to the Secretary of State and for publishing regulations in the California Code of Regulations.

The next month, the American Board of Anesthesiologists, representing forty-thousand doctors, stated it would revoke the certification of any member who participated in an execution by lethal injection.

Amid the controversy and debate surrounding the lethal injection protocols, the California Office of Administrative Law accepted the clarifications added by the Department of Corrections and Rehabilitation and the state adopted the department's protocols on August 29, 2010 even though the protocols continued to stipulate the use of the three-drug cocktail. This immediately freed superior court judges to assign new execution dates and a judge in Riverside County acted to set Albert Greenwood Brown's execution date for September 29, 2010 at 12:01 a.m.

On September 24, 2010, Judge Fogel attempted to end the moratorium on executions by authorizing Brown's execution, now just five days away. (Brown was convicted of raping and strangling to death fifteen-year-old Susan Jordan in 1980. He also taunted her parents afterwards.)

Judge Fogel, who is based in San Jose, ruled that Brown could avert the potential for pain inherent in the three-drug cocktail by opting for a one-drug overdose of the anesthetic sodium thiopental. The judge noted that Ohio and Washington State had used the one-drug protocol on nine executions without reported problems. In essence, Judge Fogel was attempting to skirt the continuing controversy of the three-drug cocktail by allowing Brown to opt for execution by anesthetic.

One of Brown's attorneys, John R. Grele, appealed for relief to the Ninth Circuit Court of Appeals. The Ninth agreed to stay Brown's execution, ruling that Judge Fogel's clearing the way for Brown's execution was in error because it placed an undue burden on Brown to select his own means of execution, something another one of his lawyers, David Senior, said he refused to do.

The Ninth's ruling not only postponed Brown's execution, but it had the effect of postponing any future executions in California for at least several more months because the state's supply of sodium thiopental expired that same week. The three-judge panel of the Ninth Circuit took sharp exception to the fact that the state was attempting to execute Brown before its supply of sodium thiopental expired. "It is incredible to think that the deliberative process might be driven by the expiration date of the execution drug," the panel wrote in its ruling. In his order staying Brown's execution, Judge Fogel wrote that he "was blindsided" by the state's eleventh hour admission about the drug's expiration date.

To complicate matters further, the sole U.S. drug company that manufacturers the anesthetic, Hospira Inc. of Lake Forest, Illinois, had made it clear it does not want its products used in executions. "The drug is not indicated for capital punishment, and Hospira does not support its use in this procedure," the company said in a statement in September of 2010.

With Hospira a reluctant supplier of sodium thiopental, California prison officials, according to records obtained by the Associated Press, tried unsuccessfully to get private doctors to procure the anesthetic. The state also struck out with dozens of hospitals and general surgery centers, VA hospitals, and the Federal Bureau of Prison. The state even explored getting the drug from Pakistan.

Like Arizona a few months previously, California prison officials then turned to the U.S. Food and Drug Administration for assistance in obtaining the anesthetic from overseas suppliers. The AP uncovered documents showing that the FDA assisted both states "obtain a quick overseas source of a hard-to-find execution drug [sodium thiopental] even as the agency declared it would not regulate or block imports, records show."

The AP article quoted California prison officials saying the FDA released a supply of the drug from England during the first week of January, 2011. The report was based on a court filing the department submitted, stating California had obtained five-hundred-twenty-one grams of sodium thiopental from a company based in England. The filing said the supply, which cost California $36,415, was sufficient to execute nearly one-hundred condemned inmates. The drugs received have an expiration date of 2014. When the state might next try to use the drug in an execution was left up in the air. State officials, enjoined against conducting executions by Judge Fogel, have agreed not to reschedule any more executions until the resolution of a federal law suit challenging the constitutionally of the state's lethal injection protocol is resolved by Judge Fogel.

The FDA refused to comment on its role in assisting either Arizona or California obtain the new supply of sodium thiopental. Providing a foreign drug to be used in state executions was an odd role for an agency commissioned to oversee drug safety in the United States. One of the FDA's roles is to give prior approval to any drug imported to the United States. A spokesperson for the agency, Christopher Kelly, attempted to explain away this conflict by stating, "Reviewing substances imported or used for the purpose of state-authorized lethal injection clearly falls outside of FDA's explicit public health role." In other words, death row inmates are not a part of the agency's public health mandate.

The ACLU's Northern California chapter accused the agency of hypocrisy. "The FDA is actively assisting these states, but they're not enforcing the law, and they're not doing anything to determine that the drugs are what they're claimed to be and that they work properly," according to Natasha Minkser, the chapter's death penalty policy director.

The very point that Minkser made was advanced in a law suit pending in federal court in Arizona. The suit contends that the sodium thiopental obtained by the state from a company in England "may be substandard and could lead to botched executions if they don't render an inmate properly unconscious," the AP reported. The supplier for both California and Arizona was Archimedes Pharma of Great Britain.

Once it became known that a British company was supplying sodium thiopental to prisons in Arizona and California, a nonprofit, anti-penalty group based in England – called Reprieve – filed suit in London challenging foreign shipments of the drug. Shortly after the suit was filed, the British government announced plans to ban thiopental exports to prisons to underscore its "moral opposition to the death penalty." *The Wall Street Journal* reported that the entire European Union, following Great Britain's lead, was considering banning the export of any drug for use in capital punishment.

Amid this negative background, Hospira announced on January 21, 2011 its decision to terminate production of sodium thiopental. In a front page article, *The Wall Street Journal* reported that Hospira's decision was a result of "a broad global campaign by opponents of the death penalty."

"The move by Hospira Inc. came after months of pressure by activists through a new campaign aimed at pressuring pharmaceutical companies whose products are used in lethal injections," the *Journal* reported. "The final decision came in the face of opposition from government figures in Italy, whose Constitution prohibits the death penalty, after Hospira announced plans to shift production of the drug to a plant in Italy."

It is not known how the state will overcome the hurdles blocking any future executions, but it is known the state is determined to do so. It is also known that anti-death penalty forces in California will work hard to thwart any reinstatement of state-sanctioned and state-conducted executions. The expenditure of nearly $1 million in taxpayer money for the new death center at San Quentin speaks to the state's commitment, particularly during a time of financial crisis that has already caused severe budget cutbacks in numerous state programs. With a budget deficit of $26 billion at the end of 2010, the state was in the midst of its greatest financial crisis in history with no clear way out. Will it continue to make sense, in these times of budget austerity, for the state to spend $184 million a year to incarcerate death row prisoners and litigate their protracted post-conviction appeals in state and federal courts compared to the $11 million it would cost to place the seven-hundred death row inmates in the general prison population with sentences of life without the possibility of parole?

A study of capital punishment costs in California since the state reinstated the death penalty in 1978 revealed the state had spent more than $4 billion on capital punishment, or about $308 million for each of the 13 executions performed during that period.

"Executing the Will of the Voters: A Roadmap to Mend or End the California Legislature's Multi-Billion Death Penalty Debacle," was written by Ninth Circuit Court of Appeals Judge Arthur L. Alarcon and Loyola Law School professor Paula M. Mitchell.

The three-year study, released in June of 2011, predicted the cost for continuing capital punishment would rise to $9 billion by 2030.

The *Los Angeles Times* reported on several of the study's findings:

• The state's seven-hundred-fourteen death row prisoners cost $184 million more per year than those sentenced to life in prison without the possibility of parole.

• A death-penalty prosecution costs up to twenty times as much as a life-without-parole case.

• The least expensive death penalty trial costs $1.1 million more than the most expensive life-without-parole case.

• Jury selection in a capital case runs three to four weeks longer and costs $200,000 more than in life-without-parole cases.

• The state pays up to $300,000 for attorneys to represent each capital inmate on appeal.

• The heightened security practices mandated for death-row inmates added $100,663 to the cost of incarcerating each capital prisoner last year, for a total of $72 million.

The *Times* reported that the study provided three options for voters to curb the escalating costs and infrequent executions: "fully preserve capital punishment with about $85 million more in funding for courts and

SCAPEGOAT   325

lawyers each year; reduce the number of death-penalty-eligible crimes for an annual savings of $55 million; or abolish capital punishment and save taxpayers about $1 billion every five or six years."

The study by Judge Alarcon and Professor Mitchell was similar in its findings to those advanced in 2008 by the bipartisan California Commission on the Fair Administration of Justice, chaired by former California Attorney General John Van de Kamp. None of that commission's remedies were adopted by the state legislature.

Things might be different this time as Governor Brown and the General Assembly grapple with a new age of austerity in government spending. From the time he resumed the governor's office, Jerry Brown has demonstrated a determination to cut the state budget. In March of 2011 the state legislature approved his partial budget plan that knocked $9.6 billion off the state's deficit. Deep cuts in public education expenditures, in programs for the poor, and the elimination of thousands of state jobs drove that budget. In May of 2011, Governor Brown proposed the elimination of more than forty state boards, commissions and task forces, cuts that would pare another five-thousand-five hundred jobs from the state payrolls.

The prospect of saving the state $1 billion every five or six years by abolishing capital punishment would seem to mesh with the governor's overall thrust to eliminate "inefficient" deployments of state resources.

A precursor to what might be in store for capital punishment in California occurred on April 28, 2011 when Governor Brown canceled a controversial plan promoted by Governor Schwarzenegger to construct a new death row at San Quentin. The new building, which anticipated a rapidly growing death row population, would have increased cell capacity from seven-hundred to 1,152. The projected cost was $356 million. Governor Brown said it was "unconscionable" to spend massive amounts of money on a new death row while making major budget cuts in scores of other state services.

"At a time when children, the disabled and seniors face painful cuts to essential programs, the state of California cannot justify a massive expenditure of public dollars for the worst criminals in our state," the governor said. "California will have to find another way to address the housing needs of condemned inmates."

For Kevin Cooper, who turned fifty-four years old on January 8, 2012 and has spent half of his life on death row, the state's determination to kill him for crimes he did not commit is no different than San Bernardino County's pinning the Ryen/Hughes murders on him. It is no different to him than Federal Judge Huff's sham of conducting evidentiary hearings the Ninth Circuit Court ordered to determine if the state framed him. It is simply the final part of the same endless loop of a nightmare that began when, running away once too often, he learned in Tijuana, Mexico that he was wanted for questioning in connection with the most horrific murders in San Bernardino County history.

—David Negus retired from the San Bernardino County Public Defender's Office in 2004, at age sixty-one, after spending his entire thirty-year career there. After the Cooper trial, he became chief of its West Valley branch and in 1992 headed up the newly created Death Penalty Unit, a clearinghouse for coordinating capital cases for indigent defendants. He left trial work in 2001 to become the assistant public defender, an administrative post.

—Dennis Kottmeier retired as the district attorney of San Bernardino County in 1994 after twenty-five years in the D.A.'s Office. He went into private practice, but soon abandoned that when he found he could not "stomach representing defendants...who lied all the time." He quit practicing law and became a law professor at Cal State in San Bernardino. In 2004 he ran for the San Bernardino Superior Court. A month before the election, Cooper was granted a stay of execution by the Ninth Circuit Court of Appeals. "I don't think the stay was related to my losing so badly. I lost big time," the former district attorney said.

—Dr. Mary Howell, Peggy Ryen's mother, was forced into retirement in 2006 after practicing chiropractics for fifty-four years. Cellulitis, a bacterial infection on her legs, disabled her the last two years of her life. She died on Memorial Day, May 26, 2008, at age ninety-three from complications brought on by septicemia, an inflammatory response to the infection in her legs.

In 2000 she appeared on a "48 Hours" segment entitled "A Grandmother's Mission," where she told interviewer Erin Moriarty she did not accept that one person could have killed her family and Chris Hughes. "I still can't believe that one person could do all that to my family...My family didn't stand in line and say 'I'm next.' Peggy was strong. Doug was strong... Peggy was a fighter. Doug was an MP in the Marines."

Dr. Howell told Moriarty that she wanted the state to allow Kevin Cooper the tests he contended would prove his innocence. "I'll never be satisfied till they give the DNA test, and let's prove it one way or the other. I want to know why my family was killed. Who did it. And I don't want to die without knowing it."

—Josh Ryen lived with his grandmother on her horse ranch in Temecula until well into his twenties. For high school, he attended a military academy. He worked as an independent contractor in the housing construction industry; his specialty is crafting spiral staircases. Like his father, he is an avid surfer. He returned to Temecula to live with and take care of his grandmother during the final two years of her life. In the local obituary for his grandmother, Josh was listed as her only relative.

—Diana Roper died on August 14, 2003 at her home in Mentrone. She was forty-six. Her death certificate listed her cause of death as cardiovascular disease and morbid obesity; her occupation as bus driver. She, too, appeared on the same segment of "48 Hours" as Dr. Howell. She called Lee Furrow "an evil, evil man," mentioned his missing tan T-shirt and his bloody coveralls that she turned in and the sheriff's department destroyed.

—Lee Furrow moved to the Philadelphia, Pennsylvania, area in the early 1990s. There he married Renee DeStephano and lived with her in Upper Darby. He worked periodically as a handyman and for a while taught shop at a high school for troubled students. He separated from his wife and teenage daughter in 2010 and moved back to Southern California.

—The medical examiner, Dr. Irving Root, died on June 28, 1995.

—Superior Court Judge Richard C. Garner died on August 2, 2008 in San Diego at age 83.

—Sergeant Billy Arthur, the lead detective, died of a heart attack in 1992. After Cooper's conviction, Arthur did slide presentations of the Ryen crime scene to demonstrate to rookie deputies how not to control a crime scene.

—Former Sheriff Floyd Tidwell has two new hips and a new wife and is going strong in the high desert in Phelan, in the Victor Valley of the Mojave Desert, north of the San Gabriel Mountains.

—William Baird, the acting manager of the San Bernardino County Sheriff's Department Crime Lab, was fired shortly after Cooper's trial concluded in 1985 for stealing five pounds of heroin. Like Sheriff Tidwell, Baird had his own pipeline to the property room at the sheriff's department. Instead of guns, he was stealing significant quantities of heroin from the evidence lockers. He admitted he stole the heroin to supply his own addiction and to sell it back to drug dealers for profit. The five pounds he was caught stealing had a street value of over $150,000.

Baird would not be prosecuted. "The Sheriff's Department screwed up the case on purpose so he could never be tried, so he was just fired," said former San Bernardino County D.A. Dennis Kottmeier, the lead prosecutor at Cooper's trial, when asked in 2010 about Baird's drug thefts.

Baird was the deputy who developed the two most important pieces of evidence linking Cooper to the crime scene: a lone drop of Cooper's blood – A-41 – he testified that he had spotted on a wall down the hallway from the Ryens' bedroom and by matching a bloody shoeprint lifted from a bed sheet in the Ryens' master bedroom to a pair of Pro-Keds Dude tennis shoes he had requisitioned from the California Institute of Men. The prosecution made these two "discoveries" the centerpiece of its evidentiary case against Cooper.

Baird currently works for the Kennewick Columbia River Nuclear Hydro Electric facility, a federal government installation in Kennewick, Washington.

—Daniel Gregonis's career as a criminalist for the San Bernardino County Sheriff's Department sailed on. In 2001 he was elected president of the California Association of Criminalists. On March 28, 2008, shortly after resigning from the San Bernardino County Sheriff's Department Crime Lab to take a similar post as criminalist at the Los Angeles County Sheriff's Department Crime Lab, Gregonis received the San Bernardino County Sheriff's Department Frank Bland Medal, a lifetime achievement award named in honor of a former sheriff.

In reporting on the award, the *Press-Enterprise*, a newspaper head-quartered in Riverside, said the award cited Gregonis for his role in the conviction of Kevin Cooper in 1985. The article said that Gregonis "used a then-new protein typing system to determine a blood type from a small stain in a home where a man had killed three members of a Chino Hills family and a houseguest.

"The blood type led to the arrest and conviction of Kevin Cooper, who has been sentenced to death. Gregonis then went on to develop the department's DNA work, which cracked many cold cases, officials said.

"If there is such a thing as a most valuable player in the Scientific Investigation Division, it is Dan,' read the department's script announcing the award."

At the time Gregonis was receiving the Frank Bland Medal, the San Bernardino County Sheriff's Department was unaware that a case Gregonis had been instrumental in providing evidence that led to a murder conviction was less than a year-and-a-half away from tarnishing its "most valuable player."

When William Richards returned home from work on the night of August 10, 1993, he found his wife, Pamela Richards, brutally murdered in the yard of their secluded Hesperia, California, home. Mrs. Richards had been severely beaten with fist-sized rocks and manually strangled. Her assailant had used a large cinder block to crush her head.

Prosecutors for San Bernardino County charged Richards with first-degree murder. His first two trials ended in hung juries and the next one in a mistrial. On their fourth attempt in 1997, prosecutors finally got the conviction. A jury sentenced Richards to twenty-five years to life. The two pieces of evidence the prosecutor introduced to convince the jury of Richards's guilt were a bite mark on Mrs. Richards's hand and one tuft of fiber found in a tear in one of her fingernails.

In 2001, the California Innocence Project at the Western School of Law in San Diego took up Richards's case. Over the next eight years its investigation ran DNA tests on a hair removed from one of Mrs. Richards's fingernails and some blood on the murder weapon. The results excluded Richards as his wife's killer. Forensic experts hired by the California

Innocence Project found that the bite mark on Mrs. Richards's hand was similar to other injuries on her body and that the shape of those injuries matched tools found at the crime scene. The bite mark was not a bite mark.

What project investigators found out about the tuft of fiber was jaw-dropping. Shortly after her autopsy, the coroner took various photos of Mrs. Richards's corpse, including her hands. The photos clearly revealed that no fibers were present in her fingernails. A few days later, the coroner severed some of Mrs. Richards's fingers and sent them to Daniel Gregonis at the San Bernardino County Sheriff's Department Crime Lab for testing.

Gregonis had a video made of himself in the crime lab that showed him removing a rather large, light-blue tuft of fibers from a crack in the fingernail of one of the severed fingers. The tuft contained fifteen fibers.

At a habeas hearing before San Bernardino County Superior Court Judge Brian McCarville, attorneys for the California Innocence Project argued that the fiber evidence "may have been falsified by someone employed by the county." Professor Justin Brooks, director of the California Innocence Project, told the court that "the fiber evidence was critical to Richards's conviction and it was not present on Pamela's fingernail when it was initially examined."

Defense attorneys also presented the DNA evidence excluding Richards and expert testimony that the bite mark was actually made by a tool.

In reversing Richards's conviction on August 10, 2009, Judge McCarville said the new evidence presented points "unerringly to innocence." The exoneration came sixteen years to the day of Pamela Richards's murder.

"In my twenty years of handling post-conviction cases in California, I have never seen a case that went wrong on as many levels as the William Richards's case," said Professor Jan Stiglitz, the founder of the California Innocence Project and the attorney who presented the closing argument that led to Richards's exoneration. "From the inadequate crime scene work, to the failure to investigate other suspects, to the use of false evidence – this is a conviction that never should have happened."

Richards's exoneration was short-lived. On November 19, 2010 the California Court of Appeals for the Fourth District vacated Judge McCarville's ruling. In doing so, Associate Judge Thomas Hollenhorst ruled that the bite mark and hair evidence presented before Judge McCarville was "supplementary," not new. Because he viewed it as supplementary, he ruled that it could not be considered as exoneration evidence. Finally, without specifically explaining why the blue fibers were not present in autopsy photos, the court rejected such evidence as clearly demonstrating innocence.

The California Supreme Court, on December 28, 2010, agreed to hear Richard's appeal of Judge Hollenhorst's ruling, specifically stating it would review Richards's claim that false evidence was introduced at his trial by the state's expert witness.

—The $10 million wrongful death suit Bill and Mary Ann Hughes filed in 1984 in Los Angeles Superior Court against various state agencies came to an end in 1985 when the California Supreme Court upheld the lower court's rejection of the suit on the grounds of government immunity.

—Lori Stahl, the teenager who claimed Cooper kidnapped and raped her after he escaped from Mayview State Hospital outside Pittsburgh, Pennsylvania, filed a damage suit against the state mental hospital shortly after Cooper's indictment in Ontario. The hospital settled the suit out of court.

December 20, 1970: Doug and Peggy Ryen marry.

November 9, 1972: Jessica Ryen born in Olympia, Washington.

September 5, 1975: Josh Ryen born in Santa Ana, California.

Late 1975: The Ryen family moves to Chino Hills.

1977: Kevin Cooper imprisoned for burglary in Pennsylvania.

1982: Cooper released from prison.

Later in 1982: Cooper arrested for a string of burglaries in Pittsburgh, Pa. and sent to Mayfield State Prison for mental evaluation prior to sentencing. There he steals the driver's license of fellow inmate David Anthony Trautman.

October 8, 1982: Cooper escapes from Mayfield State Hospital.

Late 1982: Cooper moves in with new girlfriend in Hollywood, California.

January of 1983: Cooper, using the Trautman alias, arrested for burglary in Los Angeles.

3-21-83: He pleads guilty to two burglaries.

April 19, 1983: Cooper, under the name David Trautman, is sentenced to four years.

April 29, 1983: Cooper arrives at the California Institute of Men under the name David Trautman.

June 1, 1983: He is placed in minimum-security section of CIM.

June 2, 1983: Cooper escapes CIM.

June 2, 1983: Cooper holes up in vacant house directly below the Ryens' hilltop house for next two days.

June 4, 1983: Before 9 p.m. he leaves hideout house and hitchhikes to Mexico border.

June 4, 1983: Doug and Peggy Ryen, their 10-year-old daughter, Jessica, and 11-year-old houseguest, Christopher Hughes, are brutally murdered around midnight. The Ryens' 8-year-old son, Josh, is left for dead with his throat slashed. The Ryens' station wagon is stolen.

June 5, 1983: Cooper enters Tijuana in the morning, steals a purse from a woman that contains over $100 in quarters, and checks into a downtown hotel that afternoon.

June 5, 1983: Bill Hughes, the father of Christopher Hughes, discovers the murders and finds Josh alive around 11 a.m. Josh is airlifted to Loma Linda University Hospital.

June 7, 1983: The district attorney orders the dismantling of the crime scene. Over the next two days all the blood-stained doors, walls, and furnishings have been removed to a warehouse.

June 7, 1983: A citizen finds a blood-stained blue shirt not far from Canyon Corral Bar.

June 7, 1983: Cooper's fingerprints are detected at the hideout house.

June 8, 1983: A blood-stained tan T-shirt and towel from Ryens' bathroom is found not far from the Canyon Corral Bar.

June 9, 1983: Cooper, now aware that he is wanted for questioning in connection with Chino Hills murders, travels by bus 70 miles south to Ensenada, Mexico. A man with a sailboat hires him to help him paint the boat in return for a food and a place to stay.

June 9, 1983: San Bernardino County Sheriff Floyd Tidwell names Cooper as lone assailant of Ryen/Hughes murders. The largest manhunt in California history is launched for the fugitive.

June 9, 1983: Diana Roper, believing her boyfriend may have been involved in the Chino Hills murders, turns over a pair of blood-stained coveralls to a sheriff's department deputy. She also tells the deputy that when her boyfriend returned to their house in the early a.m. of 6-5-83 he was no longer wearing a tan T-shirt

June 11, 1983: Ryens' station wagon is found in Long Beach, California.

July 31, 1983: Cooper arrested at Pelican Cove, 25 miles from Santa Barbara, on rape charge.

August 1, 1983: Cooper arraigned on four counts of first-degree murder, one count of first-degree attempted murder, and for escaping from prison.

August 11, 1983: At continuation of his arraignment, Cooper enters a plea of not guilty to all capital charges.

November 11, 1983 -- January 5, 1984: Preliminary hearing finds enough cause to try Cooper on all counts.

October 23, 1984: Cooper's trial opens in Superior Court in San Diego, with Judge Garner presiding.

February 19, 1985: Cooper found guilty on all counts after jury deliberates for over a week

February 22, 1985: Jury imposes death penalty after four days of deliberations that produced two deadlocks.

May 15, 1985: Judge Garner sentences Cooper to die in gas chamber.

May 21, 1985: Cooper enters death row at San Quentin.

May 6, 1991: California Supreme Court confirms Cooper's conviction.

December 16, 1991: U.S. Supreme Court declines to review Cooper's case.

August 11, 1994: Cooper files first habeas corpus petition with Federal District Court in San Diego.

April 24, 1996: U.S. Congress passes Anti-Terrorism and Effective Death Penalty Act that greatly reducing death-row inmates' access to relief from federal habeas corpus review.

August 25, 1997: U.S. District Court Judge Marilyn Huff denies Cooper's habeas corpus petition.

April 30, 1998: Cooper files second habeas corpus petition with Federal District Court in San Diego.

June 15, 1998: Judge Huff again denies habeas to Cooper.

2003: Superior Court Judge William Kennedy sets February 10, 2004 as Cooper's execution date.

January 20, 2004: Governor Arnold Schwarzenegger denies clemency to Cooper.

February 6, 2004: Cooper files petition for habeas corpus with the Ninth Circuit Court of Appeals.

February 8, 2004: A three judge panel of the Ninth denies Cooper's petition, 2-1.

February 9, 2004: Eight hours before Cooper's scheduled execution, the Ninth Circuit Court of Appeals, meeting en banc, issues Cooper a stay of execution and grants him another habeas corpus hearing.

April 2, 2004: Judge Huff opens the habeas corpus evidentiary hearings that will proceed intermittently for just over a year.

May 31, 2005: Judge Huff, in a 159-page ruling, denies all issues raised by Cooper's defense, invoking the severe restrictions of the Anti-Terrorism and Effective Death Penalty Act.

October 5, 2005: Cooper files request for a certificate of appealability with the Ninth Circuit Court of Appeals, requesting another habeas corpus proceeding. The next month, the Ninth certifies Cooper's claim for review by a three-judge panel of the Ninth Circuit Court of Appeals.

February, 2006: U.S. District Judge Jeremy Fogel suspends executions in California, ruling that the manner in which the state administers its lethal-injection protocol violates the Eight Amendment of the Constitution on the grounds of "cruel and unusual punishment."

January 9, 2007: A three-judge panel of the Ninth Circuit holds oral arguments on the certified claims.

December 4, 2007: By a unanimous 3-0 vote, the Ninth denies habeas to Cooper.

December 18, 2007: Cooper files a petition for rehearing en banc with the Ninth Circuit.

May 11, 2009: Ninth Circuit denies Cooper's en banc petition. Judge William Fletcher issues his dissent.

January 3, 2011: Jerry Brown inaugurated governor of California.

November 2, 2011: The California Attorney General's Office agreed to postpone its legal efforts to end the federal court's moratorium on executions until September of 2012, a move that will push back the scheduling of any executions until at least 2013.

In most instances throughout the book, sources are cited infra. Unless otherwise noted, descriptions of the crime scene and its aftermath are taken directly from the trial transcripts. The trial testimony of the various witnesses, including Kevin Cooper, is taken from the trial transcripts. The courtroom and in-chamber utterances of the attorneys and the judge are taken from the trial transcripts. All juror communications are taken from the trial transcripts.

FOREWORD
8. Since 1973: "Death Row Exonerations Point to Flaws in System," by Allison Bath, Jan. 24, 2010, citing the three most prevalent reasons for exonerations: prosecution withholding evidence favorable to the defendant; perjured jailhouse snitch testimony; and faulty eyewitness testimony at trial.

CHAPTER ONE
Information about San Bernardino County and Chino Hills was taken from Wikipedia and from the San Bernardino County and Chino Hills's web sites.
12. Over the preceding ten years: "Scudder's Dream Prison Becomes Chino Nightmare," Don Green, *Daily Report,* June 21, 1983.
12. Its first warden: "California Institution for Men: A Historical Perspective," by R. Palta, March 15, 2001.

CHAPTER TWO
15. Peggy had owned horses: Details about Peggy Ryen's background

are taken from in-person and telephone interviews conducted by the author in 2010-2011 with her half-sister, Lillian Shaffer.

16. For eighteen months: Letter from Dr. Lorna M. Forbes to California Department of Adoptions, June 6, 1985.

16. At one point: Ibid.

16. The hand-written letter: Letter from Peggy Ryen to Lillian Shaffer, December 27, 1973.

16. When the Ryens' neighbors: Dr. Forbes's letter to Department of Adoptions, June 6, 1985.

16. In another letter: Letter from Peggy Ryen to Lillian Shaffer, May 8, 1974.

17. "A gorgeous barn": Ibid

19: Around 9:30 p.m.: Various police interviews with Josh Ryen.

CHAPTER FOUR

23. "I thought, my God": *Daily Bulletin*, June 6, 1983.

24. "as a number of loose hairs": Coroner's report.

25. the killings were in no way "ritualistic": *Daily Report*, June 6, 1983.

CHAPTER FIVE

28. "another Manson defense possible": Author interview with Dennis Kottmeier, June 7, 2010.

CHAPTER SIX

32. Doug's sister, Cindy Settle: Author interview with Cindy Settle, October 15, 2010.

32. Other tidbits that popped out: Deputy Dale Sharp's report, June 7, 1983.

33. According to the office manager: Detective Tim Wilson's report, June 15, 1983.

33. Asked by Wilson: Ibid.

33. "The lady was quite upset": Deputy Dale Sharp's report June 7, 1983.

33. "I received information": Detective Mike Hall's report, June 8, 1983.

34. Hall asked her why: Ibid.

34. The Ryens' clinic: Detective Tim Wilson's report, June 15, 1983.

34. In May of 1984: Sergeant Billy Arthur's interview of Caryn Rhiner, May 21, 1984.

34. Peggy Ryen originally hired her: Ibid.

35. Arthur's first substantive question: Ibid.

35. The issue of the dogs: Ibid.

36. Larry Lease, who lived four-hundred yards down the road: "Ryens Characterized as Jolly and Good-Natured," *Daily Report*, June 7, 1983.

36. "No, but they were real good": Arthur's interview with Caryn Rhiner, May 21, 1984.

36. Although, according to Rhiner: Ibid.

36. Doug's drinking was something: Ibid.

37. Arthur also wanted to ask: Ibid.

37. The big question: Ibid.

C<small>HAPTER</small> S<small>EVEN</small>

39. This possibility was soon: Detective Tim Wilson's interview of Linda Edwards, June 7, 1983.

39. Further down Peyton Road: Lieutenant Knadler's report, June 7, 1983.

40. Two hours after Josh: Sergeant Rick Roper's report, June 5, 1983.

40. The hatchet was: Ibid.

40. The next day, June 6: Police dispatch log dated June 6, 1983.

40. A sheriff's department log: Ibid.

41. On a cross-country trip: Author interview with Lillian Shaffer, March 30, 2010.

41. "Peg went to the closet": Ibid.

41. "The stallion reared up": Ibid.

41. "big and strong": Author interview with Cindy Settle, October 15, 2010.

C<small>HAPTER</small> E<small>IGHT</small>

43. On Saturday night, June 4: Detective Tim Wilson's report, June 7, 1983.

43. "May the force be with you": Ron Forbush interview with Pam Smith, May 12, 1984.

43. They ordered one round of beers: Detective Tim Wilson inter-

view of Kathy Royals, June 8, 1983.

43. One of the places Royals mentioned: Ibid.

44. A waitress there: Detective Phil Dana's interview of Mary Risi, June 8, 1983.

44. About three hours after: Detective Wilson's interview of Kathy Royals, June 8, 1983.

44. The manager of the bar: Deputy Curtis Lee Ward's interview of Shirley Killian, June 7, 1983.

44. "very tired": Ibid.

44. Killian made no notice: Ibid.

44. "larger than the average car": Ibid.

44. When Smith heard: Ron Forbush interview with Pam Smith, May 12, 1984.

CHAPTER NINE

47. Roper had come across: Detective Jim Stalnaker's interview of Diana Roper, May 18, 1984.

48. A few days after: Detective Stalnaker's interview of Diana Roper, May 14, 1984.

49. Roper had good reason: Ibid.

49. This prompted Roper to call her father: Ibid.

49. Roper also told Stalnaker: Ibid.

50. She told him Furrow: Ibid.

50. Furrow, now quite agitated: Detective Stalnaker's recording of phone call from Diana Roper on May 17, 1984.

51. "Jesus!": Ibid.

51. "I'll be honest with you": Ibid.

51. Stalnaker began the interview: Detective Stalnaker's report of his interview with Lee Furrow, May 17, 1984.

51. "an axe to grind with you.": Ibid.

52. Furrow told the detectives: Ibid.

52. "Did you hear, at all": Ibid.

52. "Cooper to you": Ibid.

35. Stalnaker now wanted to know: Ibid.

53. Sergeant Arthur now weighed in: Ibid.

53. "I don't know that a polygraph: Ibid.

Chapter Ten
55. The prison houses: *Daily Report*, June 11, 1983.
55. L.A. police subsequently: San Bernardino *Sun*, June 8, 1983.
56. Although Etzkorn notated: *Daily Report* article about California Attorney General John Van de Kamp's report concerning how Cooper was misevaluated by his probation officer and CIM prison officials.
56. Three days later: "Murder Suspect Slipped Through System," Fontana *Herald-News*, June 11, 1983.
56. As it turned out: San Bernardino *Sun*, June 8, 1983.
57. Several hours later: Fontana *Herald News*, June 11, 1983.
57. California's vaunted public school system, Wikipedia, "California Proposition 13 (1978)."
57. In the five years since Proposition 13: "Cuts Threaten Probation System," Associated Press report, July 4, 1983.
58. By 1983 at CIM: *Daily Report*, June 11, 1983.
58. The minimum-security section: Ibid.
58. When Cooper escaped on June 2: Ibid.
58. The State of California appealed the court order: *San Francisco Bay View*, May 23, 2011.
58. "County jail expansion does not solve the underlying problems": Ibid.

Chapter Eleven
59. Cooper had been running away: Author interview with Kevin Cooper, June 30, 2009.
64. For the hyper-active Cooper: Ibid.

Chapter Twelve
66. "I didn't care where they were going": Author interview with Cooper, June 30, 2009.

Chapter Thirteen
69. On June 9, Sheriff Floyd Tidwell: *Daily Record*, June 10, 1983.
69. "We have evidence in our possession": Ibid.
70. Seventy sheriff's deputies: UPI, June 13, 1983.
70. To further tie Cooper to the murders: San Bernardino *Sun*, July

31, 1983.
70. Back in Pittsburgh: Fontana *Herald-News,* June 11, 1983.
70. "for information leading to: UPI, June 21, 1983.
70. "Cooper is a very average looking guy": UPI, June 13, 1983.
70. "Cooper is known to have associated with transvestites: *Daily Record,* June 29, 1983.
71. "a homosexual with a history": *Daily Report,* July 8, 1983.
71. Based on the assumption: Ibid.
71. The manhunt caught its first major break: "Slain Family's Car Turns Up, But It's Cooled Off as Lead," San Bernardino *Sun,* June 12, 1983.
71. "prematurely": Ibid.

CHAPTER FOURTEEN
73. They also smoked some of Handy's marijuana: Author interview with Cooper, June 30, 2009.

CHAPTER FIFTEEN
77. As a barefoot Kevin Cooper was escorted back: "Suspected Killer Caught Saturday," San Bernardino *Sun,* August 1, 1983.
77. Kevin Cooper did not find out: Author interview with Cooper, June 30, 2009.
77. "My father was always trying to prove something": Ibid.
79. As he was awaiting trial for those burglaries: The commitment order stated "Cooper is a danger to himself and others." Cooper had previously been admitted to Mayview in 1980 under a diagnosis of "assaultive," with a problem controlling his temper. Civil complaint filed in Common Pleas Court of Allegheny County against Mayview State Hospital by lawyers representing alleged rape victim, Lori Stahl, in 1983.
79. While at Mayview, Cooper stole: Author interview with Cooper, June 30, 2009.
80. Cooper went to New York City: Ibid.

CHAPTER SIXTEEN
81. They "rushed the fence and began to jeer": "S.B. Crowd Jeers, Taunts Cooper as He Enters Jail," San Bernardino *Sun,* August 1,

1983.

81. "An angry crowd jeered the manacled and barefoot mass-murder suspect": UPI, August 1, 1983.

81. "I think they should do the same thing": Ibid.

81. "We're just glad they caught that sucker": Christina Sears, San Bernardino *Sun*, August 1, 1983.

81. "That way we could save the taxpayers": Ibid.

81. "We can't afford to make any mistakes": UPI, August 1, 1983.

82 "I hope he gets the gas chamber": Ibid.

82. Cooper as "calm" and "expressionless": Ibid.

82. "I sometimes fantasize what I'd do to him": "Cooper's Arrest Elicits Rage as Well as Relief," Rob Wagner, *Daily Report*, August 2, 1983.

82. "Maybe the Ryens would have had their door locked": *Daily Report*, June 13, 1983.

83. "The thing that tipped the deliberation [about the expansion] was the escape": Ibid.

83. "In terms of consequences": San Bernardino *Sun*, July 8, 1983.

83. The California Legislature acted seven days after the warrants for Cooper's arrest were issued: *Daily Report*, June 16, 1983.

83. (In September, when $500,000 proved insufficient for a fence that high): *Daily Report*, September 9, 1983.

83. "Chino killer still sought month later": Fontana *Herald-News*, July 5, 1983.

83. "Do you want this man to be your neighbor?": San Bernardino *Sun*, August 24, 1983.

83. The treasurer of the group was Nadia Katz: Ibid.

84. "One would think families of judicial officers": Ibid. Editorial, August 25, 1983.

84. If hate mail could kill: Letters to Kevin Cooper on file at Orrick Law offices in San Francisco.

85. David Cota, an eighteen-year-old convicted murderer: *Daily Report*, September 10, 1983.

85. His public defender, David Negus: Ibid.

85. Cota had been recently convicted of murder: San Bernardino *Sun*, September 10, 1983.

85. "He was not taking a shower": *Daily Report*, September 10, 1983.

86. "Cooper isolated for his protection following assault": Ibid. Sep-

tember 13, 1983.

86. "bumper stickers reading 'Fry Kevin Cooper' have been printed": "Cooper Pleads Innocent to Chino Slayings," Richard Gray, *Daily Report*, August 12, 1983.

86. "Cooper sat quietly at the counsel table": Ibid.

86. All pretense of presuming Cooper's innocence was discarded: "Parents of Slain Boy Sue," Richard Gray, *Daily Report*, January 26, 1984.

89. "county bread": Author interview with Ron Forbush, June 9, 2010.

89. On a monthly basis: Ibid.

89. "This is the ultimate good ol' boy network in full operation": "The Good 'ol Boys," Steve Williams, editor of opinion page for *Victorville Daily*, January 9, 2009.

90. tobacco-spittin' "cowboy sheriff": San Bernardino *Sun*, January 25, 2005.

90. It would not be until June of 2003: Ibid. June 26, 2003.

90. Guess what, those guns were given to me by Floyd Tidwell": Riverside *Press-Enterprise*, May 11, 2004.

91. Before a search warrant could be issued for his house: San Bernardino *Sun*, January 25, 2005.

91. "It's necessary to investigate, Cardwell argued": Ibid.

91. "The supervisor then informed someone on a senior level": Ibid.

91. "Quite frankly, I don't think [Tidwell will] ever tell us": Ibid.

92. "We need to move on": Ibid.

92. "the case got stuck in the system": Radio commentator Barb Stanton post at www.barbstantonshow.com, December 22, 2007.

92. "several errors in judgment": Riverside *Press-Enterprise*, May 11, 2004.

92. Eleven months later, in May of 2004: *Los Angeles Times*, November 5, 2004.

92. "had been uncooperative, had sought to capitalize on his stature": Ibid.

92. "sending Colonel Sanders to a chicken coop": Ibid.

93. "Floyd Tidwell's prosecution features too much bargain": Letter to editor of Riverside *Press-Enterprise*, May 19, 2004.

93. "raiding the property room": San Bernardino *Sun,* May 13, 2004.
93. "[Tidwell] used to go through the [property] division": Ibid.
93. "I'm not guilty of anything, dang it": *Los Angeles Times,* November 5, 2004.

CHAPTER EIGHTEEN
95. "Doug is working hard – at working with Mom": Peggy Ryen letter to Lillian Shaffer, December 27, 1973.
95. Lillian knew from years of experience of her own: Author interview with Lillian Shaffer, March 30, 2010.
96. "Mom's ready for either a nervous breakdown": Peggy Ryen letter to Lillian Shaffer, May 8, 1974.
96. Over time, Dr. Howell grew to deeply resent Doug: Dr. Lorna M. Forbes letter to State Department of Adoptions, June 6, 1985.
96. "Doug came down to the park where I was with the kids": Author interview with Lillian Shaffer, March 30, 2010.
96. Lillian said in an interview that Peggy: Ibid.
97. "Hey, Josh, let's you and me have a secret": Dr. Lorna Forbes letter to State Department of Adoptions, June 6, 1985.
97. "His preferences were articulated through other witnesses": *Daily Report,* September 22, 1983.
97. "The court followed the law": Ibid.
97. "Richard Ryen felt very strongly that he had an obligation": Ibid.
97. Cindy Settle, Doug Ryen's sister: Author interview with Cindy Settle, October 15, 2010.
98. "The ruling is in our favor and in effect we won": *Daily Report,* September, 22, 1983.
98. "My mother absolutely brainwashed Josh": Author interview with Lillian Shaffer, March 30, 2010.
98. "Dr. Mary Howell was a wicked witch": Author interview with Cindy Settle, October 15, 2010.
98. The letter was an out-and-out attack on Josh's parents: Dr. Lorna Forbes letter to State Department of Adoptions, June 6, 1985.
98. "…it was clear [prior to his parents' deaths] that the boy felt": Ibid.
99. "He didn't like working too much": Ibid.
99. "Joshua's pregnancy was not wanted": Ibid.
99. "It's house-to-house with no room to play": Ibid.

99. It is evident that Joshua": Ibid.

99. "he would see this as punishment": Ibid.

99. "In my many years of consulting": Ibid.

100. "Well I can't think of anyone: Ron Forbush interview with Pam Hess, May 31, 1984.

100. "They were the best kind of people": *Daily Report*, June 7, 1983.

100. "What a shame for such a lovely, nice young couple": Ibid.

CHAPTER NINETEEN

101. "Kottmeier tried the case because he is an egoist": Author interview with David Negus, January 27, 2010.

102. "[Negus is] the most hard-working defense attorney I ever came across": Author interview with Dennis Kottmeier, June 7, 2010.

102. Negus was "brilliant": Author interview with Ron Forbush, June 9, 2010.

102. Among themselves, the jurors referred to Negus as "Columbo": Private investigator interview with a juror, June 6, 2000.

102. "Uncle Ron": Author interview with Ron Forbush, June 9, 2010.

102. "That's a question I'm afraid we'll never know the answer to": Author interview with David Negus, January 27, 2010.

103. "Kevin certainly had the opportunity being so close to the Ryen house": Author interview with Forbush, June 9, 2010.

103. "Dennis is a nut": Author interview with Negus, January 27, 2010.

103. "Kottmeier appeared to be a racist": Kevin Cooper letter to author, May 1, 2011.

104. "King Richard": Author interview with Forbush, June 9, 2010.

104. "a very religious, opinionated man, with a quick temper": Author interview with Negus, January 27, 2010.

104. "superior court judges are not necessarily": Ibid.

Chapter Twenty

105. "If Negus did not work well with other attorneys at his side": Author interview with Richard Melick, January 28, 2011.

106. "I do better if I know the material myself": Author interview with Negus, February 3, 2011.

106. "Several thousand pages of discovery immediately says": Author interview with Melick, January 28, 2011.

106. "I spent all of my time boning up on serology": Author interview with Negus, January 27, 2010.

106. "Setting the discovery aside was a major mistake": Author interview with Melick January 28, 2011.

107. "could cost me my life": Ron Forbush interview with Diana Roper, May 18, 1984.

107. "If this fits together, I will testify": Ibid.

108. that turned her into a "zombie": Ibid.

108. "There was blood all over the butt, back, everywhere": Ibid.

109. Roper told Forbush that Furrow "is a very strange person": Ibid.

109. "The bloody coveralls is the main thing": Ibid.

109. "I says you mean to tell me that them coveralls": Ibid.

109. "a whack job": Author interview with Forbush, June 9, 2010.

109. "thought she was nuts. A meth nut": Author interview with Negus, February 3, 2011.

109. "I don't recall her doing that": Ibid.

110. "I truly don't remember it very well": Ibid.

CHAPTER TWENTY-ONE

113. "I felt that a sequestered jury": Author interview with Negus, January 27, 2010.

CHAPTER TWENTY-THREE

121. To say that he was not going to prove that his client": Author interview with Melick, January 28, 2011.

122. "Again, he gives the case away": Ibid.

126. He had not written his opening down on paper and had not rehearsed it: Author interview with Negus, February 3, 2011.

127. "The absence of a clear, compelling narrative in Negus's opening statement": Author interview with Melick, January 28, 2011.

127. "had to concede that the wounds": Transcript preliminary hearing.

128. "It was his job to identify the perpetrator(s) for the jury": Author interview with Melick, January 28, 2011.

CHAPTER TWENTY-FIVE

134. Warden Carroll then promptly called one of the two lead de-

tectives on the case: Testimony of former Warden Midge Carroll at Cooper's habeas corpus evidentiary hearing in federal court in San Diego, 2004-2005.

135. "I've never met James Taylor": Author interview with Cooper, June 30, 2009.

CHAPTER TWENTY-SEVEN

147. The Ryens' white station wagon: San Bernardino *Sun*, June 12, 1983.

CHAPTER THIRTY

159. Near the end of the prosecution's presentation: Video-taped interview of Josh Ryen conducted December 9, 1984.

160. "saw like a shadow or something" by the bathroom: Ibid.

160. On his own, in an effort to make some sense of the horrible tragedy: Detective Hector O'Campo report of his interview with Josh on June 14, 1983.

161. "If I remember correctly": Negus and Forbush interview of Dr. Mary Howell, October 27, 1983.

163. Dr. Howell did not approve of the Montessori school: Dr. Lorna Forbes letter to State Department of Adoptions, June 6, 1985.

163. In December of 1983: Dr. Forbes interview of Josh, December 1983.

CHAPTER THIRTY-ONE

167. In his report, Woods wrote that Wisely informed him: Detective Gary Woods police report, covering the period December 17 through December 21, 1984.

169. Ten days later when Forbush did get around to interviewing Wisely: Forbush interview of Wisely, January 12, 1985.

170. "I made that decision because Kevin was ready to testify": Author interview of Negus, February 3, 2011.

170. "a shotgun approach or an alternative theory [approach]" Ibid.

CHAPTER THIRTY-TWO

171. Despite all of his past arrests and sentencings: Author interview of Cooper, June 30, 2009.

CHAPTER THIRTY-THREE

175. The one bit of advice David Negus gave his client: Author interview of Cooper, June 30, 2009.

175. Kottmeier would later recall: Author interview of Kottmeier, June 7, 2010.

175. "a college education" in his appearance": Ibid.

177. Something else that surprised and impressed Kottmeier: Author interview of Kottmeier, June 7, 2010.

183. "Despite three grueling days of cross-examination by Kottmeier": "Kevin Cooper Convicted in 4 Chino Hills Ax Murders – Escapee Faces Death Sentence," H. G. Reza, *Los Angeles Times*, February 19, 1985.

CHAPTER THIRTY-FOUR

193. Before working with Josh, Gamundoy had tended: Author interview with Dan Gamundoy, June 10, 2010.

194. Once the staff knew that Josh: Author interview with Marion McQuinn, June 10, 2010.

194. To make sure that he was getting accurate answers: Ibid.

195. In an interview in 2010 at Loma Linda University Hospital: Author interview of Gamundoy, June 10, 2010.

195. "The victim first advised me: Deputy Sharp's police report, June 5, 1983.

CHAPTER THIRTY-FIVE

202. Dr. Thornton was not alone in thinking: Author interview with Lillian Shaffer, March 30, 2010.

CHAPTER THIRTY-SIX

207. "tried to fight them off, tripped 'em up": Dr. Hoyle's notes from Detective O'Campo interview on June 14, 1983.

207. "They snuck up behind me and hit me": Ibid.

CHAPTER FORTY-ONE

227. "Die Cooper!": *Los Angeles Times*, January 25, 1985.

231. Unlike some juries that take an initial poll: Private investigator

interview of a juror, June 16, 2000.
231. "It was just one of those things": *San Diego Union*, March 4, 1985.
231. On the other hand, two of the jurors expressed a different take: Ibid. Quoting jurors Jetlyn Doxey and Donna Merchant, respectively.
231. "...the defense could never explain": Private investigator interview of a juror, June 16, 2000.
232. "cocky" demeanor: Ibid.

CHAPTER FORTY-TWO
234. "ineffective counsel": Legal Watch defines ineffective counsel as ineffective when an attorney's services to a defendant in a criminal case fall so far short of what a reasonably competent attorney would do that it violates the Sixth Amendment of the Constitution. The U.S. Supreme Court defined ineffective assistance of counsel in the landmark case *Strickland v. Washington* (1984). The court held that an attorney's assistance is ineffective if it "so undermined the functioning of the adversary process that the trial cannot be relied upon as having produced a just result."
236. The *Los Angeles Times* reported that her plea: "Judge Signs Death Warrant for Escapee Who Killed 4," Amy Wallace, *Los Angeles Times*, August 6, 1991.

CHAPTER FORTY-FOUR
245. A surprisingly large number of death row inmates: "Volunteering For Death: The Fast Track to the Death House by Robert A. Phillips, crimemagazine.com.

246. Over the next nine years: "A Broken System: Error Rates in Capital Cases, 1973-1995," by Professor James S. Liebman of the Columbia Law School, Columbia Law School web site. In the executive summary to the report, Professor Liebman stated: "There is a growing bipartisan consensus that flaws in America's death-penalty system have reached crisis proportions. Many fear that capital trials put people on death row who don't belong there. Others say capital appeals take too long. This report – the first statistical study ever undertaken of modern American capital appeals (4,578 of them in state capital cases between 1973 and 1995) – suggests that *both* claims are

correct.

"Capital sentences do spend a long time under judicial review. As this study documents, however, judicial review takes so long precisely *because* American capital sentences are so persistently and systematically fraught with error that seriously undermines their reliability.

"Our 23 years worth of results reveal a death penalty system collapsing under the weight of its own mistakes. They reveal a system in which lives and public order are at stake, yet for decades has made more mistakes than we would tolerate in far less important activities. They reveal a system that is wasteful and broken and needs to be addressed."

247. Although no one could have predicted it at the time: The Anti-Terrorism and Effective Death Penalty Act of 1996 is the product of legislative efforts stretching back well over a decade and stimulated to passage in part by the tragedies in Oklahoma City (1995) and the World Trade Center (1993).

Title I of the Act substantially amends federal habeas corpus law as it applies to both state and federal prisoners whether on death row or imprisoned for a term of years by providing: a bar on federal habeas reconsideration of legal and factual issues ruled upon by state courts in most instances; creation of a general one-year statute of limitations; creation of a six-month statute of limitation in death penalty cases; encouragement for states to appoint counsel for indigent state death row inmates during state habeas or unitary appellate proceedings; and a requirement of appellate court approval for repetitious habeas petitions. Summary by Charles Doyle, June 3, 1996, fas.org.

248. The task of representing Cooper in his habeas appeal was enormous: Author interview with Charles D. Maurer, June 25, 2011.
248. "I just found too many loose ends": Ibid.
248. "the most complicated criminal case I've ever seen": Ibid.
251. In the first twenty years after the passage of ADEPA: "The Effect of AEDPA on Capital Post-Conviction Litigation in the Federal Courts," in the book *Capital Punishment Issues in the Next Generation* by David R. Dow and E. Freeman, Carolina Academic Press, 2007.

CHAPTER FORTY-FIVE

253. "I would surely die a violent death in here": savekevincooper.org.

253. "I guess the bottom line is this": Cooper's clemency petition to Governor Schwarzenegger, January 9, 2004.

253. One of the first positive steps he took: Author interview with Cooper, June 30, 2009.

254. If denied, he could file a writ of certiorari: The word "certiorari" comes from Latin and means "to be more fully informed." A writ of certiorari orders a lower court to deliver its record in a case so that the higher court may review it. The U.S. Supreme Court uses certiorari to pick most of the cases that it hears, Legal Information Institute, Cornell University Law School.

254. Thanks to Alexander's belief in Cooper's total innocence: Author interview with David Alexander, June 28, 2009.

255. The petition urged the governor to consider matters: Cooper's clemency petition, January 9, 2004.

258. "This is Not My Execution": savekevincooper.org, January 29, 2004.

CHAPTER FORTY-SIX

261. Faced with the unlikely prospect of Governor Schwarzenegger granting clemency: Author interview with former Orrick attorney David Alexander, June 28, 2009.

262. The petition asserted that the state had violated Cooper's constitutional rights: Habeas corpus petition filed by Orrick with Ninth Circuit Court of Appeals, February 8, 2004.

262. Judge Rymer, writing for the majority: Ninth Circuit Court of Appeals decision denying Cooper a stay of execution and a successive habeas corpus proceeding, February 8, 2004.

263. In an extraordinary development: Judge Browning's dissent to Ninth Circuit Court of Appeals ruling denying Cooper a stay of execution and a successive habeas corpus proceeding, February 8, 2004.

264. The *Brady* violation opened the door: In 1963, the Supreme Court ruled in *Brady* v *Maryland* that the government has a duty to disclose material evidence to the defense, which could tend to change the outcome of a trial. This exculpatory evidence, often referred to as "Brady Material," could tend to prove that the accused

party is innocent or cast doubt of his/her guilt. Duty to Disclose: The landmark decision places an affirmative constitutional duty on a prosecutor to disclose exculpatory evidence to a defendant. This duty has been extended to police agencies through case law, requiring law enforcement agencies to notify the prosecutor of any potential exculpatory information, Stephen Rothlein, Public Agency Training Council web site.

264. News of the stay of execution did not reach Cooper until 6:15 p.m.: Kevin Cooper essay, "The Ritual of Death," savekevincooper. org.

264. After Jesse Jackson said a prayer for him and his friends: 188. Six guards then took Cooper to a holding cell: Ibid.

264. Cooper was told to place his back against the back wall of the cell: Ibid.

265. His pastor continued reading scripture aloud to him: Ibid.

265. "I was a nonhuman. I was just part of their job": Ibid.

265. In an interview with radio station KPFA-FM's "Flashpoints" program: SFGate.com, February 18, 2004.

CHAPTER FORTY-SEVEN

268. Anne Hawkins, the staff attorney for the Habeas Corpus Research Center: Author interview with Anne Hawkins, January 9, 2010.

268. "She smiles at everybody like she's being the most wonderful den mother": Author interview with Orrick attorney Norm Hile, December 15, 2010.

268. "I was in court in the Deep South": Ibid.

270. The reactions to Judge Huff expressed on "Robing Room" are extremely harsh: therobingroom.com.

CHAPTER FORTY-EIGHT

271. The first matter Judge Huff took up was designing a protocol: Cooper's evidentiary hearings, 2004-2005.

273. In response to the new protocol issued by Judge Huff: Dr. DeForest's letter to Judge Huff, September 3, 2004.

278. "As a result, the mitochondrial DNA testing was pre-determined": Author interview with Norm Hile, December 15, 2010.

279. Norm Hile immediately asked for discovery and testing of the swatch: Ibid.

280. "blue shirt with possible blood on it": Sheriff's dispatch log, June 6, 1983.

282. When he heard Kochis's excuse: Author interview of Hile, December 15, 2010.

284. Back in 1997, when Judge Huff was assigned Cooper's original habeas petition: Ibid.

289. Judge Huff denied all discovery the defense asked for into this claim: Ibid.

291. "Judge Huff allowing Josh to make an impact statement was totally gratuitous": Ibid.

CHAPTER FORTY-NINE

295. "somewhat disoriented": Author interview with Hile, December 15, 2010.

2295. "denies lawyers the nonverbal cues they get from the judges": *Los Angeles Times*, January 10, 2007.

295. "The interaction among the participants is just different": Ibid.

295. "I was at the courthouse in San Francisco on Tuesday": Ibid.

CHAPTER FIFTY

298. "The State of California may be about to execute an innocent man": Judge Fletcher's dissent, May 11, 2009.

299. "There's no way to say this politely": Ibid.

299. "[T]hrough a series of errors accurately described by Judge Fletcher": Judge Kim McLane Wardlaw's dissent, May 11, 2009.

299. "...the district court impeded and obstructed Cooper's attorneys at every turn": Judge Fletcher's dissent, May 11, 2009.

303. "solely those of the district court": Judge Stephen Reinhardt's concurrence with Judge Fletcher's dissent, May 11, 2009.

304. "our performance on the bench": Ibid.

304. "The case I am about to describe is horrible in many ways": Judge Fletcher's speech at Gonzaga University Law School, April 12, 2010.

CHAPTER FIFTY-ONE

308. "Unless he [Cooper] can present new evidence": Author interview with Norm Hile, January 29, 2011.

308. "investigate every lead and witness we can": Ibid.

310. If an execution date were set for Cooper: Ibid.

311. "As one of your final acts as governor": Norm Hile's letter to Governor Schwarzenegger, November 23, 2010.

311. The clemency petition that Hile filed on behalf of Cooper: Clemency petition for Cooper filed December 17, 2010.

311. Nicholas D. Kristof in *The New York Times*: Nicholas D. Kristof column "Framed for Murder"?: *New York Times*, December 9, 2010; Alan M. Dershowitz and David B. Rivkin Jr. Op-Ed column "A Time for Clemency," *Los Angeles Times*, December 1, 2010.

311. In addition, the *LA Times*, *San Francisco Chronicle* and *Sacramento Bee:* Editorials published December 24, 2010.

312. On his final day in office, the governor: Andrea Lynn Hoch, the governor's legal affairs secretary, letter to Norm Hile, January 2, 2011.

313. With Chief Justice Bird and several other like-minded justices: Rose Bird obituary, *New York Times*, December 6, 1999.

313. Rather than move into the newly constructed Governor's Mansion: "Who Was Jerry Brown"? by Robert Cruickshank, *California Northern Magazine*, Issue One: Politics, 2010.

313. "Governor Moonbeam": "How Jerry Brown Became 'Governor Moonbeam,'" Jessie McKinley, *New York Times*, March 6, 2010.

313. During the campaign for that office: "Brown's Death Penalty Stance a Likely Debate Topic" by Carla Marinucci, SFGate.com, September 28, 2010.

314. In an editorial board interview at the *Sacramento Bee* in late September of 2010: Ibid.

314. One of the last to do so in California was Caryl Chessman: Known as "The Red Light Bandit," a strong case can be made for his actual innocence. See "The Wrongful Execution of Caryl Chessman" by Randy Radic, crimemagazine.com, September 30, 2009.

314. Although California has by far the most inmates on death row: "The History of California's Death Penalty," Death Penalty Focus.

315. In March of 2011, Illinois became the sixteenth state to abolish: "Illinois Governor Signs Capital Punishment Ban," John Schwartz and Emma Fitzsimmons, *New York Times*, March 9, 2011.

315. "...after looking at all the evidence I have received": Ibid.

315. "...a real turning point in the conversation about the death penalty in the United States": Ibid.

315. California began state executions in 1893 when Jose Gabriel was hanged: "The History of California's Death Penalty," Death Penalty Focus.

316. The 1972 California Supreme Court ruling overturning the death penalty commuted: Ibid.

316. In 1976, the California Supreme Court ruled again: Ibid.

316. During the hiatus, two death row inmates were exonerated by the courts: Death Penalty Information Center.

316. In 1994, the California Supreme Court ruled the gas chamber was "cruel and unusual punishment": "The History of California's Death Penalty," Death Penalty Focus.

317. In 1996, William Bonin, dubbed "The Freeway Killer": :The Freeway Killer," J. J. Maloney, crimemagazine.com.

317. Allen would be the last to be executed in California: "The History of California's Death Penalty," Death Penalty Focus.

317. What placed all those executions on hold was a ruling: "Last-Minute Reprieve for California Death Row Inmate," Kate Randall, World Socialist web site, February 23, 2006.

317. A week before the scheduled execution: Ibid.

317. The lethal injection protocol consists of three separate dosages: Ibid.

317. The problem with the three drug-cocktail: Ibid.

318. In an attempt to remedy this possibility: Ibid.

318. Just hours before the scheduled execution: Ibid.

318. "Any such intervention would clearly be unethical": Ibid.

318. "I don't know of any other case where a physician": Ibid.

318. "To the credit of the state's medical community": Ibid.

318. Undeterred and determined to execute Morales that day: Ibid.

318. To avoid the problem of not having an anesthesiologist on hand: Ibid.

318. "appropriate clothing to protect their (sic) anonymity": Ibid.

319. Two hours before the scheduled execution: Ibid.

319. At an expense of $853,000 a new "execution center" was constructed at San Quentin: "San Quentin Unveils New Death Chamber," KTXL, fox40.com, September 21, 2010.

319. The death chamber itself is Spartan: "New Death Chamber at San Quentin Ready," Scott Shafer, *The California Report*, September 22, 2010.

320. Behind the death chamber is a control center: Ibid.

320. Amid the controversy and debate surrounding the lethal injection protocols: "With Conditions, Judge Clears Way for a California Execution." Jesse McKinley, *New York Times*, September 25, 2010.

320. This immediately freed superior court judges to assign new execution dates: "Albert Greenwood Brown Set To Die From Drug Combo," Bog Egelko, SFGate.com, September 27, 2010.

321. Judge Fogel, who is based in San Jose, ruled that Brown could avert: Ibid.

321. The Ninth agreed to stay Brown's execution: "Albert Greenwood Brown Execution Blocked by Federal Judge in California," Paul Elias, huffingtonpost.com, September 28, 2010.

321. "It is incredible to think that the deliberative process might be driven by the expiration date of the execution drug: "New Questions on Execution in California," Jesse McKinley and Malia Wollan, *New York Times*, September 29, 2010.

321. "The drug is not indicated for capital punishment": "Lethal Injections Spark Fight," Vauhini Vara and Nathan Koppel, *The Wall Street Journal*, September 30, 2010.

322. Reviewing substances imported or used for the purpose of state-authorized lethal injection: "FDA Helped States Obtain Execution Drug," Andrew Welsh-Huggins, Associated Press, January 11, 2011.

322. "The FDA is actively assisting these states, but they're not enforcing the law": Ibid.

323. Once it became known that an English company was supplying sodium thiopental to prisons in Arizona and California: "Drug Used for Lethal Injections Is Halted," Nathan Koppel, *The Wall Street Journal*, January 22, 2011.

323. Amid this negative background, Hospira announced: Ibid.

323. "The final decision came in the face of opposition from government figures in Italy": Ibid.

324. A study of capital punishment costs in California since the state reinstated the death penalty in 1978: "Death Penalty Costs California $184 Million a Year, Study Says," Carol J. Williams, *Los Angeles Times*.

324. The *Los Angeles Times* reported on several of the study's findings: Ibid.

324. The *Times* reported that the study provided three options for voters to curb the escalating costs and infrequent executions: Ibid.

325. In March of 2011 the state legislature approved his partial budget plan: "A Surprise Jump in Revenue Helps Halve California Deficit," Jennifer Medina, *New York Times*, May 17, 2011.

325. In May of 2011, Governor Brown proposed the elimination of more than forty state boards: Ibid.

325. A precursor to what might be in store for capital punishment in California: "Gov. Brown Cancels Plans to Build New Death Row," Wyatt Buchanan, *San Francisco Chronicle*, April 29, 2011.

325. "At a time when children, the disabled and seniors face painful cuts to essential programs": Ibid.

POSTSCRIPT

327. David Negus retired from the San Bernardino County Public Defender's Office in 2004: "Lawyer Who Defended Cooper Retiring," Alan Schnepf, San Bernardino *Sun*, February 4, 2004.

327. "stomach representing defendants...who lied all the time: Author interview with Dennis Kottmeier, June 7, 2010.

327. Dr. Mary Howell, Peggy Ryen's mother: Author interview with Lillian Shaffer, March 30, 2010.

327. In 2000 she appeared on a "48 Hours" segment: "A Grandmother's Mission," CBS "48 Hours," October 26, 2006. MSN.Entertainment described the episode as "A grandmother worries that a man on death row for killing her family is innocent and that the real killers are still at large."

328. Josh Ryen lived with his grandmother on her horse ranch in Temecula: Author interview with Lillian Shaffer, March 30, 2010.

328. Diana Roper died on August 14, 2003 at her home in Mentrone: Diana Roper death certificate.

328. After Cooper's conviction, Sergeant Arthur did slide presentations of the Ryen crime scene: Defense investigator interview of Vera Arthur, March 11, 1999.

329. Former Sheriff Floyd Tidwell has two new hips and a new wife: Author interview with anonymous source in San Bernardino County

Sheriff's Office, June 10, 2010.

329. "The Sheriff's Department screwed up the case on purpose so he could never be tried": Author interview with Kottmeier, June 7, 2010.

330. In reporting on the award, the *Press-Enterprise*: Riverside *Press-Enterprise*, March 29, 2008.

330. "If there is such a thing as a most valuable player": Ibid.

331. What project investigators found out about the tuft of fiber was jaw-dropping: "DNA, False Evidence Confirm Inmate Did Not Murder His Wife," California Western School of Law, San Diego, web site, August 10, 2009.

331. "unerringly to innocence": Ibid.

331. "In my twenty years of handling post-conviction cases in California": Ibid.

332. The $10 million wrongful death suit Bill and Mary Ann Hughes field in 1984: Author interview with attorney John Q. Adams, April 21, 2011.

Norm Hile and Katie DeWitt of Orrick, the San Francisco-based law firm that pro bono adopted Kevin Cooper as a client in the months leading up to his scheduled execution in February of 2004, were invaluable to me in explaining the dense legal issues that comprise such a protracted death-penalty case. I could not have written this book without their assistance. The dedication that Norm and Katie have shown in fighting for Kevin Cooper's life is as remarkable as it is rare.

From the outset, Norm opened up the complete files at Orrick to permit me to thoroughly research the case. With the aid of paralegal Max Mellenthin, I spent days sifting through pallets of boxed files in an Orrick office. The day I saw the crime scene and autopsy photos I knew, as Max already did, that I would be seeing them for the rest of my life.

Over a period of many months, Katie DeWitt meticulously went through all of the drafts of the manuscript, offering insights and guidance that were invaluable to me. I doubt if anyone understands the complexities of this case better than she.

I owe a special debt of gratitude to my friend, John Brady, the former editor of *Writer's Digest* and the author of several highly acclaimed books. More than anyone else, he helped me mold this complicated, drawn-out case into first and foremost a story of separate tragedies.

My sister, Paula O'Connor, proofread every draft and offered many suggestions, including the title. Her enthusiasm for the book's progress was a continual boost.

My daughter, Maya O'Connor, and author Marilyn Z. Tomlins also were kind to proofread the manuscript and offer encouragement.

I want to thank Amy Hall, of Amethyst Harbor, Inc. in Rockville, Maryland, for her care in indexing the book.

Richard Melick, a trial attorney with forty years experience in the Boston area, graciously agreed to read and comment on the chapters involving the public defender's trial preparation and his opening statement to the jury.

Joe Soldis, a private investigator and forme police officer, volunteered his time to help me do research and get interviews in San Bernardino County. He opened doors that would have been closed to me.

Kelly Zackmann, the local history librarian for the Robert E. Ellingwood Model Colony History Room at the Ontario City Library, was extremely kind in tracking down answers to numerous questions that arose during my research.

I also wish to thank David Negus, the public defender who represented Kevin Cooper at his trial, for his candor in speaking with me and extend the same thanks to Cooper's lead prosecutor, former San Bernardino County District Attorney Dennis Kottmeier. Both are dedicated and honorable attorneys whom I subject to microscopic analysis for their roles in the tragedy that makes up the Kevin Cooper case.

Lillian Shaffer, Peggy Ryen's half sister, and Cindy Settle, Doug Ryen's sister, provided me with insights into their siblings that I had no other way of discovering. I thank them for their willingness to discuss with such care the great loss they sustained all those years ago.

One hope I have for this book is that it will allow Josh Ryen, the sole survivor of the Chino Hills murders, to reunite with his extended family.

Finally, I wish to thank my excellent literary agent, Barbara Casey.

INDEX

Current and Forthcoming Titles from Strategic Media Books

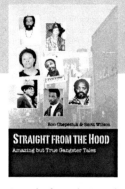

The Trafficantes
Godfathers from Tampa, Florida:
The Mafia, The CIA and The JFK
Assassination
978 - 0 - 9842333 - 0 - 4

Sergeant Smack
The Legendary Lives and Times
of Ike Atkinson, Kingpin, and
His Band of Brothers
978 - 0 - 9842333 - 1 - 1

Straight from the Hood
Amazing but True Gangster Tales
978 - 0 - 9842333 - 3 - 5

Chili Pimping in Atlantic City
The Memoir of a Small-Time Pimp
978 - 0 - 9842333 - 4 - 2

Queenpins
Notorious Women Gangsters of the
Modern Era
978 - 0 - 9842333 - 5 - 9

AVAILABLE FROM STRATEGICMEDIABOOKS.COM, AMAZON, AND MAJOR BOOKSTORES NEAR YOU.

COMING IN 2012

Rogue Mobster
The Untold Story of Mark Silverman
and the New England Mafia

Gorilla Convict
The Prison Writing of Seth Ferranti

CPSIA information can be obtained
at www.ICGtesting.com
Printed in the USA
EDOW020426151212
255ED